A SOCIOCRITIQUE OF TRANSLATION
THEATRE AND ALTERITY IN QUEBEC, 1968–1988

THEORY/CULTURE

Editors:
Linda Hutcheon, Gary Leonard, Jill Matus,
Janet Paterson, and Paul Perron

ANNIE BRISSET

A Sociocritique of Translation: Theatre and Alterity in Quebec, 1968–1988

Translated by Rosalind Gill and Roger Gannon

UNIVERSITY OF TORONTO PRESS
Toronto Buffalo London

English translation
© Rosalind Gill and Roger Gannon 1996
Published by
University of Toronto Press Incorporated
Toronto Buffalo London
Printed in Canada

ISBN 0-8020-0533-0

Originally published in French as *Sociocritique de la traduction: théâtre et altérité au Québec (1968–1988)*
© Les Éditions Balzac, 1990
Tous droits réservés. L'édition originale a été publiée par Les Éditions du Préambule, Montréal, Canada

Printed on acid-free paper

Canadian Cataloguing in Publication Data

Brisset, Annie
   A sociocritique of translation : theatre and alterity in Quebec, 1968–1988

(Theory/culture)
Includes bibliographical references and index.
ISBN 0-8020-0533-0

1. Drama – Translating – Social aspects – Quebec (Province) – History – 20th century.   2. Drama – Translating – Political aspects – Quebec (Province) – History – 20th century.   3. Translating and interpreting – Social aspects – History – 20th century.   4. Translating and interpreting – Political aspects – History – 20th century.   5. Theater and society – Quebec (Province) – History – 20th century.   6. Canadian drama (French) – Quebec (Province) – History and criticism.*   7. Canadian drama (French) – 20th century – History and criticism.*   I. Title.   II. Series.

P306.B7413 1996   418'.02'0971409045   C96-930048-4

University of Toronto Press acknowledges the financial assistance to its publishing program of the Canada Council and the Ontario Arts Council. This book has been published with the help of a translation grant from the Canada Council.

In memory of André Belleau

Contents

TABLES AND FIGURES xi
FOREWORD *by Antoine Berman* xiii
ACKNOWLEDGMENTS xxi

Introduction 3

1 The Foreigner in the Theatrical Institution 11

The Image of the Foreigner in Published Translations 12
    The Need for Adaptation 13
    No to the Anglo-Canadian Repertoire, But ... 17
    Tremblay, Translator Laureate 18
    Lysistrata, in the 'Répertoire québécois' Series 20
    For Euripides, Signed: Marie Cardinal 21
    Tremblay, Translator Laureate (Continued) 26
    The Québécois Content Rule 27
    The Faceless Foreigner 30
    The Foreign Work: No Introduction Necessary? 31

The Foreigner Upstaged 32
    Selection Criteria 33
    Origin and Proportion of Foreign Plays Produced 34
    Which Languages? Which Authors? 39
    American Tragedy versus French Comedy 47
    Politics and the Theatre 50

viii   Contents

2 At the Other's Expense: Iconoclastic Translation   59

The Scourge of Alterity   60
The Other Defaced: Imitation and Parody   70
    Gogol in 'La Grande Noirceur': Michel Tremblay's *Le Gars de Québec*   71
    Machiavelli in Underpants: Jean-Pierre Ronfard's *La Mandragore*   73
    The English, or Evil Incarnate: Antonine Maillet's *Le Bourgeois Gentleman*   74
    Rodriguemachine: Réjean Ducharme's *Le Cid maghané*   79
    Sensational Shakespeare: Jean-Pierre Ronfard's *Lear*   87
    Redefining the Boundary of the Foreign: Jean-Claude Germain's *Les Faux Brillants de Félix-Gabriel Marchand*   91
    Vive la Différence!: Bertolt Brecht's *A Respectable Wedding*   98
    A Ghost Who Speaks Our Language: Robert Gurik's *Hamlet, prince du Québec*   101
Towards a New Canon   105

3 Shakespeare, Québécois Nationalist Poet: Perlocutory Translation   109

Translation as a Perlocutory Operation   109
A Dynamic Equivalent: Scotland = Not'pauv'pays   113
The King of England in the Trash-Cans of History   119
    'I omitted lines 38 to 47.'   119
    'I didn't translate lines 139 to 161.'   127
Shakespeare Bemoans the Québécois Paradise Lost   142
The Translating Subject   158

4 The Search for a Native Language: Translation and Cultural Identity   162

Issues of Language in the Theory of Translation   162
'Translated into Québécois'   165
Québécois in the Market of Symbolic Commodities   169
The Distinctive Function of Québécois   170
The Enigmatic Québécois Language   174

The Myths of 'Québécois' as a Language of Translation   180
Why Translate into Québécois?   188

Conclusion   195

NOTES   201
BIBLIOGRAPHY   225
INDEX OF PROPER NAMES   233

Tables and Figures

Tables

1. Origin of Foreign Plays   35
2. Distribution and Percentage of Foreign Works and Québécois Works, by Theatre   36
3. Source Language of Foreign Works, excluding French   39
4. Numerical Distribution of Foreign Plays, by Theatre   40
5. Percentage of Foreign Plays, by Theatre   41
6. Distribution of Plays in Languages Other than English and French, by Theatre   42
7. Italian-Language Repertoire   43
8. German-Language Repertoire   44
9. Russian-Language Repertoire   45
10. Spanish-Language Repertoire   46
11. French Repertoire   48
12. American Repertoire   49
13. Annual Distribution of Foreign and Québécois Plays   51
14. Annual Distribution of French and American Plays   54
15. Annual Distribution of Québécois and French Translations   56
16. Proportion of Translations and Adaptations, Compagnie Jean-Duceppe   58
17. A Comparison of Settings in Stage Directions (*Macbeth*, tr. M. Garneau)   114
18. A Comparison of Place-names: Shakespeare and Garneau   115
19. References to Scotland (Nouns, Phrases, and Determiners): Shakespeare and Garneau (*Macbeth*, Act IV, Scene 3)   131

xii Tables and Figures

20 A Comparison of References to Scotland: Shakespeare and Garneau (*Macbeth*, Act IV, Scene 3) 132
21 References to Scotland: Leyris, Bonnefoy, and Déprats (*Macbeth*, Act IV, Scene 3) 133
22 A Comparison of References to Scotland: Shakespeare, Leyris, Bonnefoy, and Déprats (*Macbeth*, Act IV, Scene 3) 134
23 Common Nouns Referring to Scotland (in order of occurrence): Shakespeare and Garneau 135

Figures

1 Québécois Plays, by Year 52
2 Québécois Translations, by Year 57
3 Spatio-temporal Configuration of the Québécois Translation of *Macbeth* 112

Foreword

It is not easy for a Frenchman to introduce a work that takes a critical approach to the subject of translation and language in contemporary Quebec – and, for a reason that this present work makes abundantly clear: the Québécois search for an identity is conducted as much against the French claim to possess the 'truth' where the French language is concerned as it is against Anglo-Saxon linguistic hegemony. Indeed, in the wake of political and ideological ferment, some people in Quebec have gone so far as to posit the existence of a 'Québécois' language that could no longer be called 'French' and to assert that Quebec French is substantially 'different' from the French of France. But how exactly does it differ? Supporters of a Québécois language point, for example, to its lexical and idiomatic differences. Yet it might easily be objected that the sum total of such differences does not a language make. Then, how, in fact, do we define the *identity* of a language? This is not an easy question.

Notwithstanding the somewhat loose argumentation of supporters of a Québécois language, the French of Quebec may, indeed, not be exactly the 'same' as the French of France, in respect of a number of characteristics having to do with its *mode of being a language*. For every language has its own, unique mode 'of being a language,' and this mode is intrinsically historical and not linguistic.

The main characteristic distinguishing Québécois from French is its relation to the *dialectal*. While it might be said that, with the exception of a few variants, Québécois speak and write 'International French,' Québécois French nevertheless maintains a close link to the dialectal aspect of the French language. This is certainly not true of the French of France, as is demonstrated by its literature, and literature is the most reliable means of identifying the mode of being of a language. Whereas Québécois literature draws heavily upon oral dialects, only one writer in twentieth-century France, Armand Robin, a Breton who learned French later in life, does so. He also happens to be one of our most distinguished translators.

If its relation to the dialectal is what distinguishes the French of 'La Belle Province' from the French of France, then it is comparable to Caribbean French, the French of Black Africa, and even the French of Switzerland. This relation to the dialectal is, however, most evident in Quebec; witness the constant creation of neologisms and turns of phrase.

The second characteristic distinguishing Québécois from French is that it is an *American* language. But what does this mean? 'American' refers to all those languages of European origin brought to the Americas. By moving, by *migrating*, these languages changed their mode of being. Once again, this becomes apparent if we look at the language of literature. The link between a Québécois novelist, a Caribbean novelist, and a Brazilian novelist is closer than the link between a novelist from these regions and a European novelist writing in the 'same' language. And this is true irrespective of themes and influences. However, what is Americanness, with respect to language? This is not an easy question. The fact that Americans of both continents have managed to perceive their 'own identity' only at the ideological or mythical level does not mean that this 'identity' is in itself a fiction.

Quebec French is American in yet another sense. Despite the implementation of 'francicization,' Québécois often seems (if the reader will pardon my presumption) to be a *French version* of North American English. This is readily apparent in contemporary Québécois publications whose modes of signifying and expressing 'reality' tend to be Anglo-Saxon (American). But is it not highly disparaging to say that 'Québécois' is a French version of American English? Not at all. English is a definite threat, but it could be said that, as a threatened language, French in Quebec has acquired a new status and, with that, has become *an original way of keeping the French language alive.*

French in Quebec is further differentiated from the French of France in that it is overwhelmingly a *language of translation*. We can use the term 'language of translation' to describe a language–culture whose textual productions are principally products of translation. The French of France, in this sense, is not a language of translation; that is to say, translation (no matter how widespread it is in France) does not play a central role in the overall production of written text. This is not the case in Quebec, where translated texts play a major role. However, precisely because translation plays such a major role in textual production in Quebec, and is a major component of Quebec's 'self-awareness,' it is experienced as a multiple threat, the threat of 'doing nothing but translating.' Translation is thus seen as a threat to the creation of original works in an unreal world of copies, imitations, and mirror images. In a world of *pure secondariness*, translation reflects and heightens the 'secondariness' of a Québécois culture lost in a sea of Anglo-American influence. The threat is terrifyingly real – translation, despite a mass of terminological, grammatical, and stylistic filters, may well act as a vehicle of linguistic pollution in Quebec.

The major role played by translation in Quebec therefore *results* in a mode of translation whose whole objective is to *stave off* these threats.

Translation practices in Quebec clearly reveal that translation is systematically given the responsibility of *erasing* the Foreigner.

It is against this background that Annie Brisset's book makes its appearance. The book is so richly layered, raises so many questions for those in the theatre, for translators and translation theorists, for historians, and for sociologists, that I can take up only a few of these questions in the limited space available to me.

Annie Brisset's subject of analysis is translation in the Quebec theatre during the period 1968–88. This would appear to be a clearly defined body of material, but it is highly *symbolic* in nature. For, of all the types of translation practised in a culture during a given historical period, theatre translation is the *only* precise indicator of the profound relationship of the culture to itself and to the Foreigner. It was Goethe who taught us that translation is like a mirror. Theatre translation is the mirror that reflects the most and the most intensely. This is the case because (in the Western world) the theatre provides the community with a representational image of its being-in-the-world. The theatre achieves this representation of being-in-the-world through the *hic et nunc* realization of a *text*. Thus, the theatrical repertoire of a community is made up of the system of texts available for realization. The existence of such a repertoire is critical; without it, no representation of the Self of the community is possible and, correspondingly, no self-affirmation. For Germany in 1800, for the Ireland of Yeats and Synge, the creation of a theatrical repertoire was essential; the very existence of the (future) nation depended on the creation of a 'national' theatre. The authors discussed by Annie Brisset give this same central role to the theatrical repertoire.

But a community's being-in-the-world is just as much its being with other communities as its being with itself; the creation of a repertoire raises *ipso facto* the question of coexistence of 'native' elements and 'foreign' elements within the community, just as it raises the question of coexistence of new and old elements, translations, adaptations, and quotations. At present (1990), for example, the theatre in France is in the process of renewing its repertoire. At stake in this renewal is nothing less than the relation of our culture to oralcy, to tradition, and to the literal.

Theatre translation in Quebec (which is also attempting to create a repertoire) is guided by the principle of resistance to the Foreigner, as we mentioned earlier. This resistance is further accentuated by the fact that, as a genre, theatre translation traditionally employs adaptation. The theatre translations discussed in this book create a repertoire through annexation of certain foreign works considered suitable for heightening Québécois 'self-awareness.' At the same time, something that, strictly speaking, does not yet exist will be created: a Québécois *koine.* In this context, 'to translate' is to adapt original texts so that they can be absorbed into the Québécois repertoire, and a Québécois language created.

This type of translation is totally foreign to the discourse on 'the relation to the Other' in France, for example. In Quebec, the Foreigner, whose various representations Annie Brisset describes systematically, is the negative image against which one can define one's own identity. If the Québécois repertoire is to be created through absorption of foreign works (and no repertoire can be purely local), it will do so by removing all trace of their origin, of their *alterity*! As a result, theatre translation is returning (without apparently being aware of it) to the very practices of classical *French* translation, to an ethnocentric translation that adapts and naturalizes. The *irony* here (and indeed, it is ironic) is that the culture that is annexing and distorting is not the powerful and authoritarian culture of the Grand Siècle, but a culture that sees itself as dominated and oppressed, a culture that, moreover, rejects classical French culture. However, the creation of a *national* repertoire, although it may imply some form of linguistic naturalization of foreign works, does not necessarily require an ethnocentric mode of translation. A.W. Schlegel's translation of Shakespeare is certainly a *Verdeutschung,* a Germanization, and in this sense an annexation, but in no way is it an 'acculturating transformation' of the English playwright.

This leads us quite naturally to Michel Garneau's translation of *Macbeth* into 'Québécois.' Of all the 'translations' analysed by Annie Brisset, this is the only one that has its own poetics and its own significance as a translation. We note that Annie Brisset describes it as being 'equally powerful but different' from the original (p. 159). We may well ask why Garneau's *Macbeth* is 'equally powerful' as Shakespeare's. It would not occur to anybody to claim that the translations of *Macbeth* by Leyris and Bonnefoy (two distinguished translators whose work is as faithful as Garneau's) are equally powerful as the original.

In her rigorously clear analysis, particularly in the chapters devoted to *A Canadian Play ...* and to the 'native' language, which constitute the heart of the book, Annie Brisset reveals 'the textual and discursive ensemble of which the translation will become a part' (p. 158). But her analysis does more than simply show how the *system* of transformations introduced by Garneau produces a *Macbeth* capable of reaching the Québécois public (of awaking its 'self-awareness'). In addition to showing how the Québécois *Macbeth* conforms to a certain 'doxa,' the author demonstrates *why* Garneau's translation is a genuine translation, and not just an ethnocentric adaptation.

Annie Brisset devotes considerable space to a comparison of 'the images in this Shakespearian elegy' and 'those of Québécois poetry in the 1960s and 1970s.' She shows that they 'correspond word for word, ... as if they were literal translations of each other' (p. 149). Such perfect correspondence is rather surprising. This does not, however, mean that Garneau 'utilized' Québécois poetic imagery of the period to translate Shakespeare. Rather, he worked within *the same poetic space*, which is not the same thing. The adequacy of poetic vision in the translation is, paradoxically, what makes the work ring *true*. A translation derives its truth from a broad context. The *truth* of a translation does not lie, as is too often believed, in an *exact* rendering of the original, but in its *self-consistency*, which ensures, not faithfulness, but *correspondence* to the original. A translation becomes 'self-consistent' only by becoming a 'text' (or a 'work'), and this can happen only if the translation is based on the contemporary literary or poetic state of the language.

Garneau produced a 'true' translation by working within Québécois poetic space. Yet, his translation is highly original. While it remains within Québécois poetic space, it is, nevertheless, written in a language that is neither French nor contemporary Québécois. The language of Garneau's translation is an approximation of the 'native language' sought by Gaston Miron. Garneau's Québécois is not a dialect. He has not translated *Macbeth* into 'Québécois dialect' in the way one might translate a work into Berrichon dialect, for example. Rather, he has translated it into a *dialectalized* French. At its best, this dialectalized French gives the impression of being *closer* to Shakespearian English than the poetic French of Leyris or Bonnefoy. Why?

I remember reading an extract from Garneau's translation in *Le*

Monde, in 1986. The author of the article poked fun at Garneau's experiment. I, myself, found it amusing at the time, but eventually my laughter gave way to perplexed silence, as I began to sense that this translation had achieved something quite distinct. But what exactly? The amused reaction that greeted the Québécois *Macbeth* is somewhat reminiscent of Schiller's response when Voss read to him, in Goethe's presence, Hölderlin's *Antigone*. According to an eyewitness, Schiller 'roared with laughter' while Goethe remained silent. A memorable event. But how does this relate to Garneau? There is at least one connection between the two translations – a certain use of the dialectal, a use rarely found in translations. Usually, translation involves two dedialectalized languages; it might even be said that translation is a powerful anti-dialectal agent. Moreover, as Annie Brisset points out, the ideological objective of translators translating foreign writers into 'Québécois' is to dedialectalize Québécois and to turn it into a language. One gets the impression that Garneau was attempting *to exploit the poetic power of the dialectal and to ensure that the dialectal nature of the language was maintained*. Thus, it could be said that his translation goes beyond the ideological context which produced it. We may well ask, however, what characteristic of Garneau's Québécois could suggest a closeness to Shakespearian language, which is not itself dialectal? One possible explanation is that the raw oralcy of the dialectal in Garneau's play corresponds directly to what Rudolf Pannwitz called the 'barbarity' of Shakespearian verse, or more accurately, its 'majestic barbarity.' Obviously, Garneau's language does not render the characteristic 'majesty' of Shakespeare's English, which is based on a certain 'royal principle.' But what it does capture is the immanent 'barbarity' of Shakespeare's English, 'barbarity' meaning here the brutal immediacy of the language. This is perhaps the 'épreuve de l'Etranger' (the experience of the Foreign) that is realized in Garneau's work. He has given the language of 'La Belle Province' the *power* to match the language of the 'enemy' (as in a tennis match, when two players of equal skill 'respond' to each other).

We will now briefly consider the epistemological dimension of Annie Brisset's work, since it is, in its own way, an *epistemological treatise on translation*. The author clearly shares the principal tenets of the so-called Tel Aviv School and uses 'polysystem theory' as a point of departure, but she extends its framework of analysis:

Translation, like any writing, reflects the institutional norms of a given society ...

Thus, translation theory should concern itself as much, if not more, with contrastive analysis of *social discourses* as with contrastive linguistics or comparative stylistics. (p. 158; emphasis added)

Through careful analysis and the use of an extremely refined conceptual apparatus, the author removes any trace of the formal and mechanistic from 'polysystem' theory. Thus, her work becomes, in itself, a *sociocritique* of translation, 'sociocritique' meaning, in this case, sociology *and* criticism. This book is, in effect, a work of sociology, in so far as translation practices and their end-products are viewed in their 'social' context. But to reveal the 'doxical' forces that make theatre translation in Quebec *what it is*, Annie Brisset makes use of *criticism*, in this case, criticism as defined by the Frankfurt School. Her sociological, discursive, and semiotic analysis is also a *denunciation* of the 'closing in' of a whole culture at a certain historical period. Annie Brisset does not indulge in abstract, 'prescriptive' criticism; her aim is to shed light on the ideological basis of translation. To be sure, the very nature of any sociocritique that is not totally positivist is to be critical, as we see in the writings of sociologists such as Bourdieu and Touraine. Brisset does not base her criticism on the reverse 'ideologeme,' which in this case would be the correct relation to the Foreigner (dialogue, openness, etc.). But, surely, to speak of 'isolation,' 'exclusion,' and 'narcissism' is to employ categories that are just as *ethical* as they are *sociological.*

If sociocritical discourse is, in its way, 'demystifying,' how is it *radically* different from what has been termed, in recent times, the *ethical discourse* on translation? In a brief note, Annie Brisset outlines her opposition to Meschonnic's analysis. With respect to Meschonnic's criticism of Vialatte's translations of Kafka, she writes:

This type of analysis, which is purely normative, fails to take into account the various institutional constraints that influenced Vialatte's translation. (Ch. III, note 51)

What Annie Brisset is objecting to here is the type of *direct* criticism of translations that fails to take account of the context that determines them and makes them 'what they are.' We agree that ethical discourse on translation rarely provides a detailed, systematic analysis of this context. This may well be a flaw, in some instances.[1] But ethical discourse is not based so much on an abstract concept of translation as on the way in which not only translation but also language, literature, and culture *necessarily appear to us* today. If translation is viewed as being 'ethical' (even if the word itself is inadequate, and does not correspond in any way to 'moral'), it is not *we* who have termed it such but, literally, the passage of history, and its *imperative*. Sociocriticism encounters the *same* imperative when it denounces, however soberly, the relation to the Foreigner, the driving force of ethnocentric Québécois translations. But the imperative of history will have its way, and residual ideologies of isolation and annexation are powerless in its wake.

The success of Annie Brisset's book lies in the fact that she has been able to combine ethical analysis, poetic analysis, sociological analysis, and historical analysis within a seemingly purely factual work. It is to be hoped that Québécois readers will seize, as they should, the opportunity to look into the translucent mirror that is being held up to them.

ANTOINE BERMAN
Paris, July 1990

Acknowledgments

This book is dedicated to the memory of André Belleau, a committed Bakhtinian scholar, in fond remembrance of our fascinating exchanges on the Québécois experience of the Other. My research owes much to him.

I should like to express my deep gratitude to Professor Bernard Andrès, of the Département d'Études Littéraires, Université du Québec à Montréal, who gave so freely of his time and provided such thoughtful advice. My exchanges with this specialist in Québécois literary institutions, particularly the theatre, were most illuminating. I should also like to thank Régine Robin, and Jean Delisle, José Lambert, Jean-Marcel Paquet, and the late Antoine Berman, who, each in his or her own way, provided the inspiration for this work and were the first to read it.

Establishing the programs of the main theatres in Quebec over twenty years was not an easy task. My research frequently ran up against a lack of archival material and information on the origins of foreign plays or their translators. I am thus very grateful to those who helped me put together the pieces of the puzzle. I would like to thank especially Josette Féral, of the Département de Théâtre, Université du Québec à Montréal, who allowed me to make use of her research; Monique Forest, of the National Theatre School library; Pierre Lavoie, former director of the theatre library at the Université de Montréal and editor of the journal *Jeu*; and Daniel Gauthier and Danielle Bergeron, of the Centre d'Essai des Auteurs Dramatiques.

Special thanks go to the many people in various theatres who so kindly answered my queries: Dominique Racine, of Le Théâtre d'Aujourd'hui; Ginette Leroux, of La Compagnie Jean-Duceppe; Carole Hamelin, of La Nouvelle Compagnie Théâtrale; Lison Poulin, of Le Théâtre de

Quat'Sous; Francette Sorignet, of Le Théâtre du Rideau-Vert; Christian Beaulieu, of Le Théâtre du Nouveau Monde; and France Pelletier, of Le Théâtre du Trident.

I am also very grateful to those actors and directors who graciously provided me with information not available in the archives: Louison Danis, Danièle Suissa, Paul Buissonneau, André Brassard, Guillermo de Andrea, Paul Hébert, Albert Millaire, Olivier Reichenbach, Jean-Louis Roux, Jacques Thisdale, and the late Yvette Brind'Amour and Jean Gascon.

Finally, the book owes much to the kind encouragement of Mr Gómez-Moriana, co-director of the Collection L'Univers des Discours, the series in which this book was originally published in French.

ANNIE BRISSET
1989

A SOCIOCRITIQUE OF TRANSLATION

Introduction

How should one translate? Writings on translation, by their very nature, revolve around this question and inevitably give rise to dogmatic but contradictory rules. Ironically, these rules often conflict with the very procedures used by translators.[1] We must therefore phrase the question differently. The nature of a text, be it literary or 'pragmatic,' to use Jean Delisle's distinction,[2] does not entirely govern the choice of translation procedure; translation is a discursive act and, as such, it is fundamentally bound to the time and place of its realization. This time-worn truism becomes a little less banal if we interpret it to mean that translation is subject to 'the order of discourse' of the target society. Michel Foucault defines discourse as 'a body of anonymous, historical rules, always determined in time and space, that have defined for a given period, and for a given social, economic, geographical or linguistic area, the conditions of operation of the enunciative function.'[3] The question with which we began can thus be rephrased as follows: *what are the conditions of operation for the translative function in a given society at a given time?* When viewed as a form of discourse, the act of translation must be 'defined by the conditions under which it is produced.'[4] According to Régine Robin, Foucault's conditions involve not only 'a simple context and "circumstances" which in turn produce simple constraints on the discourse'; they also involve everything that constitutes and structures discourse: 'the institutional setting, the ideological framework and other underlying factors such as the political situation, the forces at play or the desired strategic effects.'[5]

When theorists like Itamar Even-Zohar and Gideon Toury[6] began analysing the role of foreign works in a given literature, translation theory took a step forward and freed itself from the prescriptive contradictions in which it had been mired. Their functionalist hypothesis does, however, have its limitations, in so far as it deals only with the *literary* function of translated works; but if we begin with the principle that literature is itself a *discursive practice*, and that it is also *a representation of other discourses*,[7] we can broaden the hypothesis. Thus, rather than focusing solely on a study of the literary function of translated works in the target milieu, we shall examine *how and under what conditions the 'discourse' of the foreign text becomes an integral part of the 'discourse' of the target society*. Phrased in this way, our previous question can be applied to any type of text, literary or pragmatic. In the present study, we remain within the literary genre, but we focus on the *discursive* nature of the dramatic text.

If we broaden functionalist theory, we can say that, in a given society at a given time in its history, literature in translation constitutes *a discursive formation, rule-governed like any other discourse*. To gain entry into the target social discourse, the translated text must be subject to the same institutional constraints as the original literature of the target milieu. These discursive constraints have a bearing on which foreign texts are selected for translation and on the changes these texts undergo before they can enter a new literary system and become accepted and consumed as fully fledged literary works in a new sociocultural environment. Literature in translation, like the literature of the target milieu, is shaped by the 'organizing function' of the institutional apparatus and the 'regulating function' of discursive norms, functions which, according to André Belleau, are characteristic of literary institutions.[8] This apparatus forms the visible 'material basis' of the literary institution. In the theatre, it includes such things as production houses, programming, directors, set designers, actors, publishers, critics, awards and distinctions, and teaching programs. Discursive norms are not as easily identified. They are best defined as the implicit rules to which the production and reception of the text are subject.[9]

No matter what equivalencies the source text may potentially impose, a translation is constrained by the language, literature, and *discourse* of the target society; it is shaped by what Meschonnic calls 'le possible d'une époque' (time-bound acceptability), thereby underlining the fact that translation is inherently bound to history.[10]

A foreign text, like a foreigner who settles in a new country, is 'naturalized' by the translation that introduces it into the new society. Through translation, the work undergoes many and varied changes, and these changes have to be such that the work becomes *acceptable*, that is to say, follows the set of codes that govern, to various degrees, the discourse of the target society. 'The act of writing,' according to André Belleau, 'involves not only a selection of words and utterances but also, and perhaps above all, a choice of codes.'[11] 'Code' should be understood to mean 'that which in a message (or in a text) is identified as a function of choice, an imposition of constraints of various kinds at various levels.'[12] Each discourse type draws its specificity from the set of codes that govern it – linguistic, social, cultural, and ideological codes – to which must be added, in the case of dramatic art and as a function of the genre, actantial, narrative, dialogic, stage-direction, and set-design codes. A successful translation – in other words, a translation that has managed to gain entry into the target institution – cannot but be subject to these codes. Like any piece of writing, a translation employs selected strategies. But translation differs from writing in that the selection is doubly constrained. Translation involves a number of choices. These are activated (and limited) as much by the reading or decoding of the original text as they are by what is available in the discourse of the target milieu – in other words, by what the target society *permits* the translator to write. Translation establishes its priorities between the given of the source text and the pragmatics of the target milieu, constraints from which it cannot escape. In a given society, these priorities constitute a system, and they can be identified, both individually and as part of the system, by comparing the target text with the source text. However, to reveal this systematic regularity of translation choice, the comparison must be extended to a whole body of texts belonging to a single discourse category. The present study focuses on the dramatic text. Theatre grows directly out of a society, its collective imagination and symbolic representations, and its system of ideas and values: 'The theatre, a social art, addresses a group in a particular place, at a particular time. Other literary genres are interpreted by individuals, at their own pace and in their own manner, but the theatre must stay close to the collectivity.'[13] Dramatic dialogue is thus closely linked to societal discourse, especially when, as is the case in Quebec during the period under discussion, the theatre is in a realist phase and forms part of a collectivity that is actively searching for its own identity.

Translated literature can be seen as a replication of pre-existing texts, and, as such, it provides a privileged point of observation. A comparison of translations with the original texts will reveal what adjustments have been made by the translator.[14] Discursive norms are usually concealed by the original literary text, which abstracts them from 'the immediate social milieu' and internalizes them. These norms can, therefore, be revealed only 'through negation or differentiation, that is to say, through obstacles, tensions, and contradictions, the unstated and the overstated, all those factors which govern the realization of codes activated by the "reading pact."[15] Translation is, *par excellence,* a process fraught with obstacles and tensions. By its very nature, it creates difference.[16] It thus provides a privileged observation point for research into discursive phenomena and their institutional basis. The norms of social discourse, which is the raw material of literature, are discernible in *displacements* made to works in translation. It is the very frequency, systematicness, and statistical nature of these norms that make them observable. Analysis of the regularity of certain translation choices will reveal the constituent elements – in particular, the discursive make-up – of the target literary institution. The norms that govern translation strategies intervene before, as well as during, transfer. They do so to varying degrees, but they are largely determined by the function that the texts to be translated must play in the target-literature polysystem, that is to say, by the place assigned them by the institution. It follows, then, that the translation norms governing the transfer of foreign texts correspond to the institutional norms which determine the configuration of the target literature and which also ensure that these texts, rather than others, are imported.

The act of translation functions institutionally in the same way as the act of writing: 'the writing subject transports, transposes, and transforms within his own literature, within a new textual body in the process of formation, elements already encoded in and by a multitude of other discourses.'[17] Translation theory, particularly the theory of so-called pragmatic texts, has traditionally ignored, and even denied, the link between literature and other discursive forms. It can even be said that it has attempted to keep the two apart by demonstrating that literature is essentially different – subjective, individualistic, solipsistic, floating above history and society.[18] Literary theorists view the issue differently: 'the writer's basic material is the language of society. It is provided in a form which is now commonly referred to as social discourse.'[19] Bakhtin points out that 'the organising centre of any utterance, of any experience, is not within, but outside: in the social milieu surrounding the individual being.'[20] Translation is a re-enunciation mediated by a subject. As an utterance, translation cannot detach itself from the discourse of the specific society in which it is realized. Social discourse, which is formed from the many utterances produced in a society, is subject to, among other things, 'ideological configurations.'[21] These configurations organize 'l'opinable' (what can be said) in a given society, from a given perspective. They fuse the diverse discursive formations such as literature, journalism, law, medicine, science, and technology.[22] Translation, which replicates these discursive formations, is no less subject to these configurations.

The present study will focus on the ideological regulation of translation processes in a given society. By 'ideology' we mean 'the system – more or less organized – of knowledge, images, and "values" that enable a collectivity or an individual to organize in an acceptable whole the diversity of their experience.'[23] For François Châtelet, ideology, in this sense, corresponds to a view of the world, that is to say, to a conception of 'relations of the "subjects" (of the ideology) with nature, with others, with their imaginary (sacred or profane), or with themselves.'[24] These relations are realized by 'ideologemes.' Marc Angenot defines the 'ideologeme' as a presupposition of discourse, a shared postulate, a common ground, or an ideological maxim 'underlying an utterance, whose subject-matter covers a particular field of relevance (be it "moral value," "the Jew," "the mission of France," or "the maternal instinct").'[25] For Angenot, 'ideologemes function, like Aristotelian *topoi*, as regulating principles underlying the social discourse to which they impart authority and coherence.'[26] Here, Angenot is developing Michel Foucault's thesis that the unity of discourse 'does not lie in the visible, horizontal coherence of the elements formed; it resides well anterior to their formation, in the system that makes possible and governs that formation.'[27] The ideological presupposition, 'common to interlocutors, whatever their outward differences,' is not necessarily visible on the surface: 'the presupposition is always a given, it is an active component but is absent from the discourse itself, because it requires no demonstration.'[28] In the present study, we will see how translation of foreign texts is dominated by the discourse on identity, within a field of relevance referring to 'Quebec.'

The translating subject is a collective being, a spokesperson for a society that has created its own system of representations or what is known as 'the imaginary':

All imaginary is imagination, not only of something but for something. Ideological discourse, general translation of a dissatisfaction itself general, expresses in its content the nature of this dissatisfaction. The system of representation indicates, by its very omissions, the source of its dissatisfaction.[29]

Québécois society of the late 1960s, at the end of the Quiet Revolution, provides a good illustration of this definition of the imaginary. In the discourse of this society, independence is 'the projection' of a sociopolitical ideal 'onto a longed-for paradise.' The discourse of independence is a discourse of compensation. It compensates for the ethno-linguistic inferiority of Quebec within the Canadian federation. Underlying this discourse is an ideologeme that on the surface can be expressed as 'Vive le Québec libre' (Long Live a Free Quebec). Moreover, the backdrop to this discourse is a symbolic narrative in which we find the same actors, the colonizer and the colonized, locked in an antagonistic relationship. Alterity is defined in terms of this relationship. Otherness is negative and threatening; it symbolizes the assimilation of the Québécois collectivity, the inevitability of its dilution in a 'sea of anglophones.' At the time of the Quiet Revolution, the renewal of national consciousness found its voice in the search for identity. Imperceptibly, the Quiet Revolution ushered in the change from *French Canada* to *Quebec*, 'the one corner of the earth where we can be completely ourselves,' in other words, the change to a sovereign Quebec.[30] The assertion of '*québécité*,' awareness of Québécois distinctiveness or 'difference,' has its negative side, '*québécitude*,' or victimization by the Other, and such a status could be abolished only if the territory and the group inhabiting it gained sovereignty. But the resurgence of the nationalist ideal at the end of the 1960s gave rise to a new configuration of alterity. It would no longer be just the English, the conquerors, the victimizers, who would be used to validate the search for an identity. From now on there would also be the French and the immigrant. Both these groups were now identified as the Foreigner against whom the Québécois identity asserted itself. Now that 'allophones' or 'ethnics' had swelled the ranks of the Foreigner, it was no longer sufficient to struggle against Anglo-Canadian hegemony. The time had come to break with the cultural and linguistic legacy of France, a remnant of colonial times that prevented *homo quebecensis* from flourishing. Similarly, the time had come to get rid of the duality of the literary institution where 'although the Apparatus is Québécois, the Norm is still French.'[31] Elimination of this duality was to be more visible in the theatre than in other genres. Moreover, in Quebec, the theatre, of all the genres, makes the most frequent use of works in translation.[32] We will thus use theatre translation to examine the new Norm, the Québécois Norm. What are the rules governing translation strategies? Under what conditions does a foreign play gain entry into the discourse of Québécois society? What are the literary and doxological parameters of its discursive acceptability? Such are the questions that the present work will attempt to answer.

In Quebec, 1968 was a pivotal year. Politically, 1968 saw the founding of the Parti Québécois, with its distinctive independence option. In literature, the same year witnessed the birth of a type of drama that also described itself as being 'Québécois,' to indicate its difference from the 'French Canadian' drama that had preceded it. This new drama, whose emergence coincided with the staging of Michel Tremblay's *Les Belles-Soeurs* at Le Théâtre du Rideau-Vert, distinguished itself by its use of a realist aesthetic based, in large part, on a rejection of the 'French of France,' which until then had been the language of literature. The use of the realist aesthetic brought *joual*, the vernacular French spoken in Quebec, to the fore. The year 1968 also saw the first use of a Québécois sociolect as a language of translation, with Éloi de Grandmont's translation into *joual* of the cockney dialogue in *Pygmalion*.

The present study begins with this pivotal year and covers the next two decades. The period was punctuated by a series of events which stand out in the history of the struggle for independence in Quebec: the election in 1970 of the Parti Québécois to the National Assembly, followed in the same year by the October Crisis (an uprising by the FLQ [Quebec Liberation Front]; the rise to power of the Parti Québécois in 1976 and its re-election in 1981; the 1980 referendum; the repatriation in 1982 of the Canadian constitution from Britain without ratification by Quebec; the defeat of the Parti Québécois in 1985; and the federal government's attempt in 1987 to bring Quebec into the constitution through the Meech Lake Accord, which would finally be rejected in 1990 by two anglophone provinces. These events became part of the social discourse, and this discourse was echoed by the theatre.[33] Our research focuses specifically on the *discursive* elements of dramatic texts, rather than on their production. Since little evidence remains of actual productions, such analysis would be problematic and would have to be based on a different type of semiology. Accordingly, the present study is restricted to interlingual translation of the text proper. However, stage directions are treated as a paratextual element and are included in the analysis, along with forewords and afterwords.

Our study is based on a double corpus. We examine theatre translations published in Quebec between 1968 and 1988. However, during this period, barely fifteen such translations were published, and that number is based on a generous interpretation of the term 'translation.' Accordingly, we expanded our corpus to include the programs of the major theatres in Quebec during the same period. Out of a total of more than 700 productions, approximately 250 were translations. The major source language was English, followed at a considerable remove by Italian, and then by a sprinkling of translations from German, Russian, and Spanish. The change in the number of Québécois and foreign plays produced in Quebec, as well as the change in the number of French translations and Québécois translations produced, reveals a great deal about the relation to the Foreigner throughout the period under discussion. Who is the Other? How is the Other portrayed? This relation to the Other was expressed in three modes of translation: iconoclastic translation, perlocutory translation, and identity-forming translation.

Iconoclastic translation is situated at the juncture between creation and translation proper. This ambiguity stems from the fact that this translative operation breaks up the structure of the source text, and uses fragments of it to produce a different work. But it still retains too much of the original to be considered a new work in its own right. Iconoclastic translations assume the form of adaptation, imitation, and parody: *Le Gars de Québec* is an imitation of Gogol's *The Government Inspector*; *Le Bourgeois Gentleman* admires an Englishman rather than Molière's Grand Turc; *Le Cid* is just a found object, 'maghané' (battered) to produce a sort of *Rodriguemachine*; the gloomy wit of the *petits bourgeois* in Brecht's *A Respectable Wedding* becomes kitsch in translation; and Hamlet monologues like a 'Prince of Quebec.'

Perlocutory translation is a form of propaganda: 'Propaganda is an active form of ideology; similarly, dramatic texts and their production are media in which ideology can be perceived by the general public and the critical reader.'[34] Analysis of translation strategies can provide a revealing picture of the ideological forces at play in a given society. Our case-study of Michel Garneau's translation of *Macbeth* shows, for example, how his choice of translation strategies reflects the ideology of the committed writing that typifies Québécois poetry of the 1960s and 1970s.

The basic material of any translation is language. However, in Quebec, the target language is far from being a given, at least as far as theatre translation is concerned. With the emergence of the new Québécois theatre, the vernacular language acquired the status of a literary language and replaced the 'French of France.' How was translation going to adjust, or even contribute to the rejection of the old identity? The final chapter of the book takes up this question.

While it may be possible to analyse the new Norm in the Québécois theatre in terms of these three translation modes, we should make it clear from the outset that the aim of the present work is not to analyse theatre translation as a field in itself, nor even the institution of Québécois theatre; rather, our aim is to analyse the *relation between translation and social discourse* in a field which happens to be that of the theatre in Quebec.

1

The Foreigner in the Theatrical Institution

Accused of not being a genuine national writer because his writings lacked local colour, Borges replied that one would search in vain for a camel in the Koran.

We propose here to examine the status of the Foreigner in the major areas of the theatre: the dramatic text and the stage. Our study will focus on institutional practices such as the publication of dramatic works in translation and the production of foreign plays by theatre companies. The decision to publish or stage one foreign play rather than another is an arbitrary one. Yet, together, such decisions constitute a system:

> The literary act, said to be individual and unique, suddenly becomes part of collective phenomena. We become aware of a process of exchange – symbolic exchange, material exchange – that must be located in the social structure, while taking into account forms of stratification and separateness that the structure implies, constraints that it presupposes.[1]

Our analysis will attempt to reveal how these diverse constraints function. First, we will examine how the publication apparatus creates an image of the Foreigner. To that end, our study will include the paratext, that is, texts that are published along with the actual translation of a play – prefaces, biographical notes, and reviews – and illustrations, all of which are another semiotic form of textuality. We will then examine the repertoire of the major Quebec theatres. Our analysis will show how the relation to the Foreigner crystallized during the period under examination. We will also determine to what extent this process paralleled the discourse on the Québécois identity, a discourse which, in turn, ushered in the major political events of the time – the October Crisis of 1970, the rise to power of the Parti Québécois, and the referendum on independence.

The Image of the Foreigner in Published Translations

Plays in translation represent a very small percentage of publications in Quebec. It took considerable effort to come up with fifteen foreign plays in publishers' catalogues and, even then, we had to broaden our definition to include Anglo-Canadian works and all types of adaptation, from re-actualization to imitation. Categorizing such translations is a difficult and risky task. Translation, in our corpus, does not necessarily imply translation of a whole work. It may imply translation of only certain parts; other parts will vanish or undergo various types of alteration. Among the different types of 'adaptation,' a term that often includes translation, we will distinguish between re-actualization and imitation.[2]

Re-actualization entails the spatial, and sometimes temporal, transposition of a foreign play. The degree of transformation varies, depending on whether the scene of the action, the name and function of the characters, or even the dramatic situation itself – which can be replaced by a situation considered equivalent in the new context of the target culture – is changed completely or partially. In theory, re-actualization preserves the structure of the work, its content, and the sequence of the dialogue. For example, Robert Lalonde's Québécois translation of Chekhov's *Three Sisters* preserves the structure of the original play – three Côté sisters living in Abitibi in the 1950s are dying of boredom; they dream of one thing, moving to Montreal, which at the time was a safer place than Stalin's Moscow!

Imitation is a radical form of adaptation, the equivalent of what is called a 'remake' in the cinema. This type of rewriting also adapts the play to the new context in which it is produced, and presupposes that selected elements from the original will be rearranged and combined with new elements. This reconstruction with borrowed materials produces, none the less, a new work in its own right. Michel Tremblay's *Le gars de Québec* follows the plot of Gogol's *The Government Inspector*, Antonine Maillet's *Le Bourgeois Gentleman* imitates Molière's comedy, and Jean-Pierre Ronfard's *La Mandragore* is inspired by Machiavelli's play of the same name. In these three Québécois imitations, the original work survives only as an intertext.

Between 1968 and 1988, about fifteen translations of plays, including different types of adaptation, were published in Quebec – a small number over a period of twenty years, considering that, during the same period, the major theatre companies alone mounted more than seven hundred theatrical productions. If to this figure we add productions by experimental theatre, regional theatre, touring theatre, and children's theatre, and exclude amateur theatre, the number of productions rises to well over a thousand. By comparison, the number of foreign plays translated *and* published in Quebec is negligible. Plays in translation, by their very nature, lend themselves to reinterpretation with each new production. Their life expectancy tends, thus, to be shorter than those of translations of novels or poetry. Moreover, an audience prefers to experience a play *live*, rather than read it. A published play is therefore likely to be less lucrative than other literary genres, for which the printed word remains the sole outlet. Given the small number of translations of foreign plays published in Quebec, we may well ask why particular plays were canonized in this way. Which authors and which texts were selected? Which translations were published? How were these translations introduced to the reader? Answers to these questions should throw light on how foreign works are selected and validated in the Quebec theatre.

The Need for Adaptation

The small number of translations published in Quebec gives the impression that Québécois theatre is inward-looking and isolationist. However, a number of factors suggest that this is not entirely the case. The major French publishing houses exercise considerable control over the already limited market for literature in Quebec. French publishers are often granted exclusive rights, and this limits the number of foreign works that Québécois publishers can publish. For example, Les Éditions de l'Arche in Paris holds all the translation rights for Brecht, which precludes Québécois publication of works such as Gilbert Turp's translation of *Mutter Courage* or *Der guter Mensch von Sezuan*. For similar legal reasons, involving authors' rights, several translations by Michel Tremblay, notably that of Dario Fo's *Mistero buffo*, remain unpublished. It is possible for publishers in Quebec to acquire translation rights, but often, when the opportunity does arise, they cannot afford it, hard-pressed as they are to compete with the powerful French publishing houses. We should not lose sight of these financial realities, as they determine, in part, which foreign works are translated and published in Quebec, and perpetuate a certain cultural dependence on France, the traditional source of translations for Quebec. French theatre, like Québécois theatre, is protectionist. In France, translation of foreign works is subject to the same constraints as the dubbing of foreign films, which must be done in France before they can be shown. Similarly, in the theatre, only translations produced in France can be staged. As a result of this protectionism, Québécois translations have no access to the French market. René Dionne, one of the most prolific translators for the theatre, describes the situation as follows:

> When a play already translated in France is translated here, we are forced to split the fee with the French adapter. It is impossible to publish our translations in France, impossible to sell adaptations of American or South American works.[3]

The fact that this market is closed to Québécois publishers largely explains why so few foreign plays are published in Quebec and, consequently, why only a few publishing houses operate in this highly specialized area. Aside from a few works occasionally made available by publishers such as VLB, theatre translation is a quasi-monopoly of Les Éditions Leméac, which has introduced a series entitled 'Traduction et adaptation' (Translation and Adaptation). During the period under discussion, this was the only drama series of its type to be published in Quebec. Approximately ten titles appeared during the period. Below we reproduce the list that appeared on the back cover of each new publication of a translation, each time with appropriate additions. To give a clear picture of chronology and publication intervals, we provide dates of publication, in parentheses:

(1970) 1. Paul Zindel, *L'Effet des rayons gamma sur les vieux-garçons* [*The Effect of Gamma Rays on Man-in-the-Moon Marigolds*], traduction et adaptation de Michel Tremblay;
(1971) 2. John Herbert, *Aux yeux des hommes* [*Fortune and Men's Eyes*], traduction et adaptation de René Dionne;
(1971) 3. Paul Zindel, ... *Et Mademoiselle Roberge boit un peu* [*And Miss Reardon Drinks a Little*], traduction et adaptation de Michel Tremblay;
(1974) 4. John T. McDonough, *Charbonneau et le Chef*, traduction et adaptation de Paul Hébert et Pierre Morency;
(1974) 5. Mordecai Richler, *Les Cloches d'enfer* [*The Bells of Hell*], traduction et adaptation de Gilles Rochette;
(1975) 6. Roberto Athayde, *Mademoiselle Marguerite* [*Miss Margarida's Way*], traduction et adaptation de Michel Tremblay;
(1976) 7. Peter Shaffer, *Equus*, adaptation québécoise de Jean-Louis Roux;

(1976) 8. Victor Lanoux, *L'Ouvre-boîte* [*Le Tourniquet*], adapté et interprété par Yvon Deschamps et Jean-Louis Roux;
(1981) 9. Bernard Slade, *Chapeau* [*Tribute*], traduction de Luis de Céspedes;
(1983) 10. Anton Chekhov, *Oncle Vania*, traduction de Michel Tremblay, avec la collaboration de Kim Yaroshevskaya;
(1985) 11. Michel Tremblay, *Le Gars de Québec*, d'après *Le Revizor* de Gogol [*The Government Inspector*].

One would expect a foreign series[4] to carry a title referring to the outside world, to a *world to be discovered*. We are reminded, for example, of series such as 'Du monde entier' (From All Over the World), published by Gallimard, and 'Cosmopolite' (Cosmopolitan), published by Stock. In contrast to these exocentric titles, the title 'Traduction et adaptation' proclaims a Québécois reterritorialization of foreign works. Morever, inclusion of these two terms in a single title presupposes that the two operations overlap. The linking of the two items also *validates free translation*. In other words, the target milieu *would expect* a translation to be a naturalization. The ethnocentrism implicit in the term 'adaptation' can be seen as an inherent principle of transformation, a principle that must take precedence over the integrity of a work brought in from outside. Thus, for the institution, the value of the foreign work becomes a functional one, and elimination of its alterity becomes the primary condition of its acceptance into the theatrical system that will absorb it. We will now examine the function of the foreign text in this system.

According to the publisher's list cited above, eleven plays were brought into the repertoire; of these, as the descriptions in the list would suggest, only two are translations, the remainder being adaptations. The number of adaptations clearly indicates that publishers accord a truly ambiguous status to imported works. The foreign work is 'summoned' into the Québécois theatre system, but once there, its alterity is immediately expunged. When a foreign play is selected, a rare event, it is chosen less for the play itself and more as a vehicle for the emerging national theatre. This must be the case; otherwise, why are foreign plays almost always adapted or imitated? The local production absorbs the foreign play, which, cut off from its origins, is now added to the list of Québécois plays, thereby increasing the institutional stature of the emerging Québécois theatre. At the beginning of the period under review, foreign works were accorded greater exchange value than local works and the former dominated the field that was to be reserved, henceforth, for authentic, Québécois productions. The institutional primacy accorded foreign plays returns again and again as a leitmotif in studies of Quebec theatre. Angèle Dagenais was asked by the Institut Québécois de Recherche sur la Culture to do a 'diagnostic' (a revealing term in itself) study of the theatre in Quebec.[5] In her study, she describes the situation of the theatre in terms of the struggle for market share: on its own territory, Québécois theatre is forced to compete with foreign plays; underlying this analysis is the presupposition that foreign competition is, by its very nature, illegitimate and a threat to theatrical production in Quebec. In her assessment of the respective institutional roles played by the two repertoires, Dagenais begins by emphasizing the 'bias' or predilection of the major companies 'in favour of foreign plays.'[6] She adds that the institutional theatre, represented by these major companies, 'is more or less engaged in a truly *Québécois* endeavour, but these companies are not *all* open to Québécois plays and to creative thought in Quebec.'[7] In her analysis of the situation, she denounces the guilty parties:

The major companies produce mostly foreign plays – classical or contemporary, European or American – and if they had no moral obligation to include Québécois works in their programming, so as to become eligible for public funding, a number of them would probably not produce any today.[8]

Whereas theatre companies supposedly had to be forced to use Québécois material, it would appear that the publishing industry was a primary promoter of Québécois theatre. As part of its 'Théâtre canadien' series, in 1969, Les Éditions Leméac introduced a collection entitled 'Répertoire québécois.' Curiously, the second title in the new series was *Lysistrata*, an adaptation of Aristophanes' play by André Brassard and Michel Tremblay. It was also the first time a foreign work had been listed in the Québécois repertoire, but we should remember that this repertoire existed only in embryonic form in 1969. Thus, the dividing line between a Québécois work and a foreign work was not well defined. And for that matter, neither was the line between 'canadien' theatre and 'québécois' theatre. Works by writers such as Dubé or Tremblay could be listed as either 'québécois' or 'canadien,' as no obvious criteria existed for assigning a play to one series rather than another. The same inconsistencies are to be found in the 'Traduction et adaptation' series: the cover of *L'Effet des rayons gamma* ... attributes the play to Michel Tremblay, although it is scarcely more than a translation, with very little adaptation. One thing is clear, however; with the almost systematic naturalization of foreign works, institutional values were being overthrown and the publishing industry was playing a major role in this change. Québécois works were acquiring an exchange value greater than that of foreign works.

No to the Anglo-Canadian Repertoire, But ...

The definition of a foreign work began to change and was extended to include French works, which sometimes had to be modified linguistically. For example, Victor Lanoux's *Le Tourniquet* became *L'Ouvre-boîte* in its Québécois adaptation. Anglo-Canadian works, on the other hand, required a total change of language, like any foreign work. According to the Social Science and Humanities Research Council's 1977 survey, only three Anglo-Canadian plays were translated and published in Quebec:[9] *Aux yeux des hommes* (*Fortune and Men's Eyes*) by John Herbert, *Charbonneau et le Chef* by John T. McDonough, and *Les Cloches d'enfer* (*The Bells of Hell*) by Mordecai Richler. It is interesting to note that, as against these three titles, the same bibliography records some twenty Québécois plays translated into English for the Canadian market. This imbalance is in part attributable to the fact that the play was a less prominent genre in Anglo-Canadian literature. Nevertheless, so great is this disproportion that it cannot but be viewed as evidence of indifference, and perhaps disdain, on the part of the Quebec literary institution for Anglo-Canadian theatre.[10] Since P. Stratford's 1977 survey, the situation seems to have changed very little. By the end of the period under study, no new translation of an Anglo-Canadian author had been undertaken by established Quebec publishers such as Leméac or VLB, who published most of the (very few) foreign plays that did appear in Quebec – clear evidence of Quebec's lack of interest in Anglo-Canadian plays. In contrast, the Anglo-Canadian literary institution was highly receptive to Québécois plays. A list prepared by the Centre d'Essai des Auteurs Dramatiques in May 1987 records 123 Québécois plays translated into English.[11] Given the total number of plays produced, the figure is impressive. Moreover, 54 of these translations were published in Canada, mostly in Toronto and Vancouver.

Let us examine the three Anglo-Canadian plays that were favoured with publication in Quebec. It is easy to understand why *Charbonneau et le Chef* was chosen for publication. The play is about an important event in the recent history of Quebec, one of the first events in the struggle for independence which would ultimately lead to the Quiet Revolution. McDonough's play retraces the conflict between the premier of Quebec and the archbishop of Montreal during the Asbestos strike, 'the unparalleled drama which unfolded in "La Belle Province" in 1949 and which gripped all French Canadians ... the Asbestos strike shook Québécois to the very foundations of their identity.'[12] During this period of renewed nationalism, the play touched the very fibre of contemporary Québécois society.

Why the other two plays were chosen is not so obvious. Mordecai Richler's reputation and the success in Quebec of films based on his books, especially *The Apprenticeship of Duddy Kravitz*, could explain why he was translated and published. Richler is, of course, a Montrealer who writes about a particular milieu in that city. His publisher could expect that his play, which had already appeared on television, would be well received by francophone audiences. Torontonian John Herbert's play brings to mind some of Michel Tremblay's plays, both in its theme of homosexuality and in its portrayal of the alienation of prison life. The characters use a type of language that is easily translated into *joual*. Moreover, the play was published at a time when homosexuality was a popular theme:

Homosexuality will thrive this year: with or without touch ups. Natural flavour or enriched! Besides 'Staircase,' 'La Duchesse de Langeais,' 'The Boys in the Band,' and 'L'Escalier,' to name just a few, there's 'Aux yeux des hommes,' which deals yet again with what is now fashionably known as 'that delicate problem.' As interest from the theatre-going public increases, this new trend is beginning to look like some form of collective introspection ...[13]

We could say, then, that these three Anglo-Canadian plays were published in Quebec because they echoed certain discursive codes dominant in Quebec society. As such, they could act as a mirror, providing Québécois society with an image of itself, a basic function of the new Québécois theatre.[14]

Tremblay, Translator Laureate

When *Les Belles-Soeurs* was written in 1968, a 'Québécois' theatre was only just emerging. With the production of his play, Michel Tremblay was immediately consecrated by the establishment as the first authentic 'Québécois' playwright. Today, he is still the uncontested major figure of the new theatre, surrounded by the young writers who will be his worthy successors. Michel Tremblay's works have become 'classics' and he enjoys supreme respect in the Quebec theatre. Moreover, Tremblay translated and adapted half of the works published in the 'Traduction et adaptation' series, the only foreign-theatre series in Quebec during the period under review. Thus, a third of all the foreign plays *published* in Quebec were translated and adapted by him. Publishers of literature, ever attentive to the demands of the public, which they not only reflect but to a large extent create, hold Tremblay up as the most competent translator in Quebec. They also portray him implicitly as being the most skilled at making foreign works conform to the new norms of authentic Québécois theatre. Clearly, in the Quebec publishing industry, the line between local works and imported works is a fluid one. Foreign works are merely an extension of, and sometimes a substitute for, local works. In actual fact, foreign works are borrowed and used to increase the creative capital of the Québécois theatre. In the market for symbolic goods, which includes dramatic works, the use value of translations and adaptations by René Dionne is considerably greater than that of translations and adaptations by Michel Tremblay, if only in terms of their number and their more frequent production in Quebec. Yet Leméac's catalogue contains only one of René Dionne's translations. The commercial imperative cannot be ignored. Despite its having a lower use value, Michel Tremblay's fame has a greater exchange value than that of other translators; the Québécois playwright's name is a guarantee of success.

The aforementioned list of translations published by Les Éditions Leméac opens and closes with works by Michel Tremblay. While he is referred to as the translator and adaptor of the first play on the list, his name is quite brazenly substituted for that of the author of the last play. At a minimum, this elevation in status reveals that, in Québécois society, the institutional value of Michel Tremblay surpasses that of Gogol. It is, however, conceded that the Russian author, who now plays a secondary role, acted as a catalyst for the theatrical genius of the Québécois writer – 'D'après (after) *Le Revizor*' appears as a subtitle to the play 'by' Michel Tremblay. However, the publisher's decision to replace the author's name with Tremblay's is not totally unethical. By listing *Le Gars de Québec* in the 'Traduction et adaptation' series rather than in the 'Théâtre canadien' series, the publisher gives Gogol his due as the original author of the play. The inherent contradiction in listing the play as an original work written by Tremblay and then placing it in the foreign-drama series indicates that, in Quebec, there is no clear dividing line between writing and translating for the theatre.

Lysistrata, *in the 'Répertoire québécois' Series*

Aristophanes was not accorded the same consideration in 1969 as Gogol was in 1985. In all fairness to the publisher, we should point out that the foreign-drama series did not yet exist. *Lysistrata* was included in the series entitled 'Répertoire québécois' within the larger series entitled 'Théâtre canadien.' Authorship of the play was attributed to André Brassard and Michel Tremblay. The reason for crediting them as authors is provided on the back cover: 'From the Greece of Aristophanes to the Quebec of Brassard and Tremblay, humanity, through successive conquests, has sought Peace ... but has never attained it.'[15] The two societies, Quebec and Greece, are placed side by side, the alpha and omega of the fate of humanity. This self-serving perspective of humankind's inexorable fate makes it possible to equate these two societies that would normally be viewed as radically different: Quebec and Greece each have their own great playwrights, their own great portrayers of their society's culture. Brassard and Tremblay are to Aristophanes what Quebec is to ancient Greece, are they not? Implicitly at work here is a projection in which the first term in each analogy elevates itself to the level of the second. In this equating of the Québécois adaptation with the original *Lysistrata*, the Québécois identity 'positions' itself vis-à-vis the founding civilization of the West and assumes its place in the cultural paradigm whose initial term is ancient Greece. Here, we see clear signs of 'affirmationism.' Ironically, Michel Tremblay's dramatic output was still very modest at this time – in terms of actual publications, it consisted solely of *Les Belles-Soeurs*. Nevertheless, similarity between the two societies is established by emphasizing their comparable situations, which were created 'through successive conquests.' This key word (conquest), which is the basis of one of the principal tenets of Québécois discourse, indicates *ipso facto* equality between the two societies. With its experience of conquest, Québécois society has affinities with Greek society and, individual fate being tied to collective destiny,[16] there is no difference between the Québécois *phenotype* and its Hellenic counterpart: 'From the tragic to the farcical, man finds himself unchanged, incomplete, a solitary animal ... Aristophanes-Brassard-Tremblay present us with an image of woman VICTORIOUS! Lysistrata!' Is this the unconscious metaphor of a longed-for victory for 'La Belle Province'? Whatever it may be, in the fusion of the three names, Aristophanes' play is no longer distinguished from the Tremblay–Brassard play, and they become interchangeable. Indeed, on the first page, just above the heading 'Collection théâtre canadien,' there is an attribution of the 'text' of *Lysistrata* to Michel Tremblay. And the typography clearly indicates the relative institutional importance of Aristophanes and Tremblay: Aristophanes' name appears in small letters, whereas Tremblay's is repeated twice in capital letters.

For Euripides, Signed: Marie Cardinal

The same substitution of authors occurs in *La Médée d'Euripide* (*Euripides' Medea*), which was published and distributed as a work by Marie Cardinal, although, in this case, it was a genuine translation rather than an imitation or an adaptation. However, the actual text, about sixty pages long, makes up only half of the book. The translator reserved the other half for herself. In a foreword of approximately forty pages and in a twenty-page interview following the translation, she speaks of her own life. Euripides and Medea are discussed, but only as they relate to Marie Cardinal's life. This is how the translator, 'in all modesty,' begins her preface:

Medea, Cardinal!
Those two!
First, I thought there was some woman's thing going on between them. Medea giving Cardinal a whole tissue of words created for her by Euripides more than two thousand years ago. Cardinal draped in this respectable garb, then unleashing her violence ... Stories of lovers, spouses, mothers and daughters ... Cardinal, using Medea's voice, vents her murderous impulses. Today, people no longer murder in such a fashion, they no longer scream in such a way; today, lightning is diffused by lightning conductors and passions are looked upon as illnesses ...

This is how I explained the voracity with which she who is in me wrote down her screaming and her dreams, and then turned to Euripides' text. I identified with his Medea, I saw myself as that woman in his tragedy about women, I was the principal character in a play written by a Mediterranean. Cardinal was going to learn how to evolve with the syntax and the memory of her soil, because this syntax and this memory have been within her since her conception.[17]

The institutional transfer of ownership of the play from Euripides to Cardinal was reinforced and perhaps facilitated by the novelist's identification of herself with Medea. Her comment on Euripides' tragedy can be summed up in the phrase 'Medea is me,' echoing Flaubert's famous comment on *Madame Bovary*. Drawing on her own Mediterranean experience and on her feminist struggles, Marie Cardinal underlines the relevance of *Medea* and, by virtue of her own past, passes herself off as the true interpreter of the heroine in Euripides' mythical tragedy. Here, translation becomes a *prise de parole*, a way of speaking out, in the militant sense of the word, and, in the literal sense, an appropriation of the original text. For Marie Cardinal, 'a translation is a work in its own right.' Thus, she claims autonomy for the target text and consequently the right to sign her name to it as her own creative work. When she adds: 'I have been translated into eighteen languages'[18] to demonstrate, as an author, her knowledge of translation, she lets her public know that she is aware of her institutional position and the weight and legitimacy conveyed by her name as an author. She nevertheless insists on respect for the original, a respect that guided her own translation:

I was always conscious of trying to remain close to Euripides ... I neither removed, nor added any dialogue. The text that I produced is, nevertheless, very different from the original Euripides text, since I totally suppressed the metre; at the same time, however, it is very close, extremely close in spirit.[19]

This apparent concern with accuracy and faithfulness is belied by the book's cover. The title, *La Médée d'Euripide*, stands out in bold white letters against a black background between the name of Marie Cardinal, underlined with a heavy red rule, and a colour photograph of the novelist, which alone takes up two-thirds of the page. The bold lettering and the large photograph overshadow the reference to Euripides in the title. The title, allegedly designed to highlight the connection between Euripides and *Medea*, in actual fact erases it. When asked about her treatment of the play, Marie Cardinal stated that it was neither a translation nor an adaptation. However, she did add:

This is why the work is entitled *La Médée d'Euripide* and not simply *Médée*. I explain in the preface why it is not a translation (there is no metre). And neither is it an adaptation, because my text follows Euripides' text faithfully.[20]

The cover mentions the name of the publisher but does not ascribe the play to Euripides. Quite clearly, the publisher decided to substitute authors and give credit for the play to Marie Cardinal. There is no indication that the work is a translation, either in the ascription or in the format. On the contrary; everything leads one to believe that *La Médée d'Euripide* is an original work, a monograph, a fictionalized study by Marie

Cardinal, based on the theme of Euripides and Medea. The flyleaf does nothing to dispel this first impression:

LA MÉDÉE D'EURIPIDE
Text by Marie Cardinal
is the Two Hundredth Work published by
VLB ÉDITEUR

Two comments are in order here. First, in the case of such an adaptation, we would expect to find the ascription '*French* text by ...,' the converse of the customary 'translated by ...' Suppressing any reference to the language of translation, source language, or target language suggests that the text is an original one. Thus, the traditional expression used to indicate the foreign origins of a work undergoes an ethnocentric transformation.[21] The absence of the word 'français,' a word we might expect to find, may also indicate that its use would be problematic. In the Québécois context, the word 'français' has a negative value. However, it cannot be replaced by the word 'québécois,' a word that connotes 'joual.' This connotation and the 'naturalist' use of 'québécois' by playwrights would thus have made it difficult to print 'Québécois text by Michel Tremblay' on the cover of *Lysistrata*. Conversely, however, the expression 'French text by Michel Tremblay' brings together two apparently incompatible terms.

Second, Euripides, through the intervention of Marie Cardinal – or is it the reverse? – enriches the catalogue of Québécois publications of a publisher whose growth parallels the emergence and increasing independence of a specifically 'Québécois' literature. The local literary institution gains two credits for this single work. Euripides' *Medea* is exploited to bring prestige both to Marie Cardinal and to her publisher. This translation of *Medea*, with its lengthy commentary that overshadows the original on the pretext of bringing it out of oblivion, now becomes part of the novelist's cultural legacy. At the same time, it enriches the cultural legacy of Les Éditions VLB. The translator's name, itself a selling point, becomes more important than the transhistoric, but locally unrecognized value of the source text. This coalescence of interests underscores a reality of Québécois society. In itself, the classical play has almost zero value in the Québécois market of symbolic goods – hence, the need to erase all trace of its origin and identity. This institutional situation stands in marked contrast to that of a country with a long cultural tradition like Germany, where Greek plays are regularly produced. For example, the Berlin production of *Orestes* by Peter Stein, an extremely long production in which

Stein tried to be as faithful as possible to the Greek theatrical tradition, contained passages in the original Greek. The value of the work was tied to the preservation of its alterity, to its 'foreignness.' To gain acceptance in Quebec, Euripides had to be brought in on a 'carrier' discourse, feminism. Marie Cardinal's support was also essential, since she was a local, more prestigious writer whose exchange value was superior to that of Euripides. This institutional piggybacking was also essential for *Lysistrata*. Similarly, Brassard and Tremblay, prestigious local writers, took Aristophanes under their wing.

This appropriation of classical Greek works can be attributed to the cultural and temporal distance of ancient Greek authors from contemporary Québécois society. These works have a transhistorical value; thus, when a producer like André Brassard or Jean-Pierre Ronfard decides to stage them, he endeavours to produce or have produced a translation 'adapted' to the new context and thus acceptable to the public;[22] for example, alterations will be made to compensate for changes in context and for the resulting semantic changes. Marie Cardinal had this to say about her adaptation:

... so that the audience is not distracted from the action, I removed a considerable number of invocations to the gods and replaced them with expressions such as: 'May the gods protect you,' or 'forces of the universe, listen to me!' It is essential for the presence of the gods to be felt, but they should hold the attention no more than they did in the original work. I tried to avoid the well of mystery we always fall into when we hear unfamiliar names.[23]

Here, translation distances itself from the 'language system' of the source text and attenuates its 'foreignness,' enabling it ideally to enter the arena of mass consumption. Yet, the theatre remains the preserve of a minority. The idea that translation should make a work transparent and accessible to all is seen here as a given, even though such a goal is far from being an absolute, as the history of translation attests. The translator cannot simply choose from the alternatives traditionally presented in the discourse on translation – literality as opposed to interpretation, 'faithfulness' to the text as opposed to 'faithfulness' to the reader. But one cannot escape from these absolute alternatives without recognizing that translation is a function of a particular literary institution within a given society at a given time.

In its attempt to dominate the theatre scene, the new theatre in Quebec, characterized or accepted as 'Québécois,' espoused the principle of maximum accessibility. Its aim was to be accepted and recognized by as many people as possible. Translation, which played a role in shaping the new theatre, either through direct substitution or through recycling of elements from the original, focused on the same goal:

A dream: thousands upon thousands of theatre-goers, with their Cokes, their chips, and their popcorn, coming to see *La Médée d'Euripide* at the Théâtre du Nouveau Monde in Montreal in 1986 after Jesus-Christ ...
- Impossible!
- Why?
- !!!??

Why is this theatre reserved for an élite when it was written to be understood by everybody? Why is it that the theatre that was for the people, no longer is?[24]

To meet the 'popular' horizon of expectations, Cardinal had to simplify the original text, yet she none the less says that her objective was to be faithful to the original. We are not talking here of a rewrite, such as Jean-Paul Sartre's *Les Troyennes* (*The Trojan Women*) or Eugene O'Neill's *Mourning Becomes Electra*, where the classical tragedy merely provides a thematic and symbolic matrix for a work that reinterprets contemporary society in a radically different way. Québécois transformations of Aristophanes and Euripides attempt to make the original work transparent, accessible to as many people as possible. In these transformations, the original may, on occasion, be modified considerably, but surely this fact alone does not justify replacing the name of the author with that of the translator! This phenomenon is indicative of an institutional constraint and reflects the society's laws of reception, laws that override the classical work: if the classical work is to be accessible to the general public, it must be modified to conform to a discourse that can be 'received' by Québécois society.

These same laws of reception that rob the foreign author of his work and reassign it to the Québécois translator have also been applied to more recent works. Even a Québécois work did not escape the new strictures and was rewritten to conform to the new aesthetic dominating the theatre. Félix-Gabriel Marchand, a nineteenth-century Québécois politician and vaudeville playwright, was dispossessed of his own work by his adapter, Jean-Claude Germain. In this type of adaptation, the original author, be it Euripides or Marchand, is given prominence, but a false prominence, in that the author's name is mentioned only as part of the title of the work, which hardly gives him due credit for authorship. When the author's name is absorbed in this manner, the institutional autonomy of the adapted play is reinforced. *Les Faux Brillants de Félix-Gabriel Marchand* was published as if it were an original work by Jean-Claude Germain, and like Marie Cardinal's *La Médée d'Euripide*, it has become part of the 'Québécois' cultural legacy: first, it brings credit to the author-translator and to the publisher; secondly, it becomes an asset in an emerging literature that needs to bolster itself by posting each and every acquisition to the ledger:

LES FAUX BRILLANTS
DE FÉLIX-GABRIEL MARCHAND
by Jean-Claude Germain
is the Twentieth Work Published by
VLB Éditeur

Tremblay, Translator Laureate (Continued)

The original text of Michel Tremblay's *L'Effet des rayons gamma sur les vieux-garçons,* which introduced the Éditions Leméac series entitled 'Traduction et adaptation,' won the Pulitzer Prize for its author, Paul Zindel. However, on the cover of the book, it is Michel Tremblay's name that stands out. It appears in large black letters on a white background positioned where the name of the author would normally appear; the author's name is relegated to a position under the title of the play. The reversal of the roles of translator and author is emphasized by the difference in size of the letters used to print their respective names. In the typographical hierarchy on the cover, Paul Zindel's name is as hard to read as the minuscule letters that hover at the bottom of an optician's chart. The true authorship of the play ceases to be an issue when we turn to the spine, where his name disappears completely! It has simply been replaced by Tremblay's name. Yet we are dealing with a *translation.* Granted, the action of the play has been moved to Montreal and the place-names are Québécois; but Tremblay points out that, these changes apart, he stayed very close to the original text: 'I added no more than three or four lines and only because there were some plays on words that I could not translate. That is all the adapting I did. That, and changing the street names.'[25]

The writer of the preface has a slightly different view of the play, which, he claims, was 'made truly Québécois by Tremblay's treatment that involved more creation than adaptation.'[26] The word 'translator' is not used. Traditionally, the transparency of the translating subject is assumed:

the translator will not tamper with the original text, given that it is someone else's. But, in these Québécois adaptations, it is assumed, on the contrary, that translators must leave their mark. The original text is treated as nothing more than raw material, because its characteristics may well get in the way of the realization of an authentically Québécois work. The genius of the translator is the ability to equal or, better yet, surpass the work of the foreign writer. This is reminiscent of the old cliché of the translation being an improvement on the original text. The original is treated as if it never had a real existence outside of its Québécois regeneration, its merit being its ability to pass as a local work. This is how the work is presented to the public and how it is received. When the institution gives artistic awards, the work is judged as a Québécois work. When asked about the danger of the public taking an adaptation for a local work, Jean Duceppe gave a surprising and revealing response: 'The danger exists. The year I received a Méritas prize, Michel Tremblay also received one for "his" play *Les Rayons gamma* ...'[27]

The Québécois Content Rule

If some trace of the author remains by virtue of his name appearing, however minimally, on the cover of the translation, the reader is still left without the slightest indication as to the author's origins, language, life, or previous works. What country does the play come from? When was it written? Where and when was it produced? In what circumstances? What language was it written in? Where, when, and how did the author live? Such questions have to do with foreign works and with foreigners. They are irrelevant as far as the Québécois theatre-book market is concerned and, no doubt, for the Québécois literary institution, too. Shakespeare and Chekhov, if need be, can get by without introduction. Paul Zindel, John Herbert, Peter Shaffer, and Roberto Athayde are hardly so well known that they need not be introduced. Of all the authors translated and published in Quebec, the two Québécois writers, Mordecai Richler and Félix-Gabriel Marchand, were the only ones given a biographical note. But even here there is a hierarchy. Mordecai Richler, an anglophone writer, is accorded a few lines on the back of the book, while the life and career of 'L'honnête M. Marchand,' Québécois premier and man of letters in the last century, receives a whole chapter.[28] Mordecai Richler's biographical note reads as follows: 'Mordecai Richler was born in Montreal in 1931. His family came from Poland and

Russia and settled in Canada two generations ago.' The two sentences in this terse biography reflect the *territorial* situation of the writer with respect to Quebec. Above all, it is the author's origins that must be communicated to the reader. This is the only information provided in the brief note, apart from his date of birth. These two short sentences have a double meaning. They can be read as either reterritorializing or deterritorializing the writer. The Jewish, anglophone ring to Richler's name and his Russo-Polish ancestry are deterritorializing factors, but he redeems himself by the fact that he was born in Montreal (it is not enough for him just to live and work there) and comes from a Canadian family with roots going back two generations. But there is another way of interpreting the biographical note. Everybody knows that Mordecai Richler is as much a Montrealer and a Québécois as Michel Tremblay. Yet this identity is disputed; reference to his Russo-Polish ancestry flushes out Richler's extraterritorial origins. His name says it all: he is an anglophone, and Jewish to boot. In these two sentences, which is all the information we are given about Richler's life, there is a peculiar juxtaposition: the writer was 'born in *Montreal*' whereas his parents 'settled in *Canada*,' or as the social code would have it, 'foreign' territory as far as Quebec is concerned. In terms of the Quebec–Canada opposition, which is a strongly marked one in social discourse, the Anglo-Québécois is considered to be a foreigner in his own birthplace. The deterritorialization arising from his name and his origins, delegitimizes the writer in the eyes of the institution. Witness the minimal space Richler receives on the cover of *Les Cloches d'enfer* in comparison with the importance accorded Michel Tremblay's name on a work published in the same series. The typographical disparity speaks volumes.

In contrast, the political and literary activities of Félix-Gabriel Marchand merit an extremely long commentary, and a full-page photograph of the writer, who, in this case, is authentically Québécois. His biography is placed between the text of the adaptation, described as a 'paraphrase,' and a facsimile of the original text. Marchand is the only author accorded the privilege of a bilingual edition, an institutional mark of respect for the original work which must, on no account, be superseded by the translation. How surprising that the only bilingual edition in the list of published translations is reserved for a Franco-Québécois! In the adaptation of Marchand's text, the transformation does not involve a change from a foreign language to a national language, from the unknown to the known. There is, however, a linguistic transformation, from the French of France to the French of Quebec, from the known to what henceforth must be known. Here, the approach is reterritorializing, normative, and didactic.

To sum up: the publishing apparatus restricts the public to access to the literary legacy of Quebec; only grudgingly does it provide access to foreign works, and only to those which can enrich that legacy. These foreign works, however, must undergo changes that, preferably, will enable them to be taken for Québécois works. References to the alterity of the foreign text are suppressed, as if the original play had never existed in any other form except its Québécois adaptation or re-creation. This is true, moreover, of all translations published in Quebec. According to Sherry Simon, translations 'are not always identified as such (in catalogues, for example, and in promotional material). They are rarely recognized as a genre by publishers and are not specifically promoted as translations.'[29] At the end of her study, she concludes:

> In the last few years, a large number of translations have been published in Quebec without reference being necessarily made to their origin. Indeed, translations, like some other imports, are often considered to have a better chance of success in the local market if their origin is suppressed.[30]

Similarly, translations of plays are often presented as if they were adaptations, and the translator given the prominence that would normally fall to the author of the original text. Sometimes the name of the translator replaces that of the author altogether. On other occasions, it is given the same typographical prominence, leaving the impression that credit for creating the work is owed as much to the Québécois translator as it is to the author. With most of Leméac's published translations, the author's name and that of the translator appear on the front cover and on the spine. The two names appear in exactly the same typographical style, making it impossible to ascertain which of them is the real author of the work. But concealment of the alterity of works assumes various forms. For example, Le Théâtre du Rideau-Vert's playbill for the 1987–8 season proudly proclaims: '5 pièces, 5 auteurs de chez nous' (5 Plays, 5 of Our Own Authors). Two of the five plays are entitled *La Cerisaie* (*The Cherry Orchard*) and *Qui a peur de Virginia Woolf?* So Chekhov and Albee are now Québécois authors! Hardly! These 'pièces de chez nous' are, of course, translations by Robert Lepage and Michel Tremblay. Morever, the playbill highlights the name of the Québécois authors and translators at the expense of the two foreign writers, whose names appear in smaller letters.

The Faceless Foreigner

The tendency of publishers to suppress or minimize reference to the foreign work is found not only on book covers but in the way books are illustrated. With the exception of *Macbeth*, which is illustrated with drawings by Maureen Maxwell and an enlarged excerpt of Michel Garneau's handwritten translation, publishers use photographs as illustrations. These photographs are included to promote, not the text, which is foreign, but its local interpreters. Sometimes, a photograph of the translator appears, other times a photo of the adapter: Tremblay in *Oncle Vania*, Marie Cardinal in *Médée*, Jean-Pierre Ronfard in *La Mandragore*, Antonine Maillet in *Le Bourgeois Gentleman*. In the last two cases, there is more justification for inclusion of these photographs, since the works are not translations, but imitations. More often, however, the cover and the text are illustrated by photographs of the actors who appeared in the Québécois production of the play: Denise Pelletier and Rita Lafontaine in *L'Effet des rayons gamma ...*, Monique Leyrac in *Mademoiselle Marguerite*, Jean Duceppe and Jean-Marie Lemieux in *Charbonneau et le Chef*, Jean-Louis Roux and Yvon Deschamps in *L'Ouvre-boîte*, Andrée Lachapelle and Béatrice Picard in *Mademoiselle Roberge*, and Jean Besré in *Chapeau! ...* Only photographs of Québécois personalities appear. There are never any photographs of the foreign author, nor, needless to say, of the director or actors who would have been involved in productions of the play in its country of origin. The photographs focus attention on the *Québécois* incarnation of a work that was written outside Quebec. They help to eliminate the 'foreignness' of the work. The front cover of Michel Tremblay's translation of *Oncle Vania* is an excellent example of this. The title of the play appears in very large type on the upper part of the cover; a photograph of Michel Tremblay fills the lower two-thirds. A visual equation is established between these two black blocks set against a glossy white background: '*Oncle Vania* = Tremblay.' The connection implied in the equation erases the origins of the play, especially its real author. The author's name seems to be of secondary importance. This typographical ruse, no doubt commercially motivated, uses Tremblay's name to exploit the ideology of stardom. This is a far cry from the 'unobtrusive' translator, the transparent mediator of the original work. In the case of *Oncle Vania*, we see, literally, only the name of the translator. Clearly, Michel Tremblay is more valuable than Chekhov in the Québécois market for symbolic goods, just as the institutional value of Marie Cardinal is greater than that of Euripides. The Québécois version of *Oncle Vania*, moreover, derives its legitimacy from the cultural capital of Michel Tremblay, an author who, incidentally, does not know a word of Russian. Paradoxically, *Oncle Vania* is one of those rare plays that is actually acknowledged to be a translation.

The Foreign Work: No Introduction Necessary?

In this spirit of reterritorialization, a published translation or adaptation is almost always preceded by detailed information on the Québécois (re)creation of the foreign work: the time and place of the production, the director, the set, the costumes and lighting, the music, and the cast. In *Charbonneau et le Chef*, information on all three productions of the play is set out at great length, for its first production at Le Théâtre du Trident in 1971 and for its two subsequent productions, in 1972 in Quebec City and in 1973 in Montreal. Inclusion of such detailed information is, to say the least, unusual for a translation, or indeed for an original work. This is indicative of the cultural importance of *Charbonneau et le Chef*. Published translations of foreign works often contain such information on their Québécois re-creation, but they are rarely introduced by a preface. The Québécois reader will therefore find nothing in these books about the original plays, with the exception of *Les Faux Brillants*, in which the original is reproduced in its entirety, and *La Médée d'Euripide*. In the case of *La Médée*, however, the translator devotes as much space to her personal biography as to the original play and its author. With the exception of these two works, prefaces and postscripts are almost non-existent. On the rare occasions that they do appear, their aim is to legitimize the translation or adaptation, or its Québécois author. Here, for example, is how Victor Lanoux reacted to the adaptation of his play, as recounted by Jean-Louis Roux in his preface to *L'Ouvre-boîte*:

He was shown to his seat: he was going to see 'his' play. At the end of the performance, we were a little anxious; ... and the great man, his face drawn, began to speak: 'I didn't understand everything ... in fact, I didn't understand it very well at all [j'ai pas tout compris ... j'ai même pas bien compris]; but I sensed what you had done; it's really fantastic [c'est vachement chouette]. You changed nothing; I wrote it [j'l'ai écrit] like that so that people would have a good laugh and think [se marrent et qu'y pensent]. I am very pleased [j'suis vachement content]. Tomorrow, I'll try to understand the words, the expressions, but just for the fun of it; because, in fact, I understood everything.'[31]

Roux subtly justified the linguistic adaptation of the original text, not only by reporting Lanoux's positive comments, but by reporting his exact words 'slang'n'all' (in brackets in the excerpt above), thereby highlighting the difference between the French of France and the French spoken in Quebec. His preface is a rare example of a 'translator' showing respect for the original work by referring to its author, as if to dispel any inference that he had profaned the original French text. We find another type of justification in the postscript of John Herbert's play, where, once again, language is an essential element of the transformation. The postscript includes the various reviews of the play from the major Montreal newspapers, all enthusiastic – about the play, the direction, the actors, and the translation itself. Significantly, the last of these reviews is from the *Montreal Star* and it is reproduced in its original language, as if approval from the English were the highest accolade.

In the Québécois market for symbolic goods, the Foreigner has negative value. The paratext, the typography, and the illustration of Québécois theatre translations marginalize the alterity of the foreign or assimilated work. They also produce a discursive structure that reinforces the image of a Québécois theatre at the height of its creative powers. These strategies to suppress the Other, which naturalize the foreign text in an attempt to annex it, also help build an emerging national theatre. Based on the *deixis* 'nous–ici–maintenant' (us–here–now), such strategies reflect the self-affirmation of René Lévesque's famous statement, made when the Parti Québécois came to power: 'Nous sommes quelque chose comme un grand peuple' (We are something like a great nation). The strategies used in the new theatre proclaim, in turn: 'We have something like a great theatre.'

The Foreigner Upstaged

Only a small number of translations are published in Quebec, yet there is a great deal of translation done for the theatre. Of the 716 plays put on between 1968 and 1988 in seven large theatres in Montreal and Quebec City,[32] 392 plays were of foreign origin (including Anglo-Canadian), that is, 55 per cent of total production. During the same period, 324 Québécois plays were produced, a little more than 45 per cent of the total. If plays originating in francophone countries, thus already in French, are removed from the total, 256 foreign plays remain. Of this number, 156 were translated in Quebec, that is, 61 per cent of the foreign plays produced. The remaining translations originated in France.

The Foreigner 33

Selection Criteria

To follow the evolution of theatre translation in Quebec over twenty years and demonstrate its relation to the dominant social discourse, we had to establish the complete repertoire of the major theatres. Our corpus includes francophone professional companies in Montreal and Quebec City whose theatres had a seating capacity in excess of 100 and which existed uninterrupted from 1968 to 1988. Our criteria precluded experimental theatres like L'Eskabel (1971), Le Groupe de la Veillée (1973), and Le Nouveau Théâtre Expérimental (1976), which were founded more recently, operated out of cramped quarters, and attracted a limited audience. On the basis of the same criteria, and for the sake of consistency, the following were also excluded: travelling theatres, children's theatres, summer stock, and amateur theatres. The theatre companies that satisfied our criteria were in that sector of the theatre that public authorities conveniently categorize as institutional.[33] This typology of inclusion and exclusion incorporates most of the categories established and defined by Adrien Gruslin in *Le Théâtre et l'État au Québec*,[34] categories which are also employed by economist François Colbert in *Le Marché québécois du théâtre*.[35] Gruslin defines institutional companies as 'those receiving the most grants, the best-known and, historically, the oldest.'[36] However, he is at pains to add that the allegedly 'institutional' nature of these companies is relative. Taken individually, they are not necessarily identifiable with 'traditional repertory theatre, the theatre of fixed, immutable norms' that the notion of institutional theatre presupposes. Traditionally 'eclectic and international,' but, we note, not Canadian, the plays presented in these theatres have on occasion been 'audacious.'[37] Gruslin cites the plays performed by Le Théâtre d'Aujourd'hui as a good example of the ambiguity surrounding the category 'institutional theatre.' In the beginning, recalls Gruslin, Le Théâtre d'Aujourd'hui was a subversive, marginal theatre, but this distinctiveness disappeared with time and repeated productions of plays with the same dramatic form and content.

The following five theatres were chosen for our study: Le Rideau-Vert (1948); Le Théâtre du Nouveau Monde (1951); Le Théâtre de Quat'Sous, established in 1963 but inaugurated in 1965; La Nouvelle Compagnie Théâtrale (1964); and Le Théâtre d'Aujourd'hui, which had its first season in 1968–9. If we had followed all the criteria we had drawn up, we would have been restricted to Montreal. Therefore, we decided to include

Le Théâtre du Trident, the biggest theatre in Quebec City, which opened in 1970, just one season later than the time period chosen for our focus of study. La Compagnie Jean-Duceppe was not formed until 1973, but it is of such institutional importance that it could not be excluded. The group is based at the Place des Arts, the most prestigious and one of the biggest theatres in Montreal, with a seating capacity of 700 in Le Théâtre Port-Royal. By extending our criteria in this way, we arrived at a representative sample of the Québécois theatrical institution.

The sample extends over twenty years and provides a homogeneous yet varied corpus for analysis. It is homogeneous in that all the theatres are situated, although admittedly in varying degrees, at the centre and not on the periphery of the system. It is varied with respect to orientation; some theatres are more or less ethnocentric, while others are more or less open to foreign works.

Within the strict limitations of the study, 'foreign work' means foreign to Quebec, or written in Quebec in a language other than French.[38] Anglo-Canadian plays are included in this group, regardless of their province of origin and, here, we include Quebec. However, since the focus of our analysis is *translation*, which necessarily involves languages other than French, Anglo-Québécois plays are counted as foreign works. In contrast, the notion of a Québécois theatre includes Canadian plays written in French, even when the playwright is not a Québécois. Antonine Maillet is a case in point. She is closely identified with Acadia and New Brunswick, but her plays are none the less premiered in Quebec. The Québécois literary institution attracts French-Canadian writers from outside Quebec and tends to absorb their work, especially those who come to live in Quebec, such as novelist Gabrielle Roy. French-Canadian writers living in anglophone provinces are, however, commonly ignored by the Québécois literary institution. Roger Léveillé, a Manitoba writer, is a perfect example. His humorous, combinative writing does not fit the prevailing discursive norm. Literary criticism does not fare any better; books written outside Quebec that deal with Québécois literature can be ignored or rejected by reviewers inside Quebec, on the pretext that they are written in English.

Origin and Proportion of Foreign Plays Produced

Table 1 presents the complete repertoire of the seven theatres chosen for this study, from the beginning of 1968 (or from the year they were founded, as the case may be) to 1987–8, and provides a breakdown of

TABLE 1
Origin of Foreign Plays

Country	Number of plays	% of foreign repertoire	% of total repertoire
France	135	34.43	18.85
United States	95	24.23	13.26
Britain	66	16.84	9.21
Italy	29	7.40	4.05
Germany	10	2.55	1.39
Russia	10	2.55	1.39
Ireland	8	2.04	1.11
English Canada	8	2.04	1.11
Spain	6	1.53	0.83
Sweden	5	1.27	0.69
Greece	4	1.02	0.55
Holland	3	0.76	0.41
Czechoslovakia	3	0.76	0.41
Switzerland	2	0.51	0.27
Poland	2	0.51	0.27
Belgium	1	0.25	0.13
Romania	1	0.25	0.13
Argentina	1	0.25	0.13
Austria	1	0.25	0.13
Mexico	1	0.25	0.13
Japan	1	0.25	0.13
Total	392	100.00	54.74

plays by their country of origin. It also shows, calculated over twenty years, a breakdown for each country as a percentage of the total number of foreign plays, and then as a percentage of all plays.

With a total of 177 produced, English-language plays dominate the foreign repertoire, followed by French-language plays (France and Belgium), at 136 works. In each of these categories, the United States and France provide, as one might expect, the majority of plays. Conversely, we note the minor position occupied by Anglo-Canadian plays in the English-language category, confirming our previous observation concerning the disregard of Québécois publishers for Anglo-Canadian plays – or is it simple lack of curiosity? Even then, these figures do not represent the true picture, since they include reruns as well as new productions. In fact, only four Anglo-Canadian plays were produced: *Aux yeux des hommes* (*Fortune and Men's Eyes*) by John Herbert (Quat'Sous 1969–70; Trident

TABLE 2
Distribution and Percentage of Foreign Works and Québécois Works, by Theatre

Theatres	Total no. of plays	Québécois plays		Foreign plays	
		No.	%	No.	%
Aujourd'hui	104	95	91	9	9
Duceppe	77	18	23	59	77
NCT	70	23	33	47	67
Quat'Sous	118	76	64	42	36
Rideau-Vert	133	39	29	94	71
TNM	129	40	31	89	69
Trident	85	33	39	52	61
Total	716	324	45	392	55

1985–6), *Charbonneau et le Chef* by John T. McDonough (Trident 1970–1 and 1971–2; Duceppe 1973–4 and 1985–6), *Aux hirondelles* (*Back to Beulah*) by William O. Mitchell (Duceppe 1978–9), and *Le Bélier* (*The Battering Ram*) by David Freeman (Aujourd'hui 1983–4).

Before analysing these figures, the authors and works they represent and their frequency of production, let us examine table 2, which shows the distribution of Québécois plays and foreign plays among the various theatres.

In light of these statistics, one can no longer speak, as Michel Bélair did in 1973, of the 'marginal' position of the Québécois theatre. It is no longer possible to state that Québécois productions represent only 'a tiny percentage' of the programmes of major theatre companies and that these companies, which are also the most subsidized, 'consistently ignore Québécois texts.'[39] Bélair's use of the term 'marginal' to describe the Québécois repertoire of the major theatres is inappropriate, given that these theatres produce an average of 45 per cent of Québécois plays, and it is even more inappropriate if we take into account the number of plays that this percentage represents – namely, 324. This is a considerable number, in view of the fact that the Québécois theatre is quite young. To be sure, writers cannot always agree as to when exactly the Québécois theatre came into existence. For Jean Béraud, it dates back to the beginning of the seventeenth century, with the aquatic fantasies of Marc Lescarbot's *Théâtre de Neptune*.[40] Jean-Cléo Godin and Laurent Mailhot are more cautious in their analysis of texts and authors. They are of the opinion that the Québécois theatre has existed, at the very most, for a quarter of a century. Michel Bélair distinguishes between French-Canadian theatre and Québécois theatre: 'Before becoming Québécois, French-speaking theatre in Quebec was first of all Canadian, Canadian in its themes, in the universal problems that it dealt with, and also in a certain denial of the civilization of the context in which it appeared.'[41] Using this distinction, he could claim in 1973 that the Québécois theatre had existed for only five years and thereby ignore those texts predating 1968. Whether one agrees or not with this interpretation, which clearly reinforces the ideology of the 'nation,' the fact remains that an impressive number of Québécois plays were performed in institutional theatres; and this number is all the more impressive when the size of the population of Quebec is taken into consideration. However, we should re-examine the statistics used to compare Québécois theatre and foreign plays. Percentages shift and change when the many Québécois adaptations of foreign plays – in which the theme, the setting, and the role of the characters are transposed to Quebec – are counted as Québécois plays.

Without statistics for comparison, we cannot claim with any degree of certainty that the national repertoire occupies centre stage in countries with a great theatrical tradition, such as England, Italy, Germany, and Poland. One thing is certain, however; foreign theatre plays a prominent and diversified role in these countries and is far from being considered a threat to the national theatre. We do, however, find competitiveness and intolerance of foreign drama in many Québécois studies of the theatre. Relying heavily on statistics, such studies have created a whole discourse on the marginalization and deterritorialization by the Other of drama in Quebec. This accusatory and protectionist discourse is directed against some of the most influential institutions – namely, grant-awarding agencies. It is one of the strategies of institutionalization, strategies that will enable the new Québécois theatre to conquer the territory currently occupied by foreign drama and, in its turn, occupy the dominant position in the theatre: 'The classic repertoire reigns supreme while it ought to be merely an adjunct to Québécois theatre, a theatre that they try desperately not to recognize.'[42] Above all, Québécois theatre is expected to keep churning out productions. 'Cinq pièces, cinq auteurs de chez nous' was the commercial slogan of Le Rideau Vert for the 1987–8 season. But, as already noted, to come up with five Québécois authors, the translators of the two foreign works in the repertoire had to be counted as authors. The real author and the foreign dimension of the work were passed over, or, rather, concealed, a practice indicative of the prejudice against the Foreigner in a certain sector of Québécois culture. For a foreign work to be accepted, it had to be passed off as a local work. Similarly, on the third page of the programme put out by Le Théatre du Nouveau Monde, Québécois plays staged since 1953 were listed under the heading 'The TNM and Local Authors.' It would appear that the theatre felt it had to distance itself from the somewhat reprehensible practice of putting on foreign plays! Indeed, theatres only stopped just short of apologizing for exposing the public to writers who were not 'de chez nous.'[43] These tactics are obviously aimed at granting agencies, and their use clearly demonstrates that the institution, as a vehicle of Québécois hegemony, is working to keep the Foreigner at bay. The primary concern of the institution is one of numbers; only then is content a concern. Moreover, the issue of content is approached in an equally protectionist manner, through a territorial view of culture, whose ideological presupposition equates the notion of human collectivity with that of an autonomous political community:

Indeed the theatre has always, above all, been national before claiming to be universal; no matter how far back in history you go, you will see that, above all else, it has attempted to express the myths, needs, or characteristics of a given collectivity.[44]

In the name of the territoriality of the group and of the ideology of 'difference,'[45] foreign works are declared irrelevant to the Québécois context. For Michel Bélair, the function of the Québécois theatre is even to 'cleanse' the public mind contaminated by 'imported' culture, since the public has been '"moulded" by a theatrical tradition with all its stereotypes and contaminants.'[46] This is why, under the direction of Jean-Claude Germain, Le Théâtre d'Aujourd'hui decided to devote itself entirely to Québécois works. Its first play, *Les Enfants de Chénier dans un grand spectacle d'adieu*, was destined to sound the death knell of 'imported' theatre, to 'assassinate' repertory theatre, 'by forcing it to take second place, as it had to, if the theatre was to truly play its role of questioning the status quo.'[47]

If we exclude Le Théâtre d'Aujourd'hui, with its predominantly Québécois repertoire, the proportion of foreign works fluctuates between one-third and four-fifths of the overall number of plays produced. Looking at programs of other theatres, we note, not surprisingly, that Le Quat'Sous concentrates principally on Québécois plays and that La Compagnie Jean Duceppe, as mentioned above, produces a large number of American plays. All these theatres have an area of specialization. Older and bigger

TABLE 3
Source Language of Foreign Works, excluding French

Language	% of repertoire in foreign languages
English	69.0
Italian	11.0
German	5.0
Russian	4.0
Spanish	3.0
Swedish	2.0
Greek	1.5
Dutch	1.0
Czech	1.0
Polish	0.8
Romanian	0.4
Japanese	0.4

theatres, those that best fit the criteria of institutionalization – longevity, size, and public financing – do not specialize in this manner.[48] The ratio of foreign to Québécois plays staged by these theatres is approximately two to one. Such theatres include Le Rideau-Vert, Le TNM, and La NCT, as well as Le Trident, but the last produces slightly more Québécois drama than do the three Montreal theatres. This is perhaps attributable to its unique position, as dominant, but relatively isolated, in the capital of the province.

Which Languages? Which Authors?

Analysis of the source language of the plays produced reveals that, out of 716 plays (original and reruns combined), there were 136 French-language foreign plays; combined with the 324 Québécois plays, this makes a total of 460 plays written originally in French. We will return later to the characteristics and diversity of the French in these plays. For the moment, we will simply note that the plays originally written in French, in the French of France or in Québécois, constitute almost 65 per cent of the total number of plays staged in Quebec over a period of twenty years. Table 3 provides the percentage and distribution of the foreign-language repertoire. As noted earlier, the foreign repertoire includes 256 plays written in a language other than French.

English-language plays dominate the foreign-language repertoire by a

40 A Sociocritique of Translation

TABLE 4
Numerical Distribution of Foreign Plays, by Theatre

Theatre	English-language plays					French-language plays	Plays in other languages	Total foreign plays
	USA	UK	Irl	CDN	Total			
Aujourd'hui	1	1	0	1	3	4	2	9
Duceppe	38	7	1	3	49	1	9	59
NCT	8	5	0	0	13	19	15	47
Quat'Sous	16	4	0	1	21	15	6	42
Rideau-Vert	14	17	2	0	33	45	16	94
TNM	8	17	4	0	29	42	18	89
Trident	10	15	1	3	29	10	13	52
Total	95	66	8	8	177	136	79	392

wide margin. Far behind English, we find Italian and German, followed by a sprinkling of various other languages. All the foreign plays produced are European-language plays, with the exception of *Madame de Sade*, a Japanese play by Mishima, but the allusion to the famous Marquis and the phatic effect it must have on the public bring the play directly back into the realm of Western culture. However, analysis of the distribution of foreign plays produced in each theatre, as shown in table 4, reveals considerable variation.

The wide variation to be found in table 4 must not be interpreted in an absolute sense. The number of foreign plays is in fact relative to the total number of plays staged in each theatre: table II shows that the total can fluctuate greatly. We must also take into account the time period covered by the study, which is not exactly the same for all theatres. In most cases, statistics cover a period of twenty years, but, for the two more recently established theatres (Jean-Duceppe and Le Trident), the period is shorter. This is also true for Le TNM, which suspended operations for a short time during the period under review. The comparison is therefore valid only as a function of the percentages for the productions of *each* theatre, as shown in table 5.

In accordance with its educational mandate, La NCT produces many plays from the canon, and offers the widest selection of foreign plays. Moreover, in the NCT repertoire, there is a more balanced distribution of languages, with a preference for French. Le TNM, closely followed by Le Rideau-Vert, also displays a balanced distribution of languages. Faithful to its orientation, Le Théâtre d'Aujourd'hui places more importance on

TABLE 5
Percentage of Foreign Plays, by Theatre

Theatre	English-language plays (%)					French-language plays (%)	Plays in other languages (%)
	USA	UK	Irl	CDN	Total		
Aujourd'hui	11	11	0	11	33	44	22
Duceppe	64	12	2	5	83	2	15
NCT	17	11	0	0	28	40	32
Quat'Sous	38	10	0	2	50	36	15
Rideau-Vert	15	18	2	0	35	48	17
TNM	9	19	4	0	32	47	20
Trident	19	29	2	6	56	19	25
Total	24	17	2	2	45	35	20

French in its choice, admittedly very rare, of foreign plays. In the repertoire of La Compagnie Jean-Duceppe, which produces mainly American plays, English-language plays dominate by a wide margin (83 per cent). The theatre also produces more American plays than any other theatre (64 per cent). Le TNM produces the least number of American plays (9 per cent). Following La Compagnie Jean-Duceppe, Le Trident and Le Quat'Sous display a marked preference for English-language plays. However, while Quat'Sous's foreign repertoire clearly focuses on American plays, Trident's repertoire has a more balanced representation of English-language plays, and includes Anglo-Canadian plays. This relatively balanced distribution is found elsewhere only in the repertoire of Jean-Duceppe.

The preceding percentages, calculated in terms of the number of foreign plays produced in each theatre, demonstrate the relatively minor importance (20 per cent) placed on works written in languages other than English (45 per cent) and French (35 per cent). These works, on average, constitute a fifth of the foreign repertoire. They never represent more than one-quarter of overall production, and that includes all foreign languages except English. Even if we exclude Anglo-Canadian plays, which are notoriously ignored, these results present an image of a theatre milieu that has little curiosity about the outside world, beyond the immediately familiar. The numbers of foreign-language plays produced in each theatre, provided in table 6, give a clear picture of this lack of openness to foreign plays.

Given that these figures represent twenty years of repertoire, the low

TABLE 6
Distribution of Plays in Languages Other than English and French, by Theatre

Theatre	Ital	Germ	Russ	Sp	Swed	Grk	Czech	Dtch	Pol	Rom	Jap	Total
Aujourd'hui	0	0	0	0	0	0	0	1	1	0	0	2
Duceppe	3	2	1	0	0	0	1	1	0	1	0	9
NCT	4	1	3	2	2	2	1	0	0	0	0	15
Quat'Sous	1	3	0	1	0	0	0	0	0	0	1	6
Rideau-Vert	8	0	3	4	1	0	0	0	0	0	0	16
TNM	7	5	1	0	2	2	1	0	0	0	0	18
Trident	6	2	2	1	0	0	0	1	1	0	0	13
Total	29	13	10	8	5	4	3	3	2	1	1	79

number of foreign plays produced speaks all the more eloquently to the isolationism of the theatre in Quebec. Theatre production appears to have turned in on itself, oddly out of phase with the multicultural reality of the population at large, especially in Montreal, where the theatres in our study are concentrated. This phenomenon sheds light on the status of the neo-Québécois, that is, the immigrant within Québécois culture.[49] This tendency to turn in on oneself, on the community, in the narrowest sense of the term, is in inverse proportion to the degree of institutionalization of the theatres. Those recognized as being the most institutional, such as La NCT, Le TNM, Le Rideau-Vert, and Le Trident, are the most open to foreign plays written originally in languages other than French and English. The language distribution is greatest in these theatres, although it still remains quite limited. Moreover, the degree of cultural distance of the different foreign plays does not fully explain why some are produced less frequently than others. What would make Russian plays more accessible culturally to the Québécois than Spanish plays? Why would Spanish plays be less accessible than Italian plays? To shed light on these figures and provide a clearer picture of the foreign repertoire, we have drawn up a table of authors and their plays, ranked by frequency of production, for Italian, German, Russian, Spanish, French, and American repertoire.

The Italian-language repertoire (table 7) is almost totally dominated by three authors: Goldoni, Dario Fo, and Pirandello. Goldoni, a true representative of the *commedia dell'arte* and the comedy of manners, is performed all over the world. He is an almost automatic choice. Dario Fo's militant, working-class social comedy resembles Québécois theatre in its

TABLE 7
Italian-Language Repertoire

Frequency of Author

Carlo Goldoni	10
Dario Fo	7
Luigi Pirandello	5
Angelo Ruzante	2
Ettore Scola	2
Carlo Gozzi	1
Eduardo De Filippo	1

Frequency of Performance

Goldoni	
The Servant of Two Masters	3
The Venetian Twins	2
La Locandiera	2
Squabbles in Chioggia	1
The Impresario of Smyrna	1
The Boors	1
Dario Fo	
Archangels Don't Play Pinball	2
Accidental Death of an Anarchist	1
The Open Couple	1
We Can't Pay! We Won't Pay!	1
Throw the Lady Out	1
Mistero buffo	1
Pirandello	
Six Characters in Search of an Author	2
Tonight We Improvise	1
The Pleasure of Honesty	1
Right You Are	1

attempt to make the population aware of its social and political condition. His theatre is politically committed and popular, and reaches beyond the type of theatre that places more emphasis on production values than on content. The main themes in Fo's works are very similar to those in the new Québécois theatre. The similarity is taken up by Michel Bélair, who, in his discussion of *Faut jeter la vieille* (*Throw the Lady Out*), observes that 'even though the text is not really Québécois, Paul Buissonneau's adaptation was easily applicable to the Québécois context.'[50] Pirandello has become a classic of Italian theatre. The most canonical plays from his critical, subversive, metatheatre have been staged in Quebec. Yet *Henry IV*,

TABLE 8
German-Language Repertoire

Frequency of Author

Bertolt Brecht	7
Max Frisch	2
Heinrich von Kleist	1
Arthur Schnitzler	1
Rainer Fassbinder	1
Karl Wittlinger	1

Frequency of Performance

Brecht	
Mother Courage	1
The Resistable Rise of Ui	1
Rise and Fall of the City of Mahoganny	1
A Man's a Man	1
Trumpets and Drums	1
The Threepenny Opera	1
The Life of Galileo	1
Frisch	
Andorra	1
The Fire Raisers	1

considered his finest play, was not performed until the 1990–1 season, when Alice Ronfard directed it for La NCT. Pirandello occupies a dominant position in Italian theatre, but other Italian playwrights should not be ignored. D'Annunzio, for example, takes his inspiration from classical myth and employs a primitive, archaicizing style. His plays, considered to be polar opposites of Pirandello's works, have never been produced in Quebec, and neither have Marinetti's futurist works such as *Roi Bombance* (a boisterous imitation of Jarry's *Ubu Roi*), nor plays by writers from the theatre of the *grotesque* (Luigi Chiarelli, Rosso Di San Secondo, Luigi Antonelli, Massimo Bontempelli), a movement as important as futurism. More contemporary writers, such as Ugo Betti and Diego Fabbri, have also been ignored by institutional theatre in Quebec.

In the German-language repertoire of institutional theatres, there are very few expressionist plays (table 8). And yet, the alienation of man, urban man, and the loss of authenticity have never been described with such force as in these plays. Their highly transcultural themes, however, do not come close enough to the nationalist theme of alienation in the Quebec

TABLE 9
Russian-Language Repertoire

Frequency of Author

Anton Chekhov	8
Fyodor Dostoevsky	1
Valentin Kataev	1

Frequency of Performance

Chekhov	
The Sea Gull	3
The Cherry Orchard	3
Uncle Vania	1
One-Act Plays	1
Dostoevsky	
The Idiot (adapted for the stage by A. Barsacq)	1
Kataev	
Day of Rest	1

theatre. Major expressionist writers like Wedekind (*Earth-Spirit, Pandora's Box*), Kokoschka, and Georg Kaiser (*Gas, Alcibiades Saved*), are passed over in silence. Well-known contemporary writers such as Tankred Dorst (*Grand Tirade at the Town Hall*), who is representative of a post-Brechtian political movement, are also ignored by the institutional theatres. German plays from after 1980 are, relatively speaking, better represented in experimental theatre. Besides Brecht, who is still the most represented, we find Peter Weiss (*Marat/Sade, The Investigation*), Rainer W. Fassbinder (*Bremen Coffee, The Bitter Tears of Petra von Kant*), and Peter Handke (*Offending the Audience, The Ride Across Lake Constance*). In the fringe theatre, 1987 was an especially good year for German-language works: Büchner (*Woyzeck*), Heiner Müller (*Hamletmachine*), Botho Strauss (*Great and Small*), and Kurt Schwitters (*Merz Opera*). Thus, we have to wait until the end of the 1980s to see a much more varied interest in German theatre, an interest reflected both in the choice of plays and in their production.

When we look at the Russian-language repertoire (table 9), we are struck by an absence of satirical works by Maiakovsky, of expressionist plays by Leonid Andreev, and of social and revolutionary plays by Gorky (*The Lower Depths*). A work such as Nicolai Erdman's *The Suicide*, an attack on the excesses of the Soviet regime written in a wickedly funny style resembling that of Gogol, is completely overshadowed by *Le Gars de Québec*, Michel Tremblay's Québécois adaptation of *The Government Inspector*.[51]

TABLE 10
Spanish-Language Repertoire

Frequency of Author

Federico García Lorca	2
Pedro Calderón de la Barca	1
Tirso de Molina	1
Fernando de Rojas	1
Jacinto Benavente y Martínez	1
Juan José Arreola (Mexican)	1
Ricardo Talesnik (Argentinian)	1

Frequency of Performance

García Lorca	
Blood Wedding	1
Yerma	1
Calderón	
Mantillas and Mysteries	1
Tirso de Molina	
The Shy Man at Court	1
Fernando de Rojas	
Celestina	1
Arreola	
La hora de todas	1
Talesnik	
La fiaca	1

A number of important plays are also missing from the Spanish-language repertoire (table 10). Noticeable by its absence is Ramon del Valle-Inclán's *esperpento*, written in a quasi-expressionist style best represented by his *Divine Words* and *Lights of Bohemia*. Valle-Inclán was eventually produced in the mid-1990s, but for a very limited, experimental-theatre public. It is also surprising that the *engagé* theatre of Alfonso Sastre (*Roman Chronicles, Death Squad*), an author sympathetic to Basque separatism, has aroused no interest in Quebec, where there is such a preoccupation with nationalism. Nevertheless, we should applaud Le Théâtre du Rideau Vert, one of the theatres most receptive to foreign plays, for staging *The Bonds of Interest* by Nobel laureate Jacinto Benavente.

The picture of the foreign-language repertoire we have just painted, with its glaring omissions, demonstrates great disparity in the choice of plays. Two criteria seem to have been used: a play had to have canonical status or be a comedy, both if possible. But such criteria were employed only by institutional theatres. The fringe theatres moved beyond the canon to explore new forms of drama. Theatres like L'Eskabel, Le Nouveau Théâtre Expérimental, and La Veillée, and groups like Le Pool, Carbone 14, and Le Théâtre Ubu presented works by relatively less canonical authors, such as Kurt Schwitters, Georg Büchner, Heiner Müller, Ugo Betti, Witold Gombrowicz, and Stanislas I. Witkiewicz, to name a few authors whose works were produced towards the end of the period under study. But these experiments with foreign theatre, operating with no financial backing, were limited in number; and major theatrical trends, which revolutionized forms of dramatic expression elsewhere, have never penetrated Quebec.

American Tragedy versus French Comedy

French and American theatre are clearly the two poles of attraction in the foreign repertoire. However, each is represented by a very different genre, as tables 11 and 12 show.

Comedy is the most frequently produced genre from the French repertoire (table 11). The comedy writers chosen to be produced in Quebec are a diverse group, including authors such as Sacha Guitry, André Roussin, and Eugène Labiche. As each of these authors is represented by only one or two plays, they do not appear in the table 11, but, as a group, they add up to an impressive total. With the exception of Molière, whose status is comparable to that of Goldoni in Italy, the authors Michel Bélair calls the 'big shots' of French culture are relatively underrepresented. Classical tragedy no longer figures prominently. Four of Racine's plays are retained: *Andromaque, Bérénice, Britannicus,* and *Phèdre,* while *Le Cid* is the only work by Corneille produced by the major Québécois theatres. These works have undoubtedly 'little relevance to the tensions and conflicts that characterize Quebec.'[52] This type of French theatre is perceived as being incapable of serving the cause of national identity: plays are expected to reflect Québécois society, to speak 'about us' and 'like us.' For certain sectors of criticism, the search for an identity is a crucial criterion and a major factor in the institutionalization of any literature. According to Rudel Tessier, the ideal play is 'a play in which the public not only recognizes itself, but one in which it can learn to recognize itself – to know itself better.' He goes on to say: 'I believe that this type of play is a good play.'[53] Another critic expresses himself in similar terms: 'The public ... expects, with reason, the play to speak to them about themselves.'[54] The preoccupation with identity in the Québécois theatre is tied to the nationalist cause: we must 'reach a

TABLE 11
French Repertoire

Frequency of Author

Molière	21
Georges Feydeau	10
Eugène Ionesco	7
Jean Racine	4
Pierre Marivaux	4
Paul Claudel	4
Jean Anouilh	3
Pierre Barillet and Jean-Pierre Grédy	3
Samuel Beckett	3
Jean Giraudoux	3
Victor Lanou	3
Jean-Claude Carrière	3
Eduardo Manet	3

Frequency of Performance

Molière	
The Hypochondriac	3
Don Juan	3
The Miser	2
Tartuffe	2
The Knavery of Scapin	2
Feydeau	
A Flea in Her Ear	2
Ionesco	
The Chairs	2

public scarcely aware of its own existence,' we must make the public 'aware that they are Québécois.'[55] In this sociocultural context, where everything must be directed towards creating the national identity, the French theatre and, more generally, all theatre with a transhistorical and transcultural value cease to have a raison d'être, unless they can lend themselves to Québécois re-actualization, and thereby fulfil the same mirroring function as the Québécois theatre. American theatre does fulfil this function. Some comedies are selected from the American repertoire, but not nearly as frequently as modern tragedy, which is obviously seen as a better vehicle for the theme of Québécois alienation.

French plays performed in Quebec appear to be chosen mainly for their entertainment value. American plays (table 12), however, have a totally dif-

TABLE 12
American Repertoire

Frequency of Author

Tennessee Williams	13
Neil Simon	8
Arthur Miller	7
Eugene O'Neill	5
Edward Albee	4
Paul Zindel	3

Frequency of Performance

Tennessee Williams	
The Glass Menagerie	2
Suddenly Last Summer	2
Arthur Miller	
Death of a Salesman	4
Eugene O'Neill	
Desire under the Elms	2
Edward Albee	
Who's Afraid of Virginia Woolf?	2
Paul Zindel	
The Effect of Gamma Rays ...	3

ferent function, despite the fact that some American comedies, like those of Neil Simon, are produced in Quebec. While such plays should not be overlooked, they do not figure prominently. Their primary function is to create a loyal theatre-going audience and to ensure the commercial viability of theatre companies, objectives that can be realized by bringing in successful Broadway shows – hence, their immediate, post-Broadway appearance in Montreal. But the majority of plays chosen from the American repertoire are *modern tragedies*. Tragedy is the quintessential dramatic form. It crystallizes the national consciousness and cultural maturity of a people. It is the repository of a society's values and reflects the balance of power in society. The plays of Eugene O'Neill, Tennessee Williams, and Arthur Miller are the incarnation of everyday tragedy, what might be called *modern tragedy*.[56] Modern tragedy revolves around the family, the dominant social forces, class conflict, the search for one's roots, and alienation in its various social and psychological manifestations. These elements of the American theatre provide a suitable thematic matrix for the major preoccupations of Québécois society. In a Quebec striving to free itself from its 'alienations' and discovering its Americanness, it is easy to see the attraction of American theatre. But can one seriously speak, as Adrien Gruslin does, of an American grip on the Québécois theatre? 'Today,' Gruslin claims, 'no one can disregard the presence of American imperialism, among others: the literary and/or the theatrical parallel the economic.'[57] Contained in this cliché is yet one more allusion to Quebec as victim, enslaved by an aggressive Foreigner. But what American dictates must Québécois theatre companies obey when drawing up their programmes? There is no doubt that commercial imperatives naturally lead theatres to choose plays that have been a commercial success south of the border. But above and beyond that, the content of the theatre repertoires is well and truly in phase with social discourse and reproduces its main social themes, themes such as the discovery of the American identity of the Québécois, whose Americanness is presented as one of the main factors distinguishing them from the French. Consequently, the co-opting of American plays into the Québécois theatre system involves a choice of values. We should also bear in mind that many American plays are not translated but adapted, and, as we have seen, these adaptations can go as far as substituting the name of the Québécois adapter for the American author. Is this, then, 'American imperialism' or, rather, a sign of appropriation of American works into the axio-ideological field of Québécois symbolic order?

Politics and the Theatre

We will now examine to what extent the repertoire under discussion evolved after 1968, an interesting period in Quebec history, which witnessed a number of very important political events. These events were closely linked to sovereigntist aspirations in the province and had wide repercussions in the social discourse. How did the theatre, a subset of the social discourse, reflect this series of events? Did these events affect relations with the Foreigner in this particular cultural field?

At the beginning of the Quiet Revolution, General de Gaulle's celebrated 'Vive le Québec libre' reverberated across the country. It was July 1967. Three years later, in October 1970, the FLQ uprising took place. In November 1976, the Parti Québécois came to power. In May 1980, a referendum was held on sovereignty. In 1981, the Parti Québécois was given a second mandate, which would end in defeat in the election of 1985. In 1982, the Canadian constitution was repatriated, but Quebec refused to ratify it. In 1987, the new federal Conservative government tried to persuade Quebec to accept the Meech Lake Constitutional Accord, but the Accord would be rejected in 1990 by Newfoundland and Manitoba. Dur-

TABLE 13
Annual Distribution of Foreign and Québécois Plays

Season	Total no. of plays	Québécois plays		Foreign plays	
		No.	%	No.	%
(67)–68*	16	3	19	13	81
68–69	31	12	39	19	61
69–70	36	19	53	17	47
70–71	30	14	47	16	53
71–72	35	16	46	19	54
72–73	34	14	41	20	59
73–74	37	12	32	25	68
74–75	42	21	50	21	50
75–76	40	18	45	22	55
76–77	38	19	50	19	50
77–78	38	22	58	16	42
78–79	35	16	46	19	54
79–80	34	14	41	20	59
80–81	34	16	47	18	53
81–82	35	19	54	16	46
82–83	37	18	49	19	51
83–84	35	12	34	23	66
84–85	30	13	43	17	57
85–86	34	18	53	16	47
86–87	32	13	41	19	59
87–88	33	15	45	18	55
Total	716	324	45	392	55

*The repertoire dates from the beginning of 1968.

ing the whole of this period, Québécois political life and social discourse centred around the problem of Quebec's national identity, and each of the above dates marked an advance or a retreat. It is true that theatre programs were established in advance of ensuing political events. Nevertheless, we shall examine to what extent the theatre repertoire as a whole followed the pattern of political events and reflected the prevailing nationalism and the new relation to the Foreigner it presupposed, a relation that is revealed in the very choice of plays produced.

Table 13 demonstrates that the relative proportion of Québécois plays to foreign plays remained almost the same throughout the period under study. The dramatic increase in numbers between the first and second seasons can be explained by the fact that the period begins with the production of *Les Belles-Soeurs* in 1968, and thereby excludes that part of the

FIGURE 1 Québécois Plays, by Year

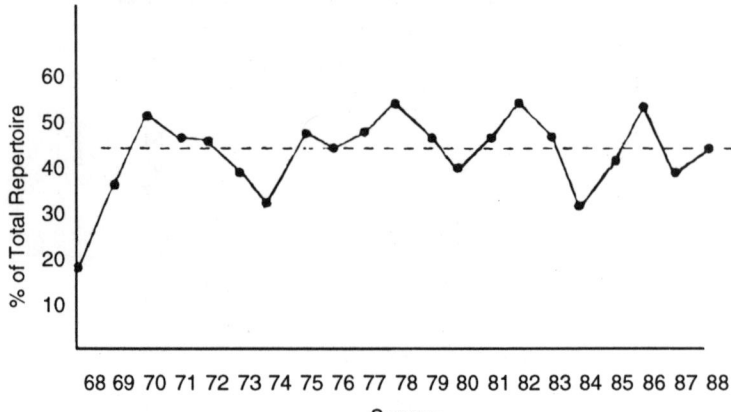

repertoire produced in 1967. We should not jump to conclusions, but the increase might well indicate that 1968–9 was a turning-point in the programming of Québécois plays. To verify this, we would have to do a comparable study for the years preceding the production of *Les Belles-Soeurs*. However, this period does not form part of the present study.

There is a striking disparity between the figures in table 13 and analysis of the Québécois repertoire in a number of studies on the theatre in Quebec. We have already quoted Michel Bélair in this regard. In 1973, he stated that the Québécois theatre occupied only a 'marginal, tiny' position in the programming of institutional theatres. The above figures clearly demonstrate that Québécois plays represented almost half of the plays put on by institutional theatres – no small achievement for a theatre going back about fifty, or even only about twenty years, if we accept the criteria used by theatre historians. It is true that the proportion of Québécois plays varies from year to year, but it reaches successive peaks in 1969–70, 1977–8, 1981–2, and 1985–6. These peaks coincide with the major political events mentioned above: the events of October 1970, the election of the Parti Québécois in 1976, the 1980 referendum, and the election of 1985 which could have resulted in the re-election of the Parti Québécois. The fact that programming precedes actual production of plays explains why theatrical events and political events do not always coincide exactly. The increase in the number of plays does not necessarily occur where we might expect it. Figure 1 gives a better idea of the extent of synchronicity between artistic production and political events. There are four periods during which the number of Québécois plays rises well above the average. At the same time, the number of foreign plays declines. The elections and the referendum were not random events. Each was preceded by a very long public debate. These events, in their turn, influenced the social discourse that had paved the way for them. The institutional theatre can be seen as a mirror of these events, supporting, in its turn, these decisive moments by promoting Québécois drama. In this way, it participated in the dynamic of Quebec's sociopolitical emancipation. At first glance, any connection between the events of October 1970 and the peak in the number of plays during the period 1969–72 may seem coincidental. However, to assume so would be to forget that the events of October marked the culmination of a sovereigntist movement which had been punctuated by acts of violence throughout the 1960s. These events were also the expression, admittedly extreme, of widely held public opinion, a point of view that may well have played a role in the emergence of a 'new' Québécois drama. The predominant position of Québécois theatre at that time and immediately afterwards is further proof of the relation between the theatre and political events. But how to explain the peak of 1985–6, a period in which the Parti Québécois went down to defeat? As the elections of 1976 and 1981 had done, the 1985 election powerfully and momentarily crystallized social discourse in Quebec around the theme of Québécois identity and nationalist aspirations. There is no reason why the theatrical field, a discursive field *par excellence*, should not also be subject to the polarizations of social discourse at a time when extreme and entrenched positions are being taken on the issue of identity, especially by artists. Interestingly, the institutional theatres were accused of ignoring Québécois plays, of being indifferent to them. For example, Michel Bélair described Québécois theatre as being a 'théâtre de revendication' (a theatre of protest) whose 'main purpose is to focus its thinking on the idea of a Québécois nation.'[58] He then points a finger at the big theatres, asking sardonically: 'How can a theatre preoccupied with the Québécois situation be as important as the International Repertoire to a public that we already have had such difficulty getting out to see the Great Works?'[59] If this lack of interest on the part of the institutional theatres was real, figure 1 should show a decline in Québécois programming in 1985–6. But, in fact, it shows an increase. Could we not conclude, then, that the so-called institutional sector is a driving force for national liberation? If this is in fact the case, the 1985–6 peak indicates that institutional theatre assumed a nationalist role at a particular time, when the elections could well bring to power a political class less sensitive to the aspirations of the independence movement. And

54   A Sociocritique of Translation

TABLE 14
Annual Distribution of French and American Plays

Season	Total no. of plays	French plays		American plays	
		No.	%	No.	%
(67)–68*	16	5	31	2	12
68–69	31	7	23	1	3
69–70	36	8	22	1	3
70–71	30	7	23	4	13
71–72	35	7	20	3	9
72–73	34	9	26	3	9
73–74	37	11	30	4	11
74–75	42	10	24	5	12
75–76	40	12	30	7	17
76–77	38	6	16	6	16
77–78	38	4	11	3	8
78–79	35	7	20	2	6
79–80	34	10	30	3	9
80–81	34	6	18	5	15
81–82	35	6	17	5	14
82–83	37	4	11	6	16
83–84	35	2	6	9	26
84–85	30	1	3	6	20
85–86	34	6	18	3	9
86–87	32	4	12	8	25
87–88	33	3	9	7	21
Total	716	136	19	95	13

*The repertoire dates from the beginning of 1968.

if the institutional theatre was so motivated, the accusations of indifference and élitism levelled at this theatre have no basis whatsoever. But it is naïve to think that nationalism was the only motivating factor; theatres depend on grants for their existence, and therefore on the powers that be. Whatever way you look at it, the chronological reality of the statistics sheds a whole new light on the critical and accusatory discourse on institutional theatre, a discourse that implicitly states that there is no room for foreign theatre, at any level. In the theatre, as in life, the ideal is to be, is it not, 'maîtres chez nous' (masters in our own house)?

Let us now examine the French and American repertoires throughout the period under examination. Table 14 reveals a slow increase in the number of American plays produced, and a corresponding decline in the number of French plays. The change in relative influence of these foreign repertoires occurred around the time of the referendum and parallels the development of a new form of national consciousness. Quebec rejected the cultural legacy of France as a remnant of colonialism: 'We must ensure that Québécois culture is no longer viewed as a sort of by-product of French culture, but rather as a culture in its own right.'[60] Once again, Quebec proclaimed that its uniqueness was tied to its American identity:

All of contemporary Quebec has constructed its identity on what is called the 'French fact,' that is to say, upon a rejection of Canadian history and of everything Canadian, and yet at the same time it finds itself forced to discard an essential part of its own history, bound up as it is in the history of French and English Canada. From such a perspective, ... the French-Canadian and native fact, or, to be more precise, our American fact, can be seen as a symbol that Quebec has rejected and still rejects.[61]

In this plea for the reterritorialization of the Québécois identity, Americanness is defined as recognition of the 'native' attachment of the Québécois to Canadian soil. The argument is interesting in that it annuls, or at least relativizes, French antecedence. It makes it easier to break ties with French ancestry, ties that were strengthened by one historical illusion at the expense of another, authentic, real tie.[62] The referendum debate was undoubtedly the catalyst for this change in the definition of the Québécois identity, a shift that was reflected in the social discourse.

At the same time, the proportion of translations coming from France as opposed to those produced in Quebec was reversed (table 15). This change clearly reveals a rejection of what was felt in Quebec to be cultural dependence on France.

The difference in the curve in figure 2 from that in figure 1 confirms the decisive role the referendum played in affirming Québécois culture. The decline in the number of French translations, which started at the beginning of the 1970s, accelerated around this time. In contrast, the number of Québécois translations soared, to a point where French translations were almost eliminated. This increase in Québécois translations represents an indisputable reterritorialization of cultural activities, including translation. Translation was repatriated to where there was a need for it. Not only were foreign plays translated, but, very often, serious alterations were made to the original, which was naturalized and thereby incorporated into the theatre that selected it. A case in point is La

56 A Sociocritique of Translation

TABLE 15
Annual Distribution of Québécois and French Translations*

Season	Total no. of foreign plays	Québécois translations		French translations	
		No.	%	No.	%
(67)–68	8	2	25	6	75
68–69	10	1	10	9	90
69–70	8	4	50	4	50
70–71	9	4	44	5	56
71–72	12	6	50	6	50
72–73	9	2	22	7	78
73–74	14	6	43	8	57
74–75	12	6	50	6	50
75–76	11	6	55	5	45
76–77	14	7	50	7	50
77–78	13	7	54	6	46
78–79	13	8	61	5	39
79–80	11	5	45	6	55
80–81	12	7	58	5	42
81–82	10	6	60	4	40
82–83	15	13	87	2	13
83–84	21	19	90	2	10
84–85	16	9	56	7	44
85–86	10	8	80	2	20
86–87	15	13	87	2	13
87–88	15	14	93	1	6

*The table includes Québécois 'translations' of French works.

Compagnie Jean-Duceppe, the only theatre to establish officially a distinction between translated works and adapted works.

As table 16 shows, since it was founded in 1973, La Compagnie Jean-Duceppe had produced fifty-eight foreign plays in translation. Translations from France made up 19 per cent of the total, as against 81 per cent from Quebec. Until 1979–80, of the translations chosen by the company, approximately 35 per cent were French translations. In 1980–1, French translations disappeared; Québécois translations, henceforth, made up 97 per cent of the foreign-language repertoire. We note that, after this date, the company produced Québécois translations of plays that it had previously staged in their French translation.

We observe also that, on average, 42 per cent of Québécois translations were adaptations. Thus, nearly one-quarter of all foreign works staged by

FIGURE 2 Québécois Translations, by Year

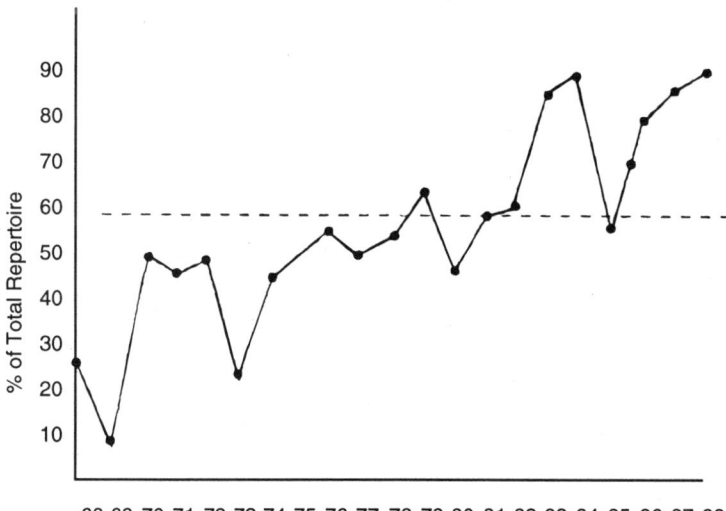

the company were, in fact, adaptations, adaptation being an ethnocentric form of translation:

> Ethnocentric will be taken to mean here that which reduces everything to its own culture, to its norms and values, and considers that which is situated outside – the Foreign – negatively or as just barely suitable for annexation, adaptation, for enriching that culture.[63]

Adaptation removes from a play any indication of its foreign origins and gives it the appearance of being a local work. It gives the public the illusion of being in the familiar milieu of its own culture and, by so doing, it increases the literary legacy of the country that produces it. In this sense, it is annexationist.[64] At other times and in other places, translation has assumed similar forms – in Rome, for example, where, according to Berman, ethnocentric translation was born. But in this powerful empire, translation did not play quite the same role it does in Quebec, a province with the more modest aim of becoming a nation-state. However, in both cases, ethnocentric translation plays a central role in literary creation. It fills what is perceived as a lacuna in the cultural field. Yet one can hardly

58 A Sociocritique of Translation

TABLE 16
Proportion of Translations and Adaptations, Compagnie Jean-Duceppe

Season	No. of trans.	French trans.	Québécois trans.	Québécois adaptations
73–74	4	2	2	0
74–75	5	2	3	0
75–76	4	2	0	2
76–77	4	1	1	2
77–78	3	1	2	0
78–79	5	1	3	1
79–80	4	1	2	1
Total	29	10	13	6
80-81	3	0	2	1
81-82	3	0	2	1
82-83	3	0	3	0
83-84	5	0	3	2
84-85	5	0	4	1
85-86	3	1	0	2
86-87	4	0	4	0
87-88	3	0	2	1
Total	29	1	20	8
Overall total	58	11	33	14

speak of imperialism when it comes to Québécois adaptations. On the contrary, these adaptations manifest a turning-in on one's own community. We will explore the various reasons for this phenomenon later. In Quebec, adaptation is based on a solipsistic ideology, which is inextricably linked to the ideology of 'difference.' This type of adaptation rejects the view that culture can be interhuman. It rejects *dialogism.* The Other has nothing to say to me. The Other is irrevocably different, just as I am. The voice of the Other silences my voice. I must therefore silence the voice of the Other.

2

At the Other's Expense: Iconoclastic Translation

> Québécois adaptation is proof of our theatre's uniqueness. Once stifled by foreign theatre, it has now shown itself strong enough to assimilate it.
>
> Paul Lefebvre and Pierre Ostiguy, 'L'Adaptation théâtrale au Québec'

The emergence of a 'Québécois' theatre coincided, as we have seen, with the emergence of a new form of national awareness that asserted itself not only against Anglo-Canadian hegemony but also against the cultural and linguistic legacy of France. The time had come to eliminate the French legacy, a remnant of colonialism. Under these circumstances, it is not surprising that a new way of translating emerged along with the new theatre. Indeed, the simultaneous growth of writing and translation for the theatre indicates that translation played an active role in the renewal of the theatre in Quebec.

The year 1968 saw the success of both Michel Tremblay's *Les Belles-Soeurs* and Éloi de Grandmont's translation into Québécois of Shaw's *Pygmalion*.[1] With Tremblay's play, the first play to use the vernacular language exclusively in its dialogue, the literary institution heralded the birth of a Québécois theatre. Grandmont's translation of *Pygmalion*, which also used the vernacular, broke with the traditional mode of expression used in translations imported from France, and also gained recognition from the institution. Two aspects of this translation are worthy of note: first, the linguistic transformation in Grandmont's *Pygmalion* differs only in certain parts from earlier French translations; the vernacular is used to translate only the cockney dialogue and transpose the action more effectively to Montreal. Second, the vernacular is used to render the humorous effect of the foreign work.

These two features of this widely acclaimed translation prompted us to look at a unique ensemble of productions from the period under discussion, plays that were on the borderline between original works and importations from foreign theatre. These plays relied heavily on translation. Indeed, translation became *the very subject-matter* of dramatic writing, as if using it as a theme could ward off this dangerous activity that daily placed Québécois in a position of dependence. The year of the Official Languages Act, 1968, saw an explosion of translation activity, centred in Ottawa. Most translation was from English to French; administrative, technical, and commercial documents originated in anglophone Canada; however, foreign literature in translation came from France. Thus, translation, a constituent element of the cultural and political situation of Quebec, was perceived as a source of dispossession, the very incarnation of the dependence of a province that aspired to be recognized as a fully fledged nation.

Under these circumstances, writing and translation for the theatre gradually started to move into the realm of parody. The time had come to 'break with edifying, imported literature.'[2] Dramatic writers made liberal use of translation and of imitation, an extreme form of translation. The new theatre thus operated on two levels. On one level, it was reacting against a textuality in which it no longer recognized itself; paradoxically, in this reaction, it opted to imitate the very model it was attempting to replace. On the other level, it was attempting to throw off the shackles of the institution, which was seen as a root cause of Québécois alienation. Indeed, the Québécois condition itself became a subject of parody. This social satire was profoundly linked to the resurgence of nationalism.

The Scourge of Alterity

Jean-Claude Germain's play, with its evocative title, *A Canadian Play/Une Plaie canadienne*, is a good example of a work in which creation and translation are interwoven. Such use of translation in dramatic writing is indicative of a problematic relation with alterity. Jean-Claude Germain's play is paradigmatic by virtue of its very title, which parodies translation and ridicules the perverse effects of institutional bilingualism. The structure of *A Canadian Play/Une Plaie canadienne* imitates the *cadavres exquis*, or hybrid forms, found in translations done for the federal government, for example, forms in which toponymic expressions fuse English and French:

Maple Avenue des Érables.³ Germain's title is clearly designed to denounce this co-presence of the two languages and the fact that French is always overshadowed by English. This metonymical phrase also brings to mind official translations from Ottawa in which the two languages are placed side by side. The position of the two languages is far from innocent or innocuous – English, given the numerical majority of its speakers, occupies the position of source language; French, the language of translation, takes second place, as weak and distorted as an echo. In these bilingual texts, French has no autonomous existence. It is marginal to English, and the more it duplicates English, the more it becomes, insidiously, a literal translation of English:

We should in fact consider that whenever there is close contact between two languages, there is inevitably an exchange, and to the extent that one dominates the other, the dominated language receives more than it gives: the dominated language is subjected to interference from the dominant language.

[... in Quebec] francophone translators are influenced by English in two ways. On the one hand, they have to provide in their language equivalents of concepts that were formed in English, and sometimes the easiest thing to do is to borrow or translate literally from English. On the other hand, because they live in contact with English, translators may sometimes unconsciously absorb anglicisms for which there are authentic equivalents that they do not know or have forgotten.⁴

The bilingualism of translation is thus a Canadian wound (une plaie). The adjective *Canadian* is significant because, as opposed to *Québécois*, it designates the federal reality, the true cause of the wound. And as we all know, the wound has its origins in history, dating all the way back to the defeat of Montcalm and the French Canadians on the Plains of Abraham, and the beginning of colonial subjugation. The 'Canadian wound' is the unhealed wound of this humiliation. The title *A Canadian Play/Une Plaie canadienne* is parodic, yet, at the same time, dysphoric with regard to the situation it is attempting to describe. It is paradoxical in form, the better to reinforce the *doxa*, the point of view, the discourse on the Québécois condition. But Germain's parody does not stop at the title, for his whole play is an attempt to exorcise, through laughter, the federalist scourge that forces the Québécois to become Canadians: 'In other words French people who speak English! ... So we end up with two borrowed cultures!'⁵

In this dual definition of alterity, cultural attachment to France is seen to be as much a source of alienation as English domination. Becoming

English-speaking French people, in other words, opting for federalism over national autonomy, is tantamount to denying one's specific *Québécois* identity and becoming assimilated – just as the Englishman who sealed Quebec's fate in the last century had desired. *A Canadian Play* puts that Englishman, Lord Durham, on trial. Lord Durham was sent out from England to survey the situation in the province following the Patriote rebellion. In his report to Queen Victoria, he described the Québécois as a people bereft of history and culture, whom the British had to assimilate in order to protect themselves against even the slightest hint of secessionism. The following is an extract from that part of the report which deals with the dependency of French-Canadian literature, in particular, the theatre:

They are a people with no history and no literature. The literature of England is written in a language which is not theirs; and the only literature which their language renders familiar to them, is that of a nation from which they have been separated by eighty years of foreign rule, and still more by those changes which the Revolution and its consequences have wrought in the whole political, moral and social state of France. Yet it is on a people whom recent history, manners and modes of thought, so entirely separate from them, that the French Canadians are wholly dependent for almost all the instruction and amusement derived from books: it is on this essentially foreign literature, which is conversant about events, opinions and habits of life, perfectly strange and unintelligible to them, that they are compelled to be dependent.

... Though descended from the people in the world that most generally love and have mostly successfully cultivated the drama – though living on a continent, in which almost every town, great or small, has an English theatre, the French population of Lower Canada, cut off from every people that speaks its own language, can support no national stage.[6]

To stifle any secessionist impulse, Lord Durham advocated the political and demographic integration of the colony, which was cut off from France and already anglicized. He recommended that an English administration be set up in the colony and that the local population be drowned in an anglophone majority.

In Germain's play, Lord Durham's ghost is tried before a court of a Québécois brotherhood whose name, 'Les Enfants de la Veuve Saint-Jean' (The Children of Widow St John), refers to the patron saint of Quebec, St John the Baptist. In this symbolic trial, Germain puts the following words in the mouth of Lord Durham:

At the Other's Expense 63

Je n'ai fait que *translater* la réalité! Je suis venu! J'ai écouté! J'ai regardé! Et dans mon rapport à sa Majesté, je n'ai fait qu'une *translation*, monsieur Caron! Qu'une *tra-duc-tion* de la réalité! Que vous avez *retranslaté*! *Re-tra-duit* à votre tour! Dans vos mots! A votre guise! Croyez-moi! Votre histoire, si vous tenez absolument à en avoir une, ne souffre pas d'une maladie des symboles, mais d'un abus, d'un *e-x-c-è-s de tra-duc-tion*!

MONSIEUR CARON – D'une *indigestion de traduction*, excellence! Pour que votre expertise soit plus complète!

L'HOMME AU BANDEAU [Durham] – Alors, si c'est le cas, *c-e-s-s-e-z* de *tra-dui-re*! Il faut se dire soi-même, si l'on ne veut pas être dit par les autres!

[I only *translated* reality! I came! I listened. I looked around! And in my report to Her Majesty, all I did was a *translation*, Monsieur Caron! Just a *trans-la-tion* of reality! Re-trans-la-ted in your words! As you like! Believe me! Your history, if you insist on having one, does not suffer from the disease of symbols, but from abuse, from an *e-x-c-e-s-s of trans-la-tion*!

MONSIEUR CARON – From *translation indigestion*, Excellency! So that your evaluation will be more complete!

THE BLINDFOLDED MAN [Durham] – So, if that's the case, c-e-a-s-e *trans-la-ting*! You have to express your own self, if you don't want to be expressed by others!][7]

Germain's play provides a paradigm as enlightening as the title suggests. The play is explicitly constructed around a metaphor of translation, a metaphor that presents translation in a negative light. Translation is a calque: *traduire* (the standard French verb) and its literal translation, *translater*, are interchangeable. Germain puts the verb *translater*, an etymologically justifiable yet incorrect form, in the mouth of the Englishman. We should therefore see the verb as an error, a bad translation and, figuratively, a pernicious, alienating, and destructive act. Translation is portrayed in the most pejorative way possible. Here again we see the old cliché – *traduttore traditore*. One of Lord Durham's Québécois judges bluntly declares: 'It's the rule, the more you are translated, the more you are betrayed!'[8] This cliché presents the Québécois with an image of themselves – they are the victims of an existence perpetually mediated by the Other and, as such, they are inexorably *betrayed* by the Other.

To understand the full impact of the translation metaphor, we must remember that the play was produced in 1979, just before the referendum that offered Quebec yet again the option of independence. The Patriotes' dream had come to the fore once more, but it was hampered by the same obstacles as before. Once again, the province was divided. The nationalists, for whom Germain now spoke, saw the attachment of part of Quebec's population to federalism as a new form of French-Canadian 'loyalism' to the British Crown. This very loyalism, together with British orders to repress the rebellion, had aborted an American-style attempt at independence in the preceding century.

On the eve of the 1980 referendum, Germain's play was a final plea, an attempt to awaken consciousness, a 'shamanistic operation,' wrote Germain, directed at a population that had to be liberated from its British (federalist) obsession and convinced it should acquire enough independence to live for itself.[9] Germain harks back to a time when imperialist England had the upper hand in the Dominion of Canada. Lord Durham's ghost is brandished as a symbol of that era which, following the repression of the first failed attempt at autonomy, saw the formation of the Canadian Union of Upper (anglophone) Canada with the former French colony, known at that time as Lower Canada. The ghost of the Englishman accused of advocating this union still haunts Quebec today, incarnated in his French-Canadian emulators: Wilfrid Laurier, Louis Saint-Laurent, and Pierre Trudeau. The three Canadian prime ministers from Quebec are tried before this same court, in the presence of an allegorical character, the 'Maumariée' (mismarried maiden) who represents the Province of Quebec. The three men are directly identified with the Englishman who advocated assimilation. Lord Durham actually assumes their physical appearance and dress. La Maumariée, the gullible inveterate dupe, is completely taken in by his resemblance to the prime ministers. Germain's message is clear: since Durham, history has repeated itself. These three men came to power in Ottawa with a mandate from Quebec to go before the majority, the inheritors of the victory of the Plains of Abraham, and defend the interests of the francophone province: 'I voted you in so you could translate what we want in their language!'[10]

These men, in whom Quebec placed its trust, these men, brought up in both languages and in both founding cultures of the Union, turned out to be poor 'translators' of Quebec's interests. They are accused of treason, of playing the Anglo-Canadian game at Quebec's expense. They put Quebec at a disadvantage, and deprived it of real power instead of fulfilling their mandate, to give it more power:

JOS – Vous traduisez toujours mieux de l'anglais au français que du français à l'anglais! [...]

SIR WILFRID – Bon! Quecé qutu veux, Jos?

JOS – P-l-u-s-s-e!

SIR WILFRID – Y a pas dmots en anglais pour ça! [...] P-l-u-s-s-e ça straduit pas en anglais, Jos!

[JOS – You always translate better from English to French than from French to English ! ...

SIR WILFRID – So! What do you want, Jos?

JOS – ... P-l-u-s-s-e! (More!)

SIR WILFRID – There are no words in English for that! ... That can't be translated into English, Jos!][11]

In Germain's play, the translator is described as a *dobbeule crosseur*[12] (double-crosser). Anglicisms such as this are tangible proof of the 'success' of Lord Durham's mission and of its continuing success in the federalist option, an option Germain attempts to discredit by superimposing the past on the present. In this way, he conveniently fails to mention the changes the Canadian Confederation has undergone, both internally and in its relations with the British Crown, whose role today is more symbolic than real.

Beyond its immediate ideological function, the translation-treason metaphor questions the identity of the *translator* – the *other name of the Québécois*. The perpetrator of pernicious translation is not the Other, but its Québécois double. A double traitor, above all to himself, he denies his own identity, then assumes the characteristics of the Other, to better dupe his own people. The double (and with it, the theme of duplicity) is associated with the definition of the Québécois, who is torn between desire for a pure identity and desire for the power and privileges of the dominant group. The theme of the double is omnipresent in the social discourse, along with a whole series of denigrating images such as the shadow, the ghost, and the distorted mirror image;[13] eloquent images of a problematic quest for identity. Lord Durham was well aware that a series of events had prevented French Canadians from creating their own identity and that this failure would facilitate anglicization, a process that circumstances were already favouring at the time. According to Germain, French Canadians have always had a tragic fascination with the conqueror; and, ever since the Conquest, they have been attempting to imitate the conqueror. They are incapable of conceiving of their own institutions without reference to an English model. Furthermore, traitors in their midst reinforce this secret desire to imitate and be the equal of the English model:

SIR WILFRID – ... it means that their institutions will become our institutions! Their laws, o-u-r laws! Their democracy, o-u-r democracy! ...

JOS – I don't see what's so uplifting about becoming a copy!

SIR WILFRID – And I don't see what's so humiliating about copying the best model in the world![14]

As fate would have it, whenever the Québécois make a real attempt to disassociate themselves from the English model, they end up, once again, as prisoners of that model. In the preface to his play, Germain develops this idea, demonstrating that nothing actually belongs to the Québécois, not even the symbols they have adopted to create their own identity. A case in point is the national holiday of Quebec, whose symbolic significance, he says, is derived from a 'translation error.' This is a surprising comparison and, as such, worthy of further consideration. The metaphor of a translation error used to criticize the Québécois desire to emulate the English is based on the historical circumstances surrounding the choice of the Feast Day of St John the Baptist as the national day of celebration, in 1834. The day was supposedly chosen in an act of provocation, to demonstrate that there was a will for independence and self-affirmation: 'English or French-Canadian, all political opponents of the Patriote movement were associated with Free Masonry, and the Masons since 1759 have celebrated St John the Baptist's day ...'[15]

However, according to Germain, French Canadians had difficulty identifying with St John as a patron saint, and this identification came about only after a historian came up with an interpretation of the saint that fitted the image Quebec society had of itself. The historian attributed the choice of that particular saint to the *liberating* virtues of the prophet. This is a clear case of mistaken identity, a translation error: St John the Baptist, whom iconography depicts with a lamb on his shoulders, had been confused with the Saviour: 'Least among the faults of this translation was the fact that it not only altered the nature and role of the Essenian Demiurge but also turned him forthwith into a sort of Québécois Panurge.'[16]

The image of a Québécois Panurge, according to Germain, is more than a fortuitous choice of words; it is the very image others have of the Québécois identity. To express the 'ethnic humiliation' of a people who have only ever known their name 'from the outside,' Gaston Miron writes, for example, 'My name is "sheep."'[17] In the social discourse, 'nation of sheep' 'nation of translators' are interchangeable expressions, used repeatedly, as if to exorcise this self-representation of Québécois society. Thus, according to Germain, the initial attempt at self-affirmation by the Québécois was derailed by an incorrect 'translation' which rebounded against them; this error foreshadowed the 'sheep-like' behaviour they would display throughout history. Was the failure of the 1980 referendum on Quebec sovereignty not final proof of this?[18]

Above and beyond Germain's political plea, what is significant here is that this *prise de parole*, this attempt at auto-translation, results in a *mistranslation* of identity. Instead of damaging the prestige of the model, thereby repelling the invading alterity, 'translation' literally takes as its *target* the society that it was attempting to support and promote. *Mistranslation* is not without consequence. It is demeaning and provokes laughter and disdain. On the other hand, the superiority of the Other is strengthened by translation, an act that makes Québécois translators the willing victims of the plan to assimilate them, and the agents of their own destruction. Translation is exposed as an involuntary act of self-derision, involuntary but inescapable because of the promiscuousness of the model. It is thus imperative to distance oneself from the model, to act as if the Other did not exist, so as to finally gain access to one's own identity. And if such distance is not achieved, in the process of asserting one's identity, of 'translating' oneself, one is destined to be nothing but a ridiculous, distorted imitation of the Other: 'a fantasy in a theatre of shadows, whose only reality is to be "l'Endroit imaginé d'un Envers imaginant" [the imagined outside of an imagining inside].'[19] For Germain, translation is a metaphor of the deformation that occurs when there is contact with the Other, so clearly demonstrated in the juxtaposition of *A Canadian Play* and *Une Plaie canadienne*. The metaphor of translation assumes a profoundly ideological function in Germain's work. His portrayal of translation as an act of duplication, controlled from the outside, on occasion coercive but always despoiling, parallels the theme of the distorted mirror image, a theme that permeates the discourse on *québécité*. As a result, when translation is put on trial, the Other is put on trial for being an inescapable model, a model that reflects back a distorted, inferiorizing image to the Québécois. The Other, whom Germain also calls the 'Foreigner,'[20] is not an abstraction: 'Wherever we look, we inevitably find the Other – in this case the English, whose gaze clouds our own vision.'[21] Omnipresent and absolute, Otherness sullies and contaminates. Alterity is an absolute: for Québécois, the sole incarnation of alterity is the anglophone world.[22] The Other is also a mirror in which one seeks to find one's own image. But the Other sends back a *reflet abîmé* (a reflection that is both distorted and, in Gide's sense of the word, 'a-bys-mal'), because this form of self-identification produces only *a double of the Other's shadow*: 'He will think he is someone else and, since he exists solely through the Other, he will condemn himself, in the same breath, to existing only for the Other: in other words, he is going to become the double of the Other's shadow.'[23] The Other is a subjugating, hegemonic figure, whose proximity leads to the degradation, and then the loss, of individual and collective identity.

In Quebec, the theme of destructive alterity is more prevalent in poetry than in drama, particularly since Gaston Miron began speaking of 'the suffering of being an other,' 'the hopeless conditions of daily otherness,' 'the polluted culture': 'l'altérité pèse sur nous comme un glacier qui fond sur nous, qui nous déstructure, nous englue, nous dilue. [...] Accepter CECI c'est me rendre complice de l'aliénation de mon âme de peuple, de sa disparition en l'altérité' (alterity weighs on us like a glacier that melts over us, that destructures us, traps us, dilutes us ... Accepting THIS makes me an accomplice of the alienation of my people's soul, of its disappearance into alterity).[24]

After Miron, Paul Chamberland spoke even more harshly of the 'ravages of alterity [les saccages de l'alterité].'[25] Clearly, the Québécois search for identity is diametrically opposed to other notions of identity such as the German *Bildung*, 'the creation of Self through the experience of Alterity.'[26] In the German *Bildung*, translation is a preferred means of building self-identity. However, in the Québécois notion of identity, the exact opposite is true. The Other is not a source of knowledge; neither is it a pole in a dialectic relationship with the Self. The Other is too close and too similar for that. And since the Self and the Other tend to be one and the same, to create the Self, one must make every possible effort to avoid becoming 'a Non-Other like before [Non-Autre comme devant].'[27] Thus, the experience of alterity is an *agonic* one, a daily struggle against assimilation. The pain of this experience is condensed in the memory of a traumatic event, the Conquest, the colonization that produced ethnic inferiority. It explains the rejection of the Other and the tendency to turn in on oneself, phenomena that have become explicit themes.[28] For example, in a 1983 study of Québécois theatre between 1900 and 1950, the author views the past from a contemporary perspective, projecting onto it the contemporary feeling of alterity, with its attendant narcissism, 'specularity' or mirroring, and its focus on the dominant Other, the English:

What this nation loved was itself as it knew itself or imagined itself to be; it believed sometimes that it loved another people (the French, the English), but it really loved itself through the image it had of other peoples. The Québécois were a different people from the others, from the English people, and they knew they were, since they were of a different origin, which did not include the 'FOREIGNER.'[29]

Refusal by the Self to replicate the Other logically leads to a claim of absolute difference, and the logical consequence of this claim of absolute difference is segregation, or negation of the Other, who must be confined to his own implacable difference. This differentiation may be needed to create a dialogue in which the Other can recognize 'me,' but the whole process is nevertheless basically anti-dialogic, as there is no reciprocity. Rejection of the Other perpetuates the preconstituted Self. This rejection of any dialogue results in an entrenched fidelity to the values and ideas passed down by one's own history.

The reader will recall the definition of translation attributed to Lord Durham by Jean-Claude Germain: to translate is not to express the Other or to want to do so, but, rather, *to be expressed by the Other*, and, consequently, to be dispossessed of one's own words. This is indeed the effect of federal bilingualism, which drowns the francophone minority in texts translated from the dominant language, whereas these texts could have been written originally in French. Being expressed by the Other can also imply that one does not yet have one's own language. Thus, along with the rejection of anglophone hegemonic alterity, there is a desire to banish the French language to the sphere of the Foreigner, making it possible for the Québécois language to come to the fore or be created. Taking refuge in the voice appears to be a consequence of the narcissistic negation of the Other; one's own identity has been dissolved in the Other's gaze and, from now on, one's own language is to be the new reality.[30]

This relation to the Other raises the question of what remodelling procedures are used to 'translate' foreign plays – or those perceived as foreign – to make them acceptable to the new Québécois theatre system and to its new canon. For example, if we take *A Canadian Play/Une Plaie canadienne* as a paradigm in which translation is a *differential* and *entropic* form of replication, what translation procedures might we expect to find in the works included in our corpus? Or rather, since categorizing procedures is of little interest, on what basis are these differential procedures selected, apart from the obvious desire to provoke laughter? The relevance of these questions becomes apparent when we examine the title of Germain's play, which fuses two mutually exclusive operations – translation and parody. In theory, translation aims at perfect coincidence between the target text and the source text, and thus, as a process, excludes any palimpsestic effect. Parody, on the other hand, requires the recognizable presence of a hypotext in a hypertext, the presence of the parodied within the parody itself.

The parody in the title *A Canadian Play/Une Plaie canadienne* is produced by a deformation of the translative operation. This skewed translation was obtained by translating phonetically a single element in the title, which is otherwise translated semantically.[31] The resulting homophony produces a striking semantic opposition between the two component parts of the title. The *lexeme* 'play,' whose denotation is euphoric and play-ful, is replaced by 'plaie' which has two dysphoric meanings: *scourge* and *wound*. The parody resulting from this phonetic manipulation makes the title *A Canadian Play/Une Plaie canadienne* self-referential. Like Magritte's pipe, but in the converse sense, this parodic title, which is not a priori a translation, nevertheless clearly says: 'This is a translation.' And since, in its duality, it refers to itself as a translation, the double utterance takes on a metadiscursive meaning, as analysed at the beginning of this chapter.

As a case-study, Germain's work raises questions about the metadiscursive function of dramatic works whose comic effect results from partial or deformed translations. What does the *grand discours*, to use an expression from the pragmatic semantics of Oswald Ducrot, consist of – the *grand discours* being the more or less illocutionary discourse that the dramatist uses to address his audience through the *petit discours*, that is to say, through the dialogue in the play?[32]

The Other Defaced: Imitation and Parody

In that grey area of Québécois theatre where creation and translation meet, we find imitation of the foreign model, pure and simple. Any translation must select along a cline between literal respect for the source text and the pragmatics imposed by the target milieu. Imitation can be considered to be an extreme manifestation of the choices in the translation process. In imitation, typical translation procedures such as expansion, reduction, and transposition are applied not only to short utterances but to the whole narrative and to the actantial structures of the original text. None the less, the original remains recognizable in the new version. In some cases, the title alone indicates that the translation is a remake. For example, Roland Lepage's debt to *La Folle de Chaillot* is easily detectable in the title *La Folle du quartier latin*. Lepage used Giraudoux's plot, but he moved the action from the Paris of the 1940s to contemporary Quebec City, with the necessary transposition of setting, protagonists, references, and language. As these transformations have been discussed by Paul Lefebvre and Pierre Ostiguy,[33] we will turn our attention to two more recent imitations to see what transformations have been made to the original texts.

Gogol in 'La Grande Noirceur':
Michel Tremblay's Le Gars de Québec

Michel Tremblay's title *Le Gars de Québec*[34] would never lead one to suspect that the play is based on Gogol's *The Government Inspector*. Tremblay's translation transforms the original through re-actualization of space and time. The action takes place in the Quebec of the 1950s, which clearly seems to function in the theatre as the Québécois equivalent of nineteenth-century Russia.[35] Only the bare bones of the plot of Gogol's play are retained. The somewhat shady public figures of an imaginary village on the north shore of the St Lawrence are in a state about the visit of an inspector, who is actually an impostor, sent by Premier Duplessis:

MADAME BOUCHARD – Ouan, mais chus sûre qu'y vous a pas dit c'qu'y'avait dit, par exemple, cher... Y'a conté à son ami de Québec qu'y'était tombé sur une gang d'habitants ignorants qui avaient l'air de le prendre pour quelqu'un d'autre pis qu'y'espérait faire une cenne avec vous autres... Vous pouvez pas vous imaginer c'qu'y'a dit, cher... De vous, pis des autres!

MARC-ANTOINE PETIT – C'tait pas l'inspecteur de Québec!

MADAME BOUCHARD – Pantoute! C't'un tout nu qu'y'avait même pas une cenne pour retourner chez eux... qui venait de perdre sa job, à Québec, parce qu'y'avait bavassé contre le cardinal Léger!

[MADAME BOUCHARD – Yes, but I was sure he didn't tell you what he said, dear ... He told his friend from Quebec that he came across a gang of ignorant locals who seemed to mistake him for someone else and who were hoping to make money off you ... You'd be amazed by what was said, dear ... About you and the others!

MARC-ANTOINE PETIT – It wasn't the inspector from Quebec City!

MADAME BOUCHARD – Not at all! He was penniless, didn't even have a cent to go back to where he came from ... he had just lost his job, in Quebec City, because he had said things against Cardinal Léger!][36]

The satire of a Russia riddled with corruption finds its equivalent in the depiction of a local Québécois event which could have taken place during La Grande Noirceur ('the Great Darkness,' a reference to the Duplessis period). Tremblay retains the main outline of the play, but he does not include the myriad of tiny details that enrich the humorous but caustically critical description of daily life in the highly corrupt Russia of Tsar Nicolas I. Tremblay's depiction of Québécois society is infinitely more benign and self-indulgent, a nostalgic evocation of days gone by. A comparison of the above extract with the equivalent passage in Gogol's play reveals the difference in the way the two societies are depicted.[37] For further comparison, let us examine the same scene as translated into English by Milton Ehre and Fruma Gottschalk:

THE POSTMASTER (reads) – 'My dear Tryapitchkin, some amazing things have been happening to me. On my way here, an infantry officer cleaned me out of my last kopeck. The innkeeper was set to have me thrown into jail, when suddenly, the whole town took me for a government inspector. It must have been my Petersburg clothes and manners. I'm staying at the mayor's, living it up, flirting like mad with his wife and daughter. I haven't decided who to start with. Probably the mother – she looks ready to go all the way at a wink ... Remember how hard up we were, the meals we sponged and the time the waiter threw me out on my ear for charging our dinner to the king of England? Now the tables are turned. They're falling all over themselves to lend me money. What oddballs! You'd die laughing. Why not put them into some of those sketches you write for the papers? Take the mayor – as dumb as an ox.'[38]

Tremblay changes Gogol's denouement, in which everyone comes a cropper, replacing it with a series of brief interchanges, focusing on events in the plot rather than on social mores. This reduction is typical of the changes Tremblay made throughout the play. One gets the impression he followed the principle of absolute simplicity, used so successfully by popular tabloids.

Machiavelli in Underpants:
Jean-Pierre Ronfard's La Mandragore

Jean-Pierre Ronfard's *La Mandragore* (*The Mandrake*),[39] a comedy inspired by Machiavelli, who in turn had based his play on the works of Terence and Boccaccio, can also be categorized as an imitation. Written in the style of a medieval *fabliau*, the plot of this Florentine comedy is built around a stratagem developed by Ligurio, a resourceful sponger: The beautiful but overly virtuous Lucrezia is led to fall in love with the young Callimaco. Gullible and obsessed with the desire to be a father, Lucrezia's elderly husband agrees to allow Lucrezia to drink a potion containing mandrake and to take a lover as an antidote to the poison. Lucrezia submits to the authority of a licentious mother and a mercenary confessor, and finally experiences the pleasures of love. In an imitation predating Ronfard's version, *La Nouvelle Mandragore*,[40] Jean Vauthier retains Machiavelli's characters, as well as their original traits, and barely gallicizes the names of the two main protagonists. But the role of Callimaco is expanded and made much more lyrical. The language becomes particularly poetic in the *finale*, when two young lovers appear. Their passionate dialogue, in a sort of *voice-off*, projects the stream of consciousness of Lucrezia and Callimaco, who are finally united but must save face. Vauthier develops the theatricalization of comic elements in the role of Sostrata, the shameless mother-in-law, and Timoteo, the 'rogue monk.' The dialogue is risqué at times, as it is in Machiavelli's play, but the characters still use the language of classical comedy, which has a distancing affect.

Ronfard's imitation, like Tremblay's *Le Gars de Québec*, is achieved through reduction. The narration is stripped down and rearranged so that it retains only elements of bedroom farce of the sort found in the light comedies of the *théâtre de boulevard*. The basic caricatural nature of the characters and situations is pushed to the extreme. What is elliptical and discrete in Machiavelli becomes explicit and crude in Ronfard's work; witness the bedroom scene. The comic effect is also derived from a disjunction between language and content. The characters are identical to those of the Florentine comedy,[41] time and space depicted in decor and costumes are still set in the Italian Renaissance, but the language follows the theatrical convention of contemporary Québécois realism: 'Bon, ça va faire! On va pas niaiser plus longtemps. Ce soir à huit heures dans le jardin. O.K., la petite porte par en arrière! Ciao!'[42] The language is made even more authentic by local allusions: 'pélerinage à Sainte-Anne de Beaupré,' 'dentellières de Pointe-au-Pic,' 'Judith Lavoie, Antoine Bérubé et Compagnie.'[43] Throughout the play, English expressions are also used to accentuate the anachronism: 'O.K! Let's go! je rentre chez nous attendre ma femme'; 'J'ai pour ami de coeur steady le cardinal Bibiena'; 'Attention, minute, caution, pas de folleries.'[44] In other words, Machiavelli is rendered in TV-sitcom language, a language aimed at the ratings and guaranteed to pull in the audience: 'Appelle-moi Callimaco tout court ou, si tu préfères, Calli, ou mieux Cal, comme ils diraient dans l'Ouest.'[45]

In Québécois theatre, imitations of the sort we have just discussed in the work of Lepage, Ronfard, and Tremblay are common. Typically, Québécois imitations utilize re-actualization, adapting the plot, as well as the names and roles of the characters, to the Quebec context. Repertoire comedies are thus replaced by 'Québécois' creations. To this end, the foreign work is *reinterpreted according to a media aesthetic*, the aesthetic of television, which uses humour based on the lowest common denominator to attract the biggest possible audience. Let us look at one of these imitations, a satire that denounces the anglomania from which the Québécois cannot escape. In this play, the relation to the Other becomes an overt theme.

The English, or Evil Incarnate:
Antonine Maillet's Le Bourgeois Gentleman

Clearly based on *Le Bourgeois Gentilhomme*, Antonine Maillet's *Le Bourgeois Gentleman*[46] transposes the action of Molière's play to the Montreal of the 1940s. A certain M. Bourgeois, from Sainte-Pétronille, has got rich selling overshoes and now has only one ambition, to live in Westmount. Central to this Québécois version of Molière's comedy is the portrayal of the English, the Other, the ultimate fantasy. M. Bourgeois 'wants to become a gentleman at all costs,' says the maidservant, 'that's why he wants to become English.'[47] The satire of the rubber-boot merchant's anglomania parallels the theme developed in *A Canadian Play*[48] – the temptation to emulate the English inevitably leads to assimilation. Naïve and uneducated, but practical and sensible, Antonine Maillet's bourgeois gentleman refuses to accept his status as a Québécois, whose fate, as the popular expression says, is to be 'né pour un petit pain' (born for a little loaf), victim of the English, who have the power and real wealth:

> The day is gone when they will explain my own business to me in a language that I don't understand; when they will treat me in a manner that is unfamiliar to me; when they will take my money to invest in a life that I will not share. Do you understand that?[49]

This line of thinking is reminiscent of arguments used by separatist politicians to sensitize public opinion. The question posed here, which is not in the least a rhetorical one, appeals to the Québécois public who share this aspiration, the legitimate desire to take charge of their own lives. Unlike the French 'bourgeois gentilhomme,' the Québécois 'bourgeois gentleman' is sensible, pragmatic, and aware of the socio-economic inferiority of French Canadians and of the political roadblocks to their freedom of action. In the Québécois version of the play, it is not so much the bourgeois himself who is derided and discredited, but the way he chooses to achieve his new status – anglicization. It is ridiculous for him to model himself after the English, because *the English are intrinsically ridiculous*.

The Englishman is represented by a character called Featherstonehaugh. The last syllable of his name is systematically repeated throughout the play, echoing the laughter he inevitably attracts each time he appears on the stage. An emblematic character, Sir Harold Featherstonehaugh is to the English what Molière's Dorante is to the nobility: the paradigm of a social category. He is an unspeakable character, his name is literally unpronounceable. 'We could only say his name if he had a real Christian name like Bouchard or Bourgeois and not ... ha-ha-haugh!'[50] Sir Harold is depraved, dishonest, and deceitful. Like his French model, Dorante, he takes advantage of the gullibility of the bourgeois to restore his own financial health. Dorante, the ruined noble, is a practical joker, but, ultimately, his deeds have positive results. He is a lover with noble intentions, to win over the woman he loves and to marry her. It is true that he gives the Marquise a ring that he was supposed to have given her on behalf of M. Jourdain, but, by doing so, he saves the licentious bourgeois from an illicit love affair that would have disturbed his household. He is also generous and goes along with the Turk's stratagem to thwart M. Jourdain's silly pretensions and make it easier for his daughter to marry the man she has chosen. In the Québécois version, Molière's tricks become nasty pranks. Sir Harold, the impecunious lover, does much more than just use the money and the house of the gullible bourgeois to seduce a beautiful woman with a fancy meal and a ring; he is also a marriage wrecker and an objectionable procurer who pushes the bourgeois into adultery. He is anxious to get rid of this extravagant woman, to push her into the arms of the father, hoping that she will become the father's mistress. His goal is to win the girl's hand in exchange, but, unfortunately, she loves someone else. However, if the opportunity presented itself, he would not be above picking up the mother. Thank God, honour is preserved, because the Québécois protagonist, who is a good husband and a good father, does not go along with the scheme. He wants to know how to say 'pécher' (to sin) in English. '"In English," replied Sir Harold, "they don't talk about that."'[51] Steadfastly moral, the Québécois continues, 'Not even in confession or to his own conscience?'[52] The Québécois bourgeois may be naïve but he is also honest, virtuous, and hard-working. The *Englishman*, however, is downright evil.

The play contains many maxims that depict the English stereotypically: 'The English don't have English maidservants';[53] 'In English you start at the top, and in French you start at the bottom';[54] and, more figuratively, 'When the dust rolls down the mountain, it's always our glasses that get dirtied';[55] 'In English you never get bogged down, you stay on the surface';[56] 'English is the language of business'; 'In English, time is money.'[57] In aphorisms such as these, the Englishman is depicted as the wealthy exploiter, the cold calculator accountable to no one, neither to God nor to his conscience. This Protestant heathen does not go to confession. He is an unscrupulous exploiter, an out-and-out scoundrel. Sir Harold is the prototypical Englishman. Financially ruined, he manages to dupe the bourgeois by selling him his mortgaged house, while the creditor is none other than the bourgeois himself!

The Englishman is evil incarnate. It is dangerous to ally oneself with him; it is harmful, indeed unnatural, for a Québécois to do so. Such an alliance constitutes a betrayal of the 'French race,'[58] to quote from nationalist language of the 1930s and 1940s. The Englishman belongs to another, totally different world, and he is thus of no interest to a Québécois. Let us listen to Mme Bourgeois, the voice of common sense, give vent to the objections she has to her daughter's plans to marry an anglophone:

Do you think I feel like going to eat roast beef and plum pudding at my son-in-law's; and listening to the mother-in-law talking to me about her childhood in Yorkshire or Winnipeg; and dangling on my knees grandchildren who call me Granny and won't understand when I sing 'La Poulette grise a pondu dans l'église'?[59]

Here the superiority and legitimacy of Québécois values are implicitly validated, while denigration and negation of the English are used to ward off alienation. The British and the Anglo-Canadians are one and the same. In contrast to the richness of Québécois history and culture, they stand out as the very incarnation of vacuousness and idiocy. The haughty, humourless anglophone, with his 'gueule gelée' (frozen expression),[60] is of absolutely no interest. The Québécois, by contrast, is depicted as a simple, unpretentious being, who enjoys life and is respectful of traditional values. It is entirely inappropriate for M. Bourgeois to proclaim, 'I want to learn English, the English style, the English way of living.'[61] He is mocked for wanting to get to know the Other; friendship with the Other is reprehensible.

In Maillet's play, one never sees the 'real' Englishman, as he is obscured by an imaginary full of self-reinforcing prejudices. And, lo and behold, behind the archetype of the Englishman, we find the archetype of all alterity: the Jew,[62] who is equated with the Englishman, as can be clearly seen in the family names used in the play. The Québécois equivalent of the marquise courted by M. Jourdain is called 'Lady Gwendolyn Twickenheim' – a name part English, part Jewish. The two cultures merge, as in the scene where M. Bourgeois's Québécois maidservant, in disguise, passes herself off as Lady Twickenheim:

BOURGEOIS – Do you like dancing?

JOSÉPHINE – I go dancing every Sunday evening ... at the Goldcloons'.

BOURGEOIS – Oh? Would you be free on Tuesdays?

JOSÉPHINE – That's my Bingo night ... at the Gold n' Golds'. And on Thursdays we hook mats at the Goldbergs', Bluebergs' and Steinbergs'.

BOURGEOIS – I might have known. And on Saturdays?

JOSÉPHINE – That's our family day. The Twickenheims, Twickenings and Twickededees come to our house to have some fun. Uncle Jérémie ... Sir Jeremy ... takes out his bagpipes, and my cousin, the head of the Cabinet, plays the harmonium, and my grandmother, Lady Twickenish, gets up and does a little step-dance for us. You should see that! Things really swing, and we eat blood pudding and hare pie, and we sing sad songs around the organ ... What they call 'Five o'clock tea' in Westmount.[63]

This caricature of life in Westmount, which reveals a whole imaginary, is based on a set of ideological maxims. The Englishman is Jewish, and the Jew is English. Is there any difference between the celebration of the Sabbath and five o'clock tea? The Englishman may be different from the Jew, but we, the Québécois, do not see the difference, and rightly so, because there is complicity between them in terms of power, money, and leisure. They form an exclusive club from which we are barred.

In the representation of the Other in the Québécois remake of *Le Bourgeois Gentilhomme*, the English and the Jew have a number of things in common, the most important of which is the power of money. Nothing, however, surpasses the ostentatious wealth of the Jews:

BOURGEOIS – Oh yes, Let's talk about houses.

HAROLD – Residences, Sir ... With a pool ...

BOURGEOIS – ... like the Goldbergs ...

HAROLD – ... tennis, golf ...

BOURGEOIS – like the Goldcloons ...

HAROLD – ... billiards ...

BOURGEOIS – ... like the Goldsmiths ...

HAROLD – ... and a bar like the Gold n' Golds ...'[64]

Jews monopolize and concentrate wealth. This is the message in the choice of the invariable root *gold*, the *English* word for capital, which is the root of all the Jewish names in the play. The Jew is thus denounced as the symbol of the double usurpation of which Quebec is a victim. Like the Englishman, whose language he shares, the Jew becomes a legitimate object of derision. The choice of the name 'Goldcloon [Goldclown]' speaks volumes. The symbolism contained in this fictitious name contaminates the other names chosen by the author, some of which are well-known family names in Quebec, such as that of the Steinbergs, the owners of the supermarket chain.[65]

Wealth accompanies power, real power, political power: 'Lady Gwendolyn is the wife of a minister and former adviser to the Cabinet of ...'[66]

We should also note the portrayal of Lady Twickenheim, a demi-mondaine who goes from her lover's (Sir Harold's) bed to M. Bourgeois's salon. M. Bourgeois is protected, thank God, by the fortress of his irreproachable Christian virtue. His wife can rest assured, he only wanted to get a little power from the Jews: 'It was not for real, my darling, only to be a gentleman, and be like the Goldbergs and Gold n' Golds, to be in charge, like the others.'[67]

Lust is the Jew's trademark, together with the monetary power he inherits at birth; but a Québecois has to earn his money, by the sweat of his brow and through his own talent: 'Are there other little guys from Sainte-Pétronille in the Conseil du Patronat? Did the Goldcloons and the Goldbergs and the Gold n' Golds start from scratch, like you, and manage to end up running a dozen factories and two dozen stores?'[68]

Characterized in this way, the Jew constitutes the prototypical Foreigner who has chosen to ally himself with the enemy in order to exploit francophones. He is doubly detestable. This characterization of the Jew maintains anti-Semitism in the consciousness of the public. The Jew is covertly accused, and humour is used as an unassailable excuse for such a portrayal; after all, it is only caricature.

We could say, then, that Molière's comedy is used as a metaphor to subtly legitimize rejection of the Other. The Québecois version of *Le Bourgeois Gentilhomme* replaces the original target of the satire with an ethnic or religious group, rather than a social group, and, as such, it is not so much an imitation as an ideological appropriation. It also can just as easily be viewed as a literary appropriation. Molière's classical comedy indirectly validates the ideological re-creation of the text. But there is evidence of false reverence for the model here. Maillet's imitation (or mockery) attempts to compensate for the inadequacy of the original play to describe the Québecois situation. This is why the original had to be replaced. Thus, in this case, adaptation destroys the original in favour of the new work, whose aim is to take over the play completely.

Rodriguemachine:
Réjean Ducharme's Le Cid maghané

Parody, at least in its traditional form, is another intrinsically humorous but 'deforming' mode of translation. In some plays, as, for example, in *A Canadian Play/Une Plaie canadienne*, only the title is affected. In Quebec theatre, there are many examples of such parodic titles, which trivialize classical canonical works and reproduce them in a minor key: *Don Quickshot, l'homme à la manque*; *Manon Lastcall*; *Émile et une nuit*; *Roméo et Julien*; *Rodéo et Juliette*; *Le Cid maghané*; *En attendant Trudot*; *En attendant Gaudreault*; and *L'Alphonse faite à Marie*. These parodies re-actualize classical plays in a Québécois context, setting the action in the milieu of marginality, with characters such as the drug addict, the bar hostess, the tramp, or the homosexual, or re-actualizing the classic in a social milieu in which the language spoken (*joual*) is disconnected from the French of France and distinctly Québécois. We note, however, that, with the exception of *Le Cid maghané*, the titles of Québécois plays cited above bear no intertextual relation, in form or in content, to the foreign literary classics whose titles they parody and whose reputation they appropriate. The foreign masterpiece becomes a mere vehicle for the Québécois play. Its status as a classic helps validate the Québécois imitation. But it validates the imitation as much, if not more, by antithesis, because imitations clearly represent the classical work as being outdated, an object of derision inappropriate for expressing the Québécois condition.

The best example of this type of parody is Réjean Ducharme's *Le Cid maghané* (*The Disfigured Cid*).[69] As its title indicates, Ducharme's parody disfigures one of the great classics of French literature, and one of the most frequently parodied plays in the French repertoire. The parodic effect in *Le Cid maghané* is mainly derived from the translation of Corneille's elegant language into a prosaic mixture of English and French:

Corneille
CHIMÈNE – Honneur impitoyable à mes plus chers désirs
Que tu vas me coûter de pleurs et de soupirs.[70]

Ducharme
CHIMÈNE – Que je suis donc bad-lucky.[71]

The famous lines from Corneille's play do not have the same cultural significance in Quebec as they do in France. Parody works only if the parodied text is a familiar one. In Ducharme's version of *Le Cid*, the parody is based less on well-known lines from the text than on the diegetic elements, or famous scenes from the play. For example, the slap scene is transformed into a bar-room brawl:

LE COMTE – You deserve a good slap in the face. She's coming. There she is! Catch her! (*Slap in the face. Don Diego falls, gets up again.*) ... (*He throws Don Diego's wig in the corner.*) You can tell the prince that you were scalped by an Iroquois. That can be an introduction to your first history lesson on America.[72]

Here, Ducharme's parody resembles *Le Chapelain décoiffé*, the first parody of *Le Cid*, by Boileau, Racine, and others.[73] But Ducharme takes particular aim at the classic Corneillian dilemma, filling *Le Cid*'s famous *stances* (stanzas) with graffiti and scathing comments. Honour is trivialized and reduced to romance-novel sentimentality:

L'INFANTE – *Léonor ma chouette, est-ce qu'il t'est jamais arrivé de te faire dévorer par les contradictions?*

LÉONOR – *Les contradictions gardent leurs distances avec moi.*

L'INFANTE – *Une chance! Il y a rien de pire. Ça me fait du mal que Chimène court la chance de perdre Rodrigue, mais en même temps, ça me fait du bien. Ça me fait du bien, parce que si Rodrigue se retrouve tout seul, c'est dans mes bras qu'il va venir se consoler. Ça me fait du mal parce que si Rodrigue vient me demander de le consoler dans mes bras, je pourrai pas dire non et je vais perdre mon honneur.*

LÉONOR – Tu es sentimentale comme une fille qui travaille dans une manufacture.

[L'INFANTE – *Léonor, my darling, have you ever been devoured by contradictions?*

LÉONOR – *Contradictions keep their distance from me.*

L'INFANTE – Good thing! There's nothing worse. I'm upset that Chimène might lose Rodrigue, but at the same time, its good for me. It's good for me because, if Rodrigue finds himself all alone, he's going to console himself in my arms. It's bad for me because, if Rodrigue asks me to console him in my arms, I won't be able to refuse and I will lose my honour.

LÉONOR – You're sentimental, as sentimental as a shop girl.][74]

Linguistically, the transformation of the text is not so much a translation as a free transcoding. The translation of Corneille's verse into *joual* and the trivialization of the language re-actualize the characters, their words, and their deeds, and put them in the realm of 'commonly prosaic daily life,' to quote Rodrigue, a daily life that is clearly Québécois: Rodrigue is portrayed as a bum, and Chimène could be a heroine from the pages of the tabloid *Le Journal de Montréal*, as could all the other characters – the Infante, who is as sentimental as a shop girl; Gormas, the killer, and his gang; or Don Fernand, the homosexual who is always begging for a 'little kiss.' Critics have interpreted Ducharme's play as an attempt to portray alienation in Québécois society: 'the author uses *Le Cid* to read – and criticize – Québécois society, more than using *joual* to reread Corneille.'[75] There are, indeed, many allusions, besides the use of *joual*, to the Québécois context in the play. However, *Le Cid maghané* is not just a satirical tableau of Québécois society. The play presents us, rather, with a grand-guignol image of a heterogeneous social environment, dwelt in by character collages in period costume. The *québécité* (Quebecness) of these characters is to be found in their identifiable geographical mode of expression, rather than in typically Québécois behaviour. The cultural references in the play are far from being exclusively Québécois. Taking your girl friend to a motel in a Cadillac, as Rodrigue does, is the dream of *any* North American 'gars de taverne' (tavern guy). The play contains far fewer references to Québécois 'heroes' than to international movie, press, and television superstars such as Cassius Clay, Rocky Marciano, Fidel Castro, Mao Tse-Tung, and Paul Newman, or to even better-known movie, popular-literature, and comic-book heroes such as Tarzan, the Three Musketeers, Al Capone, and Eliot Ness.

The blind point in parody, particularly in its modern form, is the intention that motivates it. Ducharme said of Corneille's tragedy: 'My goal was to make it more understandable, more of this place, less serious and uglier.'[76] On one level, the disfigurement of Corneille's text seems to be nothing more than a prank, like a moustache drawn on the Mona Lisa. These iconoclastic transformations deride classical tragedy, but we cannot say that they are directed against Corneille, or derived from a *polemical ethos*, to use Linda Hutcheon's term.[77] Nevertheless, the parody shatters a work belonging to the cultural legacy inherited from France. It rejects it and emphasizes its foreignness. The de-familiarization of the original text is accentuated by a functional alternation between French and *joual*. The Québécois text is interspersed with passages in which the actors must say their lines with a French accent. Bernard Andrès has demonstrated the parodic reverberation resulting from such diglossia, an effect that has an impact on content as well as on linguistic delivery.[78] This metatextual irony is to be found, for example, in the extract above and in the introductory lines of the play, which the actresses are to deliver with a French accent: here, there is a boomerang effect in which Corneille begins to parody Ducharme.

Normally, the objective of translation is to bring that which is foreign nearer. In *Le Cid maghané*, however, the translation disguises the original and has the opposite effect, distancing, or even banishing, the French classic from the Québécois field of literature. In exchange, Québécois literature is enriched with an authentically *Québécois* work. As the Québécois play replaces the French classic, there is a change of genre; the French tragicomedy is transformed into a farce, based on the model of the American sit-com. Thus, Corneille's text is rewritten in media style, using the exaggeration and absurdity of the crackpot comedy of a Jerry Lewis or a Pee Wee Herman, or of sensational newspapers such as *The National Enquirer*. Ducharme makes no attempt to hide his debt to the popular press. When asked what his influences were, he responded sardonically:

I would say Mickey Spillane ... I would say L.-F. Céline ... I would say also Ducasse ... But all those glorious wounds seem to have given me such a thick skin that I can only be moved by reading the sports pages in *Le Journal de Montréal* and the weekly installments in *Allô Police* (I take part in their Maxi-Grille crossword competition ... I've never won anything), I wonder myself what my influences really are ...[79]

The Québécois transformation of Corneille's text uses aesthetic procedures similar to those used by Roy Lichtenstein and Andy Warhol in their art – the grainy press photo, a band of prime colour framed by a black line, the naïve caricaturization of comic-books, or the blow-up. In the work of Warhol or Lichtenstein, the matrix of a painting is a visual representation of an article of mass consumption, a comic or a press photo reproduced in millions of copies. In these paintings, the meaning of repetition is inverted. Through the artist's intervention, the cliché, which by definition is banal and meaningless, assumes meaning and uniqueness, making it a work of art. Ducharme uses the same procedure with the stereotype. First he uses one of the best-known, even hackneyed plays in the repertoire: a parody of *Le Cid* is in itself a cliché as far as literature is concerned. Then he goes one step farther by using stereotypes from popular literature, or from television and cinema that either complement or replace them. The play is an obvious parody, but it is interesting to read *Le Cid maghané* in light of procedures used by artists such as Lichtenstein, for example, who makes no claim at all to parodying Walt Disney imitators. Parody is a useful literary category, but in the case of Ducharme's play, one must go beyond the parody and put aside ethnocentric interpretations that see *Le Cid maghané* as a mere calling into question of a specifically *Québécois* social context. These interpretations are questionable, as they 'provincialize' the play and fail to give it its full creative significance. A more productive interpretation sees Ducharme using the Corneillian play as basic material, in the same manner that Warhol used clichéd images, such as that of Marilyn Monroe or Mao Tse-Tung, or in the manner that Marcel Duchamp used the *found object*. In these works of art, the basic material, the model, is less important than its *aesthetic reinterpretation*, and this is exactly what Ducharme explores and exploits – the techniques and effects of the 'vulgarization' that goes along with mass consumption (communication).

There are obvious references to the media in *Le Cid maghané*. Sometimes they are direct, as in the scene where Rodrigue confronts the Comte de Gormas, who overconfidently imagines all the attention he will get from the media after his victory over his young rival:

I see the headlines of communist newspapers as if I were there. 'The Comte de Gormas Cowardly Assassinates a Child!' I can hear the radio announcer, introducing the show 'Aujourd'hui' as if I were there (*Two bars from the show's theme*). 'Can a major-general go as far, legally, as disgustingly killing a defenceless little boy in front of the disgustingly luxurious door of his king's house? This is the question they're asking in all the capitals of the world.' Really, my boy, I would prefer you went and got killed by someone else.[80]

But most allusions to the media are made in a more indirect form, in a journalistic discourse, a discourse interpreted by alienated readers whom it infantilizes. Ducharme's translation makes ample use of the sensational discourse of the tabloids, in which the news is just fodder for a story, a form of entertainment. He carries to an extreme *Le Journal de Montréal*'s famous slogan, 'Keep it simple, stupid.' For the readers of these newspapers, news gets telescoped, and history and geography are jumbled together. Durcharme's disfigurement of the classical unities owes a great deal to the media surrealism to which readers of the popular press are subjected. Rehashed and repeated by people in their kitchens, at the tavern, or in the factory, media language reaches the heights of the absurd:

All the realms, Niger and Nigeria first, are going to break into a thousand pieces at his feet, Arabs are going to depart from the deepest darkest Far East to come shine his shoes as a sign of submission. The Aragonais are going to abandon Aragon and give him a better reception in Madrid than the Québécois gave De Gaulle in Montreal. Salazar is going to come running from a far-flung corner of his country to say hello to him! Come and tell me again that it's dishonourable to love a man like that.'[81]

The play also contains after-images from popular literature and comics. Let us look again, for example, at the slap scene, where the Comte de Gormas, jealous because he was not chosen to be the prince's tutor, tells Don Diego he is too old for the job. Don Diego defends himself as follows: 'The Comte de Neipperg had only one eye and he stole Marie-Louise from Napoleon. Is there anything tougher than a pirate? And most pirates have only one leg.'[82]

We find these infantile caricatures, which come straight out of comic books, throughout *Le Cid maghané*. Like children, the protagonists model their behaviour on what they see in books or movies. Here is what Rodrigue says about the reward he should get when Don Diego praises him for bravely bumping off Chimène's father: 'I read in the Eliot Ness book that Al Capone had fixed the rate at ten thousand bucks a murder.'[83] Don Sanche refuses to make honourable amends on the pretext that 'of all the Paul Newman films, for example, there is only one where you see him apologize ... He asks an eighty-nine-year-old woman to forgive him for running his Buick over her feet.'[84] The sensational press is full of formulas designed to hook gullible readers, to whom they offer an easy, escapist form of entertainment. *Le Cid maghané* simply imitates media-style fiction. Another example is the reinterpretation of the extraordinary military prowess of Corneille's Cid, in which Ducharme uses images as exaggerated as those in any Hollywood battle scene: 'There was not a single Moslem left on a horse and there were no Moslem horses left standing. The whole horizon was awash with enemy blood, like an abattoir full of animal blood. On our side, a few soldiers had a nose bleed and a few horses had a sunburn.'[85]

We easily recognize the slapstick style of popular American television and film comedies in this reinterpretation of the Corneillian classic, but Durcharme goes beyond this and works within a modernism comparable to that of Heiner Müller. *Le Cid maghané* and *Hamletmachine* both proclaim the death of a certain dramatic iconography, but they use different registers and obviously different procedures. This iconography cannot withstand the confrontation that Ducharme's use of new cultural schema subjects it to. *Le Cid maghané* could have easily been called *Rodriguemachine*. Rodrique cannot remain the same in this new environment of 'everyday' culture, no more than the Prince of Denmark could. Corneille's hero has dropped his mask, and, like the new Hamlet, he could say:

> My drama doesn't happen anymore. Behind me the set is put up. By people who aren't interested in my drama, for people to whom it means nothing. I am not interested in it anymore either. *Unnoticed by the actor playing Hamlet, stagehands place a refrigerator and three TV-sets on the stage. Humming of the refrigerator. Three TV channels without sound.* The set is a monument. It presents a man who made history, enlarged a hundred times ... The actors put their faces on the rack in the dressing room. In his box, the prompter is rotting. The stuffed corpses in the house don't stir a hand. I go home and kill the time, at one/with my undivided self.
> Television. The daily nausea Nausea
> Of prefabricated babble of decreed cheerfulness
> How do you spell GEMÜTLICHKEIT
> Give us this day our daily murder ...
> Hail COCA-COLA.[86]

In the context of a post-industrial society, where human tragedy, interpreted by the media, is consumed with the same pleasure and the same insouciance as a soft drink, the archetypal 'problematic hero' is out of style. A unidimensional man has succeeded him, a man whose consciousness is eroded daily by the media machine. There is no longer any dividing line between reality and the fiction that depicts it. The world is merely a captionless picture book. The heroes of Shakespeare and Corneille no longer form part of the imaginary. Like *Hamletmachine*, the Québécois parody of *Le Cid* demonstrates that the masterpiece must be recontextualized. Using a procedure similar to that of Heiner Müller, Ducharme dismantles the conventions of classical theatre and reveals the limits of the Corneillian protagonist, whose problematic becomes passé when re-actualized in a new environment. Today, the Corneillian hero has no more weight than a comic-book hero; he is not even funny or ironic. Corneille's *Le Cid* has become an 'auratic' work, or we might say, a 'chromo' of literature, with the required happy ending. Ducharme's disfigurement of the play removes the chromo effect, an effect Adorno refers to as the soothing aura that comes from hackneyed reproductions, in which the play becomes a relic with no hold on reality, a creator of false consciousness. A critical intervention like Ducharme's thus has the effect of producing a cognitive impact on the consciousness of the spectator, to whom *Le Cid maghané* presents a new state of affairs, a new vision of the world and of man in the world.

Sensational Shakespeare:
Jean-Pierre Ronfard's Lear

In *Le Cid maghané*, Ducharme uses the attention-grabbing techniques of the sensational press to 'enlaidir' (make ugly) the Corneillian classic and make it better reflect contemporary reality. Parodied in this way, the play becomes part of a dramatic category that we could call *sensationalist theatre*. *Le Cid maghané* employs the basic elements of the sensationalist press – simplistic, outrageous writing and shocking images of sex and violence, but they are transformed by irony. An extreme version of this media-type sensationalism is used in the parody of *King Lear* produced in 1977 at Le Théâtre Expérimental de Montréal, and directed by the author, Jean-Pierre Ronfard. The new version, whose title, *Lear*,[87] gives no indication that the play is a parody, imitates the bawdy style of the sensationalist press, where sex and blood are the stuff of daily headlines. The use of sensationalism is clearly indicated in the stage instructions: 'Everything is to be made out of newspaper, including seating for the audience.'[88] Even more significant is the fact that, from the beginning of the first scene, the King and his three daughters become part of the décor 'concealed by giant newspapers that open and close rhythmically.'[89] This is a distorted, *en abyme* image of the royal-family scandals in which the popular press indulges. *King Lear* is a tragedy that lends itself particularly well to media sensationalism: 'Princess Cordelia Disinherited!'; 'The King of England Reduced to Begging!'; 'Forced to Flee by His Two Heirs, He Goes Crazy!'; 'The Illegitimate Son of the Duke of Gloucester!'; 'Full of Jealousy, She Poisons Her Sister, Then Kills Herself!'; 'The Tramp Was the Son of an Aristocrat!'; 'In Revenge, He Tears Out Her Eyes!'; 'Unharmed After a Several-Metre Fall!'; 'Pardon Arrives Too Late, She Is Found Hanged!'; etc.

Ronfard's *Lear* skims off sensational elements from the original tragedy – the cruelty of Regan and Goneril when they betray and abandon their father after they get hold of their inheritance; Lear becoming a beggar, and the legitimate son of the Duke of Gloucester becoming victim of a manhunt; the total madness of the King and the simulated craziness of the Duke; the masochistic fidelity of the Duke of Kent, who disguises himself and continues to look after the King despite being banished for opposing him; the fact that the bastard son is seen as the arch villain; the scenes of violence, such as the one in which we see Regan and her husband pillory Gloucester and put his eyes out; the failed suicide of Gloucester, who is led to believe that he had jumped off a cliff and managed to survive; the repentance and punishment of the traitor; and, last but not least, for good measure, a series of murders at the end of the play.

Of the many characters in the original play, the parody retains only Lear and his three daughters, renamed 'Josette' (Goneril), 'Violette' (Regan), and 'Laurette' (Cordelia). The youngest disinherited daughter disguises herself as the King's jester. The faithful Kent is replaced by a woman called Corneille, a saucy chambermaid and Lear's mistress. Corneille, the ambitious mother of the bastard named Hector (Edmond) will have her eyes put out. Apart from a few similarities, *Lear* so distorts the original Shakespearean plot that it is only nominally a parody. Since only minimal pieces of the narrative schema are retained, and in altered form, the audience is denied the double perspective essential to parody, in which awareness of the two texts is a source of irony.

Ronfard engages in a type of theatre that he calls 'hypertroped' and 'volcanic.'[90] His *Lear* turns Shakespeare's tragedy into an openly scatological and pornographic farce. The King is an old letch whom fate has made impotent. But, true to form, his two elder daughters have inherited his lustfulness, especially the younger of the two, an erotomanic character who had added to her family coat of arms 'un pénis de sinople sur fond de gueules'[91] (a red penis on a background of gules). As for the bastard, he lives in excrement, the symbol of his abjection. The bathroom is the kingdom of this ignoble simpleton. Throughout the whole play, defecation, masturbation, and other bodily acts are mimed on the stage. As might be expected, Shakespeare's poetry is replaced by bawdy language full of vulgar expressions not normally used on stage ... to put it mildly. *Lear* can be seen as a kind of end-game, revised and corrected in the anarcho-satirical style of *Hara-Kiri*, the self-proclaimed 'stupid, vicious' magazine. But this parodic version of Shakespeare's tragedy cannot be written off as marginal. The author and director of the play was at one time artistic director of the National Theatre School. The play was performed by well-known actors with international reputations.[92] Thus, the play cannot be dismissed out of hand. It is a product of the institution and is deserving of our attention.

Ostensibly, *Lear* is iconoclastic. This is not, however, all that is at work here. Distancing and irony are fully integrated into the performance. The set is framed by twin characters in Elizabethan costume, who each represent Shakespeare. They appear to be in charge of lighting, but they pay little attention to the play, drinking beer instead. For the audience, their presence is a rare tangible allusion to the source text, even though they remain on the sidelines. They do, however, participate at certain points in the play: by way of introduction, they engage in a brief 'Shakespearian dialogue' on the death of the King and the dangers of the new régime; in the middle of the play, we hear them in the background unintelligibly acting out Clarence's dream from *Richard III*; at the end of the play, they run each other through and join the other dead bodies on the stage. Their anachronistic clothing and language accentuate the outrageous, distancing dimension of this bedroom farce. We note also that throughout the dialogue and stage directions there are references to popular uprisings, specifically to the Russian Revolution:

... under the red flag ... a horde of demonstrators are shouting and chanting 'Power to the bastards,' then they move off to attack all the possible and imaginable Winter Palaces ... On their way, they meet the two Shakespeares, who emerge from their cage out of curiosity. Two worlds confront each other. Silence. Immobility. What are we all doing here? Everyone falls into this theatrical void full of metaphysical anguish.[93]

Clearly, we see here, as in the case of Réjean Ducharme or Heiner Müller, an attempt to recontextualize a literary classic, but so little remains of the source text in the target text that it becomes almost impossible to detect it. This makes it difficult even to find the parody, notwithstanding the elaborate efforts put into the production. Thus, the impact of the intervention on the original text is considerably reduced. The dialectic one would normally expect between the parodied text and the parodying text disappears beneath a veneer of obscenity and absurdity that seem to have no other function than to provoke laughter and 'épater les bourgeois.' Here, we see elements of the much-touted 'carnival' ideology. Witness, for example, the evocation of constructivism, an avant-garde proletarian movement, and the description of a world turned upside down, in the following excerpt:

THE JESTER (in an obviously contructivist style, he performs his big number on a ladder leading to his hiding place): The people are rising up. There is a revolt ... nursing babies are jumping out of their carriages and playing hopscotch with their porcelain plates. The nuns of the Sainte-Marie convent have opened a nudist camp in their congregation's cemetery. The world has gone crazy, totally crazy! ...[94]

As a dramatic work, Ronfard's parody is an apparent attempt to bring about a cultural revolution, to tear down the idols of institutional literature, whose decadence is incarnated by King Lear, with his unbelievable outbursts: '... Culture! Culture links us to the breath and blood of our ancestors like the different coloured tubes in the hospital that maintain the existence of the dying, mummified in their bandages.'[95]

Ronfard breathes uninhibited 'proletarian' renewal into this élitist, moribund culture. On the one hand, unbridled eroticism is held up as an aesthetic principle, reminiscent of the refrain that closes Peter Weiss's *Marat/Sade*: 'Revolution, copulation.'[96] On the other hand, the play has aspects of the carnival about it, elements that Bakhtin found in Goethe's description of the Roman carnival, and later developed in his work on Rabelais:

... the peculiar festive character without any piousness, complete liberation from seriousness, the atmosphere of equality, freedom and familiarity, the symbolic meaning of the indecencies, the clownish crowning and uncrownings, the merry wars and beatings, the mock disputes.[97]

Lear clearly contains carnival elements, in scenes such as the abdication of the King, whose 'throne is a tavern chair placed on top of a pile of Coke cases.' Nevertheless, this carnivalization can hardly have Bakhtin's effect on the members of the audience, since there is no audience participation. Obviously playing to a certain ideology, Bakhtin makes the people the natural source of all positive values:

... the people become aware of their sensual, material bodily unity and community.

... Carnival, with all its indecencies and curses, affirms the people's immortal and indestructible character. In the world of carnival, the awareness of the people's immortality is combined with the realization that *established truth and authority are relative.*

Popular-festive forms look *into the future.* They present the *victory of the future, of the 'golden age,' over the past.* This is the victory of all the people's material abundance, freedom, equality, brotherhood. The victory of the future is ensured by the people's immortality. The birth of the new, of the greater, of the better is as indispensable and as inevitable as the death of the old.[98]

The Bakhtinian concept of the carnival is based on an intellectual reconstruction of the working classes, tendentiously represented as a homogeneous whole, and as the sole exponents of authenticity. Ronfard's parody appears to be based on a similar concept, but this is, in fact, misleading since neither the rituals nor the purposes of the carnival coincide with those of the theatre. The theatre acts upon a captive audience and can, thus, exert an illocutionary force, or at least a form of manipulation similar to that of the media. But, in Ronfard's play, the process is ironic, or at least its purpose is to be ironic. In fact, the sensationalism used by Ronfard is nothing more than a phatic process whose underlying message is: *Lear*, like *Le Cid*, has had its day.

Redefining the Boundary of the Foreign:
Jean-Claude Germain's Les Faux Brillants de Félix-Gabriel Marchand

Sensationalist theatre, of which *Lear* is an extreme, adheres to the strict definition of 'neoculture' pursued by the new Québécois society, as it seeks to free itself from the domination of the 'old country': 'the *paleoculture*, élitist, conservative and fetishistic, is a culture of private appropriation, museums, contemplation, individual pleasure; the *neoculture* – neither a "subculture" nor a "mass culture" – is a culture of sharing, of instant consumption, of widespread communication, a culture that creates community.'[99]

The emerging Québécois theatre system followed the imperatives of this neoculture, itself institutionalized in infrastructures and in discursive norms. The existence of these norms makes it possible to categorize apparently unclassifiable isolated phenomena. A case in point is the adaptation of *Les Faux Brillants*, a late-nineteenth-century vaudeville play by a Québécois playwright who was better known as the premier of Quebec.[100] Based on French drama conventions, Félix-Gabriel Marchand's work combines the classical theatre and the *théâtre de boulevard*. Needless to say, the rhymes and alexandrines of his play seem out of place in the new theatrical aesthetic introduced by *Les Belles-Soeurs*. However, Jean-Claude Germain set things right by 'paraphrasing'[101] the play and, in doing so, made it, once again, truly Québécois. But this time round, the play has a new title that incorporates the original author's name: *Les Faux Brillants de Félix-Gabriel Marchand*. In this new guise, the play enriched the theatrical production of its 'translator,' who published the adaptation under his own name and was recognized by the literary institution as a truly *Québécois* author. Félix-Gabriel Marchand, however, cannot be classified as Québécois. This is why it was deemed necessary to translate and transform his play to make it conform to the new dramatic canons. As we shall see, the fact that this particular play was revived by the institution was not fortuitous, for it clearly had the potential to be integrated into the new Québécois dramatic system.

The plot of *Les Faux Brillants*, with some slight variation, is yet another adaptation of the story of Molière's *Le Bourgeois Gentilhomme*, set this time in the late nineteenth century. Rich but uncultured and consumed by a desire to rise above his station as an 'homme ordinaire,' Dumont allows himself to be tricked by Faquino, an Italian swindler, and his partner Trémousset. Dumont is a widower, but he has two marriageable daughters – Élise, a snob, who throws herself into the arms of Faquino, believing he is a baron, and Cécile, who is in love with a young lawyer and rejects the marriage her father arranges for her with Trémousset, alias Comte Luigi de Montebellicano. Molière's main characters play double roles in Marchand's play, two swindlers, two marriageable daughters, and two servants. Nicolas, a jack-of-all-trades, and Marianne, the chambermaid, both have the impertinent common sense of Nicole and Mme Jourdain, and the voice of reason is still that of Octave, Dumont's brother and his wise and cultured alter ego. This Québécois version of Molière's play is somewhat chaste. Captivated by a Baron and a Count, Dumont dreams ingratiatingly of the lineage of his future grandchildren. There is no upper-class woman in the offing to disturb his widowerhood. The end of the story owes more to Ponson du Terrail than to Molière. The swindlers are unmasked *in extremis* by a cousin who appears out of nowhere, having himself miraculously escaped an attempt on his life. As luck would have it, the providential cousin is a millionaire. So he marries Élise, who forthwith exchanges her rocky future with the Baron for a golden future with this new Rocambole.

Germain expands the opening lines and develops several of the scenes to take full advantage of the theatricality of the original play, but he retains all the characters and the narrative schema. We will not examine the structural changes at this time, but we will analyse two major aspects of the transformation: the ideological reinterpretation of Molière's narrative and the reworking of the language. It is significant, in fact, that from all the plays in the French-Canadian repertoire, Germain chose an imitation of *Le Bourgeois Gentilhomme*. The choice can be explained by the intertextuality linking the basic structure of Molière's comedy and its three Québécois imitations, *Les Faux Brillants* (F.-G. Marchand), *Les Faux Brillants ...* (J.-C. Germain), and *Le Bourgeois Gentleman* (Antonine Maillet). These three variations borrow their narrative structure from Molière: *a man who wants to rise above his inferior station in life falls victim to another man, whom he wishes to imitate and whose ally he wishes to become.* Once the roles have been filled by appropriate characters, the narrative activates some of the main ideologemes underlying the discourse on the Québécois condition, on relations between Quebec and Canada and the English, and Quebec and France and the French. The epilogue of Molière's *Le Bourgeois Gentilhomme* subtly introduces, in territorial terms, the social conflict between the bourgeoisie and the nobility. The French bourgeois is subjugated by Le Grand Turc, who represents, in the eyes of the bourgeois, the 'homme de qualité' *par excellence*. All three Québécois authors give Molière's narrative structure the same ideological interpretation. On the one hand, the geographical origin of the characters becomes just as important as their membership in a social class. The following divisions are used: the bourgeois is Québécois, while the person he admires is a 'Foreigner' who occupies, or appears to occupy, a higher position than the Québécois in the social hierarchy. In Antonine Maillet's version of the play, the Foreigner is an Englishman from Westmount; in Marchand's and in Germain's versions, he is a Frenchman disguised as an Italian aristocrat, or a pseudo-Italian aristocrat, with the caricatured traits of a Frenchman. On the other hand, in the three Québécois versions of the play, the relationship between territoriality and extra-territoriality is founded on antagonism – the Foreigner is the perpetrator of evil deeds, the Québécois is his victim. The Foreigner is not only a brazen scrounger, like Molière's Dorante; he is also a notorious swindler, like Antonine Maillet's Featherstonehaugh. Marchand gives the Foreigner the name 'Faquino,' a name that tells us exactly the type of person he is. The underlying ideologeme, which commonly associates Italians with dishonesty, can be seen in the following narrative structure: before fleeing with the dowry of a Québécois fiancée, whom he has no intention of marrying, Faquino manages to get his expenses, which are considerable, covered by the poor girl's naïve father. The Italian, Faquino, is a professional con man; his very name tells us that. In this version of the play, it is clear that Faquino's Italianness is as fictitious as his aristocratic title or as the name 'Montebellicano,' which he invents for his accomplice, Trémousset.[102] Marchand's Faquino is a scoundrel who normally conceals his true identity, but to no avail; the Italian suffix of his name resonates with dishonesty. Germain's version of the play adds or accentuates certain details that clearly give the character of Faquino, whom we believe to be 'Italian by birth,' the traits of a 'maudit Français' (cursed Frenchman). Witness the scene in which Oscar, his Québécois rival, appears. Oscar has just told Faquino exactly what he thinks of him, in plebeian language, then he announces that he is going to repeat the whole thing in 'bon français' (proper French). Faquino, taking a lofty tone, gives the following haughty, stinging retort: 'Parody, my dear boy, is nothing more than impersonation / You can't invent a culture for yourself far from Paris.'[103]

The Foreigner is portrayed as evil, but the Québécois are always portrayed in a positive light. They can be led astray, as Dumont and his daughter Élise are, but only temporarily. The naïve bourgeois comes out of the ordeal on top, and all the wiser for it. He was foolish to be taken in by foreigners, especially since, beneath their external superiority, their veneer of culture and elegant language, the English, the French, and the Italians turn out to be basically evil and harmful. As we have seen, these evil actants are prototypes of the politico-economic colonizer, the cultural colonizer, and the immigrant. They represent the three groups perceived as a threat to the identity and the survival of the 'peuple québécois.' In this regard, *Les Faux Brillants* corresponds interdiscursively to *A Canadian Play/ Une Plaie canadienne*. The two plays, which share the same ideologemes, also have the same author. We also find this same interdiscourse in Antonine Maillet's *Le Bourgeois Gentleman*. All these works invariably cast the Québécois in the role of victim, but willing victim: he allows himself to be easily subjugated by the Other, so much so that he wants to be like him and to ally himself with him, and this, by definition, goes against nature. This man who managed to amass a fortune is none the less a sensible man. If he allows himself to be fooled like a child, it is because of his misunderstood and misplaced pragmatism. It is also because of his inexhaustible generosity. The Other, the exploiter, takes advantage of his weaknesses. Even though he is led astray, Dumont, the prototypical Québécois, is a more or less positive hero who is, unfortunately, corrupted by the Foreigner.

In the plays of F.-G. Marchand, J.-C. Germain, and Antonine Maillet, the portrait of the Québécois hero projects the same image of the Québécois as that found in the political discourse or in news commentaries that explicitly or implicitly focus on the question of Québécois autonomy. Underlying the referendum or constitution debates, the Meech Lake Accord or the new Immigration Act, we find the same ideologemes defining the Québécois condition: the Québécois thinks, incorrectly, that he is inferior ('porteur d'eau,' 'né pour un petit pain,' 'Nègre blanc d'Amérique' ...), the Québécois is too quick to trust others, the Québécois always gets taken in by the Other (the English, the anglophone provinces, the federal government, the neo-Québécois who take sides with the anglophones, etc.), the Québécois is very generous (Quebec, a land that welcomes foreigners and gives them refuge), the Québécois identity is threatened by the Other (the English, the immigrant), the Québécois must be suspicious of a pragmatic alliance with the Other (in the Canadian federation). The political or para-political discourse centred on the Québécois condition has an implicit or avowed didactic goal. Its purpose is to *educate the Québécois*, to make them aware of the necessity of autonomy. Witness the media's insistence that, with the loss of René Lévesque, the very incarnation of the quest for independence, Quebec lost a 'great teacher.' The theatre is also called upon to play its part in the independence movement; it has a pedagogical program, to help Quebec understand the motives and consequences of its alienation, and thus opt for independence. In the next chapter, we further examine how this ideology, which underlies a whole part of the social discourse, is woven into the foreign dramatic text by the translator and how the translator becomes a didactic instrument, an instrument of persuasion, to build the 'nation québécoise.'

In Germain's postscript to *Les Faux Brillants* ..., dedicated to 'L'Honnête Monsieur Marchand,'[104] we find clear evidence of the dramatic discourse paralleling the political discourse. Marchand had a long political career in opposition before becoming premier of Quebec. Germain portrays him as an enlightened man, the last representative of political liberalism before the conservatism which plunged Quebec into 'La Grande Noiceur': 'from then on, the future belonged to the pragmatism of the Dumonts of this world,' to those who sold off the interests of Quebec, from S.-N. Parent, the flamboyant parvenu who came into office immediately after Marchand, to 'that reigning buffoon' Duplessis. Patriotism and integrity are the two axiological poles of this homage to Félix-Gabriel Marchand. Germain reminds us that Marchand was, at one time, leader of a patriotic movement and that he played a part in driving back the 'Irish agitators' during the Fenian raids of 1866. Germain portrays Marchand as an 'unrivalled' politician who 'emerges in the demagogic agitation of a turbulent sea churning with a horde of swashbucklers, corrupt officials, and fortune hunters.'[105] He adds that, 'as an author, Marchand had a clearer and broader vision than he did as a politician.'[106] Germain sees Marchand as a precursor of the Quiet Revolution, and his play as a paradigm, in that it illustrates the obstacles to the emergence of a truly Québécois society. We could say, then, that if Germain took the trouble to revive a very minor literary work, it was implicitly to realize the full ideological potential of the work; the play's narrative program already contained the basic axio-ideological tenets of the contemporary discourse on *québécité*. Indeed, in his 'paraphrase,' Germain projects a set of ideologemes from the target discourse onto the source text:

Neither strict adaptation nor nostalgic reconstitution, but a *true translation of the here and now into the recent past*, the paraphrase – through consistent distancing – attempts to be a type of double vision: in this context, the traditional visual process, which consists in re-actualizing chronological time by creating the illusion of a slice of life from that period, goes against the desired effect, which is not to bring the past back into the present *but to put the present in the past, where it was already virtually present as the future.*[107]

This translative operation, which Germain calls a 'paraphrase,' is indicative of his ambiguity towards the original text. Germain's translation is a kind of reverential translation that shapes consciousness of history and places it in the ideological framework of 'roots.' But we could also say that his linguistic transformation restored a work that was clearly out of place in the new Québécois drama. It was, in fact, his paraphrase of the work that made its ideological appropriation possible.

Germain's translation changes not only the structure but also the language of the play, which was originally written in rhyming verse. Here is how Dumont expresses himself in the original French-Canadian version, followed by its Québécois version:

Marchand

DUMONT (*très agité*) – Ouf! Je suis hors de moi!... Ces débats me surmontent.
S'il fallait s'ârreter aux histoires qu'ils content
Nul étranger n'aurait accès à nos salons.
Non, positivement...[108]

Germain

DUMONT – Spas possibbe!... Çé pas possibbe! Moué, ça mfait mourir des discussions dmême!... Çé pas possibbe... s'y fallait écouter toué-z-histouères qui sracontent sus à Grande Allée... à chaqu'fois qu'y a un étranger qui débarque du bateau, y faudrait s'embarrer dans nos maisons pis enfarmer toué filles en âge de smarier dans leu chambbes!... Pis après ça, le plus drôle, çé qutout lmonde s'étonne quant-y nous prennent pour des-z-habitants![109]

For Germain, to translate is literally to create a 'Québécois' work. His translation of Marchand's play changed not only the 'language' of the work but also the title and the author. To be repatriated, readmitted into the field of Québécois theatre, the original work, although created in

Quebec, had to undergo a change in linguistic code. Germain's translation goes beyond a mere change of register, from literary verse to everyday prose, because the idiom he uses in his new text becomes a medium for defining *québécité* as opposed to *francité*. This opposition is emphasized by alternation of lines in French and in 'Québécois.' The linguistic paraphrase is applied selectively to certain characters. Élise, Dumont's eldest daughter, and Faquino both express themselves in French in verse. Germain retains the characters' lines from the original text, but he makes some changes, shortening them, lengthening them, or replacing them with his own lines. This alternation of French and Québécois produces the same parodic effect as in *Le Cid maghané*:

DUMONT – Jl'ai invité à souper à souère à souper!

ÉLISE – Adoncques! Sans plus tarder! Je cours à ma toilette![110]

The contrast between the two languages is, however, much more pronounced than in Ducharme's play. In Germain's play, the French is marked by a ridiculous affectation (préciosité). Ducharme does not alter Corneille's language as dramatically, although the interspersion of lines in *joual* produces parodic effects. The Québécois specificity of Germain's rewritten dialogues, which is much more pronounced than in *Le Cid maghané*, lies in the actual written form, which reproduces a 'hyper-Québécois' mode of expression and pronunciation, in contrast to 'le bon parler français.' Witness this dialogue between the two Dumont sisters:

ÉLISE – Je vous entends, ma foi, mais dois-je m'y arrêter? Votre façon de parler me donne la nausée.

CÉCILE – Tu vas ptête virer dl'oeil plus vitte que tu penses, Élise, parsquàsqu'y paraît... l'Étalien... y est en train dnous pleumer ben raide, pis sus un temps rare![111]

The exaggeration and alternation of the dialogue of *francité*, on the one hand, and *québécité*, on the other, sets up an opposition between *artificial language* and *natural language* or between (borrowed) culture and (one's own) nature.[112] In the denouement, when the scoundrels are unmasked, Élise, the 'colonisée' (colonialized) returns to her 'true' Québécois nature. In a symbolic gesture, 'she frees herself from her sheath-dress,' in other words from the yoke of her borrowed 'culture.' As she does so, she also makes another symbolic rejection; she switches languages. But this rejection is ambiguous because, although she clearly abandons the artifice of French, she expresses herself with a familiar English exclamation. Élise's true nature is, then, to be a 'colonisée':

Que puis-je ajouter, sinon un mot du coeur:
   (*MAIS LE NATUREL REPREND LE DESSUS*)
SHHHHHHHHHOCCCCCCKKKKKKSSSSSSS![113]

The most significant change to Marchand's original play is the addition of a prologue that sets the play in its historical context. The new version takes place in the year of the Imperial Jubilee in a Quebec City theatre, in the presence of Félix-Gabriel Marchand. As the curtain rises, the director of a troupe of actors is paying homage to the premier, who is sitting in the royal box. This *mise en abyme* is a way of informing the public of the context of the work and of the author's career. However, it is Germain's play that is being put on before the author of the original or, more precisely, before the actor who plays the author. In this face-to-face meeting, there is a sort of didactic role-reversal. Germain discovered an affinity between the author of *Les Faux Brillants* and the thought underlying his own drama. He thus rewrote the work, not so much to revive it as to underline its value as an example. Marchand, the 'honnête homme,' who must attend the performance of *Les Faux Brillants de Félix-Gabriel Marchand*, is given a writing lesson by Germain, the substitute author. Germain's paraphrase and its accompanying prologue, in which the true author becomes a simple spectator, is a demonstration of what drama should be (should always have been) if it is to deserve the label 'Québécois.'

Germain's *Les Faux Brillants* ... is a perfect illustration of the degree to which so-called French-Canadian drama, like French drama, has become a foreign zone. For this reason, French-Canadian dramatic works can be subject to the same translative operations as those used for works imported from outside Quebec.

Vive la Différence!:
Bertolt Brecht's A Respectable Wedding

The reappropriation of foreign works, or works perceived as such, often involves not only transcoding of the original text but a whole series of other major changes, such as anthologization or expansion. Consider, for example, the following extracts from Brecht's original version and Jean-Claude Germain's Québécois adaptation of Brecht's *A Respectable Wedding* (*Le Buffet impromptu ou la nôsse chez les propriétaires de bungalow*):[114]

DER VATER – Onkel August starb an Wassersucht!

DER MANN – Prosit!

DER VATER – Prosit! Wassersucht! Erst war es nur der Fuss, eigentlich nur die Zehen, aber dann bis zum Knie, das ging schneller als das Kinderkriegen, und da war schon alles schwarz. Der Bauch war auch aufgetrieben, und obgleich man tüchtig abzapfte ...

DER MANN – Prosit!

DER VATER – Prost, prost! ... abzapfte, es war schon zu spät. Dann kam noch die Sache mit dem Herz dazu, die beschleunigte alles. Er lag also in dem Bett, das ich euch geben wollte, und stöhnte wie ein Elefant, und so sah er auch aus, ich meine die Beine![115]

Parts of the original text retained in Germain's adaptation are in italics, to indicate the extent of expansions made to the original:

LE PÈRE – Chpeux jusse en raconter une à fois, Simone! Fait que ... scomme jdisais ... mon grand-t-*oncque Hu-on* ... spas un secret ... *yé morre dla goutte*!

PAQUETÉ OSCAR INTERVIENT

LE MARI DL'AMIE DFILLE – Bon ben on va prendde une ptite goutte *à la santé dl'oncque* Yvon!

LE PÈRE – Pas Yvon! Hu-on ... Hue-donc à la rigueur ... *ouais ... fait qu'yé morre dla goutte ... ça commencé par le pied ça ... en fait pas tellement le pied comme lé-z-orteils ... pis* dé-z-orteils ... en passant par le pied ben sûr ... *çé monté dans lgenou ... pis là dans ltemps qu'on met pour faire un ptit ... ça stait répandu partout ... la peau tait toute marbrée nouère pis lvente s'est mis à gonfler ... y-z-avaient beau y faire des ponctions* ... spas aussi souffrant qudes ponctions lambert ... mais

LE MARI DL'AMIE DFILLE – Vou-z-avez ben raison, monsieur Simoneau, y a pas dmeilleure remède pour la toux! As-tu compris Gisèle?

LE PÈRE – Des ponctions?

LE MARI DL'AMIE DFILLE – Ouais! Le syrop Lambert! Dodds pour l'etomac... Madelon pour la tête... Sen-Sen pour l'haleine mais pour le rhume çé LAMBERT! Madame Simoneau, *y a un verre qu'yé veuf icitte,* pis qu'y aurait lgoût dfaire une passe à veuve!

LE PÈRE – Ouais. Fait que... scomme jdisais... *y ont eu beau syphonner l'estomac* à tour de bras... ça sarvait pus a rien... *y était trop tarre! Son coeur stait mis à sauter* dtous borres pis dtous côtés comme un lapin en chaleur pis dans ltemps de ldire y était rendu au pied de la pentte dousse comme y disent à Québec... un ben belle ville ça... çé malheureux qu'y aient eu l'idée dla construirre sus une falaise pis dfaire des rues si étrettes... entoucas... *Y était étendu dans son litte* pis y grognait comme un cochon dans l'auge... justement *dans l'litte que jvoulais vous donner...* y *splaignait comme* un cochon à l'abattoir... un cochon? *un éléphant* plutôt... pis y avait pas jusse la toune de l'éléphant, *y en avait l'air aussi... les jambes surtout...*[116]

As compared with the French version of the play published by Les Éditions de l'Arche, Germain's translation actually reworks the language, and goes beyond a simple change in register. In its attempt to reproduce the sociolect of the Quebec *petit bourgeois,* who do not speak like French *petit bourgeois,* Germain's Québécois adaptation introduces irrelevant transformations. Why write *morre* (mort), *pentte* (pente) or *tarre* (tard), since the difference, merely phonetic, is mainly in the diphthongization of the vowels? How can the graphic disappearance of the silent *e,* which is also not pronounced in standard French, be justified? These irrelevant changes can be viewed as ideological symptoms: they create a false uniqueness for the *Québécois* language, and make it appear to be much more different from the French of France than it really is. Here, the translative operation produces not only the target text but also the target language. It produces a sort of 'in' code with which members of the community can identify. But, at the same time, the language functions as a secret code of exclusion, part of the nationalist program: 'A country, a people, a language.'

Expansions in the form of puns, metaphors, and digressions function as signs of recognition in this code:

LE MARI DL'AMIE DFILLE – Ouais! Le syrop Lambert! Dodds pour l'estomac... Madelon pour la tête... Sen-Sen pour l'haleine mais pour le rhume çé LAMBERT![117]

References to old Québécois advertisements are signs that only members of the community can decipher. Germain's translation clearly introduces references designed to reinforce, through humour, the cohesion of a group that shares the same values. The original Brechtian text is treated as a consumer good for a specifically targeted audience. Alienated from itself, the original merely provides a thematic outline for a Québécois play destined for home consumption. In fact, when, at the end of *Le Buffet impromptu*, the character representing Brecht criticizes the other protagonists for not respecting his play, the bride's father retorts: 'Quand on change de pays, faut s'adapter' (When you change country, you have to adapt).[118] Nevertheless, Brecht is successful in his demand that his play be staged in the original version. But just as he is announcing to the public: 'Mesdames, messieurs, *La noce chez les petits bourgeois* dans la version originale de Bertolt Brecht,' the curtain is lowered. Germain's stage directions indicate that, at this point, the Québécois characters are to chase away the characters of the 'French version.' In other words, the foreign dramatist is categorically denied his author's rights: his text cannot be produced on the Québécois stage. What is more, the stage directions, as well as the dialogue, equate the *French translation* with the *original (German) version*. Hence the Frenchman, as spokesman for the Foreigner, has been chased off the stage and reduced to silence. In this case, Québécois adaptation censures the voice of the Other and retains only aspects of the original that can be recognized or heard by *la québécité*.

A Ghost Who Speaks Our Language:
Robert Gurik's Hamlet, prince du Québec

Hamlet, prince du Québec, by Robert Gurik, is another example of a Québécois adaptation that makes major changes to the original text. In this parody of Shakespeare's *Hamlet*, Gurik translates only specific passages of the original text (italicized in the excerpt below), selecting parts of the text according to their capacity to express a Québécois situation; that is, the usurpation of francophone power by anglophones:

Shakespeare

Hamlet
GHOST – Ay, that incestuous, *that adulterate beast,*
With witchcraft of his wit, with traitrous gifts, –
O wicked wit and gifts, that have the power

So to seduce! – *won to his* shameful *lust*
The will of my most seeming-virtuous queen.
O Hamlet! what a falling-off was there
From me, whose love was of that dignity
That it went hand in hand even with the vow
I made to her in marriage; and to decline
Upon a wretch whose natural gifts were poor
To those of mine!
But virtue, as it never will be mov'd,
Though lewdness court it in a shape of heaven,
So lust, though to a radiant angel link'd,
Will state itself in a celestial bed,
And prey on garbage.
But, soft! methinks *I scent the morning air,*
Brief let me be. Sleeping within mine orchard,
My custom always *in the afternoon,*
Upon my secure hour thy uncle stole,
With juice of cursed hebona in a vial,
And *in the porches of mine ears did pour*
The leperous distilment; whose effect
Holds such an enmity with blood of man
That swift as quicksilver it courses through
The natural gates and alleys of the body,
And with a sudden vigour it doth posset
And curd, like eager droppings into milk,
The thin and wholesome blood: so did it mine,
And a most instant tetter bark'd about,
Most lazar-like, with vile and loathsome crust,
All my smooth body.
Thus was I, sleeping, by a brother's hand,
Of life, of crown, of queen, at once dispatch'd;
Cut off even in the blossoms of my sin,
Unhousel'd, disappointed, unanel'd,
No reckoning made, but sent to my account
With all my imperfections on my head:
O, horrible! O, horrible! most horrible!
If thou hast nature in thee, bear it not;
Let not the royal bed of Denmark *be*
A couch for luxury and damned incest.
But, howsoever thou pursu'st this act,

Taint not thy mind, nor let thy soul contrive
Against thy mother aught; leave her to heaven,
And to those thorns that in her bosom lodge,
To prick and sting her. Fare thee well at once!
The glow-worm shows *the matin to be near,*
And 'gins to pale his uneffectual fire;
Adieu, adieu! Hamlet, *remember* me.[119]

Gurik

Hamlet, prince du Québec

THE GHOST (CHARLES DE GAULLE) –
Oui, ce monstre adultère qui a su gagner à sa passion le coeur de ma reine chérie, dont toutes les apparences témoignaient de la vertu. Mais *ne ranimons pas les plaies à jamais ouvertes,* je sens l'air du matin, il me faut faire vite. Endormi dans mon jardin après le dîner, ton oncle *muni d'une orange* me surprit dans mon sommeil et *força le fruit dans ma bouche jusqu'à l'étouffement.* C'est ainsi que je fus en dormant dépouillé, par la main d'un frère, de la vie, de la couronne et de mon épouse et relevé du monde sans les grâces du ciel, sans les derniers secours de la religion pour mes péchés flagrants, sans les prières implorées par les cloches des mourants et envoyé devant le juge suprême avec toutes mes fautes accumulées sur la tête. *Hamlet,* ne laisse pas la couche royale devenir celle de la luxure et d'un inceste maudit. *Ne laisse pas le Québec pourrir sous la botte de ce profiteur qui pourrait te laisser croire qu'il te comprend et qu'il t'aime.* Mais, par quelques moyens que tu te décides d'agir, ne souille point ton coeur et que ton âme ne trame rien contre ta mère. Abandonne-la au ciel. Adieu, le matin va se lever, adieu et souviens-toi *que vive un Québec libre.*[120]

Clearly, Gurik's selection of extracts for translation reflects the discursive constraints of the ideological field of *québécité*. In the translation, we find obvious referential substitutions ('*Denmark is a prison*' / 'Quebec is a prison'), Shakespearian characters are turned into allegories or *personnages à clé* who are active on the political scene in Quebec or in Ottawa, and expansions (italicized in the excerpt) re-actualize Shakespeare's tragedy: 'Ton oncle *muni d'une orange* me surprit dans mon sommeil et *força le fruit dans ma bouche jusqu'à l'étouffement.*'[121] The orange, which replaces the poison poured into the King's ear, evokes the Orangemen, the anglophone reactionary faction, those unconditional supporters of the British Crown. The fruit forced into one's mouth, then, is English, the language whose hegemony leads to the assimilation of francophones.

In Gurik's translation, parody becomes a double translative operation: as it moves from one text to the other and from one time period to the other, there is a shift from fictive narrative to experienced reality, filtered through the social discourse. From a pragmatic point of view, this operation, which is at once translative and parodic, accentuates the shift from the *petit discours* to the *grand discours*. It is easy to see what audience *Hamlet, prince du Québec* is aimed at; while it speaks to the Québécois audience, it also speaks to the latter's adversary, the English – hence, the *agonic* nature of this discourse, a discourse of action, the theme of which is the political, economic, and cultural alienation of Québécois society, a society that should free itself from the anglophone 'colonizer.'

Gurik's translation also grafts new elements onto extracts retained from the foreign text. These additions, which function as homogenizing glosses, are entirely rooted in the discourse of Québécois liberation, which is attempting to become the dominant discourse. As in *Le Cid maghané* or *Le Buffet impromptu*, these glosses 'carnivalize' the text, provoking laughter from the audience. Laughter, which is an integral part of the 'in' code, reinforces the cohesion of the group. In his history of laughter and mockery, Jean Duvignaud stresses the importance of 'the conviviality of the comic'; for him, the notion of popular laughter is a myth, the fantasy of an ideology.[122] Laughter, relies on the enclosure and warmth of a group. The theatre functions as an 'enclave of laughter,' a separate place that solicits and maintains the complicity of those who are laughing. The 'spontaneity' of popular laughter is produced by a code worked out *in camera* before the performance. Similarly, 'Carnival parades' are orchestrated and in no way escape from this principle. The enclosure and conviviality of the theatrical space combine with this 'manipulation' to create or accentuate the illocutionary force of laughter, a force that contributes to the doxological effectiveness of the performance, of the *grand discours*. As we have seen, the original text functions only as passive material support. The Other of the foreign text has no real right to his identity, no more than he has the right to speak, unless it is to express Québécois reality and to mediate the political aspirations of a group seeking to supplant the old hegemony:

Respect for the written text, for the specific thought of a dramatist, should be of interest to only servile, lazy, third-class artisans ... I would gladly pay without baulking, royalties to Aeschylus or Shakespeare for certain well-executed dramatic structures; but, as for the psychology of a sixteenth-century character or an Elizabethan *clair de lune*, or even Greek pantheism, reproducing them would be pure indulgence, for a small coterie of literary types, those voyeuristic intellectuals, a luxury, not a necessity, and the theatre comes alive only with necessities.

When Québécois dramatists find a framework, a theatrical structure which is our own, that really expresses our uniquenesss, we will have not only an authentic drama but also a country.[123]

Henceforth, the theatre had to give itself over entirely to the nationalist cause – this idea partially determined the new relation to foreign plays. Foreign theatre was no longer significant and, even worse, it was an obstacle to self-affirmation. Old buildings that were blocking construction of a new road had to be torn down. Reusable material would be retained from the rubble and used for a better cause, to build a 'national' drama.

Towards a New Canon

The new relation to foreign works was reflected in Quebec's literary system and resulted in changes to the component parts of that system. The examples analysed above show that the definition of a foreign work now included the literary legacy of France; it was even extended to include the French-Canadian repertoire, contaminated by its connection with French drama,[124] and by the resulting linguistic overlapping. Witness a theatrical production from the beginning of the period under discussion, whose aim was to have done with 'traditional theatre,' to tear down the models and create a 'truly Québécois theatrical space.'[125] This was the goal of *Les Enfants de Chénier dans un grand spectacle d'adieu*, a collective creation by Le Théâtre du Même Nom, under Jean-Claude Germain. The following is Michel Bélair's synopsis of the play, quoted in its entirety, despite its length, as the play is a perfect illustration of the *agonic* relation to foreign drama, to mainstream, classic, official theatre – in a word, to French theatre:

In the left corner, les Enfants de Chénier! (Applause. Bravos. Silence.) In the right corner, the sons of b...s (Boo!) The French champions. (More boos!) Molière, Musset, Giraudoux ... and others. The champions' coach: (silence). The champions' coach: absent or deceased. (Laughter.) The 'trainer' of Les Enfants de Chénier; J.-C. Germain! (Hurrah!). (The announcer silences the room and starts in again.) You know the rules of the game: no hitting below the belt, but annihilate each other! A fight to the death in two rounds. Go ahead and beat each other up.

FIRST ROUND

Marivaux comes out of his corner cautiously. Jean-Luc Bastien and Louisette Dussault from Le TMN watch him, amused. Assisted by Nicole Leblanc and Gilles Renault, they quickly overpower him. Marivaux is out of breath. His tongue is hanging out. He is starting to look ridiculous. The next thing is an arm lock and a pull-down. Marivaux collapses on the ground, like an old man: he doesn't get up again, as if the ridicule were killing him. The first fall of the first round goes to Le TMN. J.-B. Poquelin gets up fearfully, now, slowly regaining confidence. Dissension reigns among Les Enfants de Chénier: they all want to participate in the match. Finally, Gilles Renault and Monique Rioux are declared the winners. The fight starts again, Poquelin, known as Molière, also collapses after a couple of minutes of a one-sided fight. (And what a pleasure it is to see him destroyed!) Before he even comes out of his corner, Musset, Alfrède de, admits defeat. Gilles Renault, claiming that his authenticity resembles that of Yvon Deschamps, knocks him out by using his jaw muscles. In less than two rounds, Giraudoux succumbs to the same fate. The victory is total: the first round goes to Les Enfants de Chénier, with no resistance whatsoever from the team from France.

INTERMISSION

In collaboration with Le Centre du Théâtre d'Aujourd'hui, Le Théâtre du Même Nom managed, in this collective creation, to stigmatize all the banalities and all the clichés of conventional theatre. And also: to ridicule it completely. Inspired by the most well-known scenes of the so-called classical repertoire, Jean-Claude Germain's team demonstrates the ridiculousness of the situation. Proof by absence. Beyond the label 'théâtre engagé' and all its restrictions. Les Enfants de Chénier, beneath their facile exterior, re-pose the question of the relation of the theatre to the society that gives it birth. It is not so much *joual* that is questioned in this endeavour, but the social reality in which we live, a reality that is put at the bottom of the list by 'official' theatre. When this theatre exists. The social reality of Quebec exists concretely. It questions not only a language but a whole cultural reality that one is trying to make people forget. To bury and hide under the cloak of the few manifestations of it that one sometimes lets out of the bag. From time to time [...]

SECOND ROUND

The great tragedians and mystics come out. This is the star team. Claudel out in front, followed by Anouilh, Euripides, Aeschylus, Racine, Corneille, and Shakespeare (an Englishman!). You can see the anxiety on their faces, torn between duty (to fight) and the weight of destiny, they are going to lose. And they know it. This is tragic destiny! Les Enfants de Chénier are waiting for them, confident. Proud of their success in the first round, they will take only thirty minutes to demolish the team of classical stars. They are banking on a precious asset: ennui.

EPILOGUE

The match is over. The theatre is dead. (The 'Great Theatre'). Now all Les Enfants de Chénier have to do is take over the stage or go out into the street, and talk.[126]

The significance of unorthodox translations of foreign drama becomes evident when they are placed in the context of this iconoclastic movement. These translations demonstrate the embryonic nature of Québécois drama, a drama unsure of its own resources and of its own rules. In this first stage of development, drama builds itself against foreign works, but none the less with them. Foreign works are still the reference point against which Québécois theatre defines itself. The relationship to the Other is thus fundamentally one of 'specularity,' or mirroring. Despite the label 'Québécois,' imitations and parodies are style or learning exercises that are still bound to a 'model.' Such translations indicate that there is still a desire to equal or surpass the model, while refusing to give it access to the Québécois stage. Assimilation of foreign works does not involve a *Bildung*, respectful of their specificity. It is, on the contrary, conceived and practised as a destruction of the Other. Obsessive fear of the destruction of the group, of its own assimilation by the Foreigner, is turned against any form of alterity.

In the Québécois theatrical system, foreign drama in translation cannot be seen as a homogeneous, clearly identifiable set of plays, as translation imports the works not only in their entirety, but also in fragments. In this disarticulated form, they become reusable material for building the new Québécois theatre. In this way, translation contributes to the disintegration of the old canonic nucleus and to the formation of a new dominant theatrical canon. In the next chapter, we will see that translation is an axio-ideological factor, mediating between the particular discursive formation we call 'literature' and other formations of social discourse. It is no coincidence that this homogenization is found primarily within a specific field of the literary system, that is, the theatre. Indeed, the quest for Québécois specificity, for *québécité*, is carried out through the quest for a language distinct from the Franco-French code, on which Québécois theatre used to be based. But the difference between *franco-québécois* (French spoken in Quebec) and *franco-français* (French spoken in France) is mainly phonetic; and although this difference is relative, since it varies according to the social and cultural status of its speakers, one can readily see why an 'oral' literary genre such as the theatre, the only genre in which this difference can make itself heard, has become the preferred area of translation.

3

Shakespeare, Québécois Nationalist Poet: Perlocutory Translation

... they made up the deficiency by recommending the best productions of the past as patterns, and making them accessible to their scholars. These were chiefly the works of the Christian-Catholic school of the Middle Ages. The translation of Shakespeare, who stands on the border of this art, and smiles with Protestant clearness into our modern time, was intended for controversial purposes ...

Heinrich Heine, *Germany*

Translation as a Perlocutory Operation

As the witches are dancing on the moors, a drum announces Macbeth's arrival. This is Macbeth's first appearance in the play:

Drum within
THIRD WITCH: A drum, a drum!
Macbeth doth come.[1]

In Michel Garneau's Québécois version of the play, Macbeth's arrival is announced by a different musical instrument, a fiddle:

Violon
TROISIÈME
Le vialon, le vialon, Macbeth s'en vient 'citte![2]

By way of metonymy, the fiddle acts as an *actualizer* in this important scene, as it immediately brings to mind two characteristic features of Québécois folklore – the fiddler and the ebullient rhythm of the jig. The replacement of the drum is only a minuscule change, but it transforms the setting of the dramatic action and places the tragedy in an unambiguously Québécois framework. This change passes almost unnoticed in print, but, on stage, the sound of the fiddle is powerfully evocative, transforming the Scotland of *Macbeth*, a foreign, imaginary, and distant land, into something immediately familiar.

On another level, this typically Québécois folk music, together with other markers such as the 'Québécois language,' functions as a powerful metadiscursive operator. When they hear the sound of the fiddle, the audience realize that the place being referred to (Scotland/fiction) can be superposed on the place from which the lines are being delivered (Quebec/reality). The fusion of the content of the play and the place where it is being performed transforms the discourse of Shakespeare's tragedy into a dual semantic that works upon the consciousness of the audience. Here, translation becomes a *perlocutory* operation, to use a term from speech-act theory. The term 'perlocutory act' (or, according to J.L. Austin and J. Searle, the perlocutionary act) refers to what is commonly called the 'effect on the receiver' in translation theory:

For example, by arguing, I may *persuade* or *convince* someone, by warning him I may *scare* or *alarm* him, by making a request I many *get him to do something*, by informing him I may *convince him* (*enlighten, edify, inspire him, get him to realize*). The italicized expressions above denote perlocutionary acts.[3]

The term 'perlocutory' will thus be used to refer to those transformations that give the target text a persuasive or injunctive function. This function, absent from the source text, is designed to produce specific reactions in the receiver.

Normally, re-actualization transposes the space and time of the original play into a reality familiar to the audience. For example, Robert Lalonde sets the action of Chekhov's *Three Sisters* in the Quebec of the 1950s, changing the names, and even the roles of the characters. Michel Garneau's *Macbeth* does not re-actualize the entire text of the original play; indeed, his translation retains the essential identity of *Macbeth*. Garneau does, however, introduce changes at certain points that transport Shakespeare's tragedy to another setting, to a reconstituted past in which the play becomes an allegory of the Conquest, a real-life tragedy from Quebec's past that throws light on the life of contemporary Quebec. Thus, Shakespeare's tragedy is made to fall in line with Québécois reality as it is represented in the social discourse. The fusion of these two realities operates at two levels: space and time.

In Garneau's spatial re-actualization of the play, the fictitious elsewhereness of *Macbeth* is re-actualized in a Québécois context through the explicit use of the target language, a language whose importance, as we have seen, is underlined by the inclusion of the expression 'translated into Québécois' on the cover of the published play. Temporal re-actualization is achieved through the use of certain markers, such as the archaic form of the language of translation. These temporal markers prompt the Québécois audience to perceive the temporal distance of a Quebec that they already recognize through other markers. Although they may seem contradictory, the spatial and temporal dislocations produced by the translation realize a *historic re-actualization* of the Shakespearian play, a re-actualization *distanced in time*. This produces a much more subtle fusion of the play's dialogue and the social discourse than could ever be achieved by direct and total transposition of place and characters. By emphasizing the temporal nature of the spatial markers of the dramatic action, Garneau's translation establishes a distance between the place of reception (Quebec) and this same place at a specific time in its history. Dislocated in time, the place referred to in the play (an imaginary Scotland) and the place the translation refers to (historic Quebec) are fused in a contemporary space, that of the prevailing social discourse (present-day Quebec). It is this interaction between the theme of the play, space, and time that produces the perlocutory effect of the translation.

The concept of a 'chronotope,'[4] a term used to refer to the conjunction of a particular space and a particular time, will enable us to schematize the way in which actualizers switch the discourse from one space-time to another. We will demonstrate, in particular, how the actualizers in Garneau's translation bring about axio-ideological shifts between reality and fiction, that is to say, how they inject into the dialogue of *Macbeth* values and ideas that represent the Québécois fact in the social discourse.

Michel Garneau's *Macbeth* operates within three main space-times – the chronotope of the original: Scotland/in a mythical time; the chronotope of the re-actualized original: Quebec/historical time; and the chronotope of the audience: Quebec/at the time of reception. For each of these chronotopes, there is a discursive configuration: who is speaking, of what, and how? In the first chronotope, we find Shakespeare's dialogue. In the second, we find the same dialogue reworked by translation. In the third, the discourse of Québécois society, of which the translator and the audience are part, plays an infinitely greater and much more complex role.

112   A Sociocritique of Translation

FIGURE 3 Spatio-temporal Configuration of the Québécois Translation of *Macbeth*

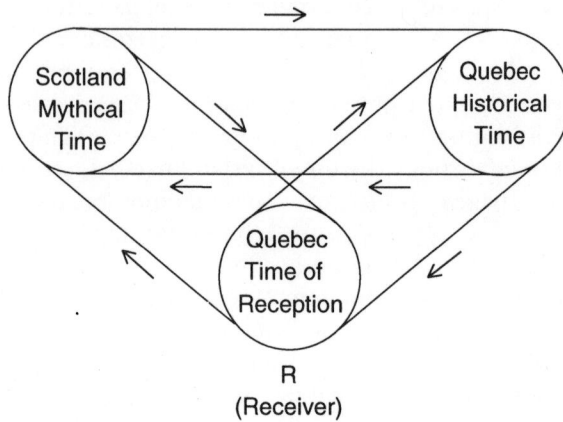

R
(Receiver)

We can schematize the interaction of the three discursive configurations around their respective chronotopes. Figure 3, in which the audience appears on the periphery, demonstrates that a variety of semantic avenues open up for the audience as the tragedy unfolds. However, the audience's choice of avenue is far from free and undirected, as the translation contains various guiding indicators, in particular, space and time actualizers. By definition, actualizers disconnect the translation from the original work; but, paradoxically, as *spatio-temporal disconnectors*, they play the role of *discursive connectors*, as they lead the audience to project the content of the Shakespearian dialogue onto one of the Québécois chronotopes (historical or contemporary). Thus, the actualizers ensure that the audience gives a particular axio-ideological interpretation to the dialogue.

Figure 3 makes it clear that some elements of the original text may facilitate, while others may hinder, the transfer of the original dialogue into a different space–time. The translator may either emphasize or suppress these elements, depending on whether they reinforce or destroy the potential axio-ideological interpretation provided by the foreign work. Even when they are not present in the target text, these markers act as indicators for the audience; their very omission allows the discourse contained in the dialogue to shift from one chronotope to the other. Conversely, if these markers are retained, they can interfere with the projection of ideologemes from the target social discourse and limit the translation to the chronotope of the source text (in this case, mythical Scotland) – at least, this will be the perception of the audience, who are at the mercy of the translator.

The translator is, however, confronted with certain limitations in this process: *Macbeth* does not lend itself uniformly to axio-ideological semanticization in terms of Québécois social discourse. Some parts of the play lend themselves better than others to the superposing of chronotopes and, consequently, to the dynamic of discursive exchange. If the entire text of *Macbeth* were translated to correspond perfectly with the discourse of Québécois society, the Shakespearian play would be unrecognizable. Thus, it is not surprising that only parts of the play are adjusted – namely, those that are the most compatible with the values and ideas manifested in Québécois discourse .

Such adjustments to the original text, which the translator is often not even aware of, can nevertheless reveal the discursive codes of the society into which foreign texts, selected by that society, enter – hence, the interest of these adjustments to translation theorists. A description of the structural underpinnings of these adjustments will enable us to understand better the institutional constraints of the translative operation, as well as the role, little known and very little studied, of the subjects of this operation, translators themselves, in their role as conveyers of the norms of the social discourse and the institution that sets them up and validates them.

A Dynamic Equivalent: Scotland = Not'pauv'pays

Our examination of a single actualizer in Garneau's *Macbeth*, the substitution of one musical instrument for another, led us to formulate a number of principles, which we will now apply to the play as a whole. Let us begin with Garneau's spatio-temporal transformations, comparing settings in the original stage directions with those of the Québécois version.

Tables 17 and 18 demonstrate the reductive simplification of the Québécois version of the play. In its defence, it might be pointed out that this simplification is dictated by the production constraints of a different theatrical aesthetic, that of an impoverished theatre, the very symbol of the Québécois as victims of history. But this only emphasizes all the more that translation and production values are products of the same society and operate within the same ideological framework. They start from the same position, and from the same historical juncture, and arrive at similar interpretations of the source text.[5]

114 A Sociocritique of Translation

TABLE 17
A Comparison of Settings in Stage Directions (*Macbeth*, tr. M. Garneau)

Scotland; England		En Écosse. En Angleterre
I.1	A desert heath	Un brûlé
I.2	A camp near Forres	0
I.3	A heath	Le brûlé
I.4	Forres. A room in the palace	Devant le château de Macbeth
I.5	Inverness. Macbeth's castle	Au loin dans la plaine
		Au château de Macbeth
I.6	Before the castle	La grande salle
I.7	A room in the castle	Une chambre
II.1	Inverness. Court within the castle	Cour dans le château de Macbeth (Inverness)
II.4	Without the castle	0
III.1	Forres. A room in the palace	0
III.2	Another room in the palace	0
III.3	A park, with a road leading to the palace	Au bord de la forêt
III.4	A room of state in the palace	Salle à manger
III.5	A heath	Le brûlé
III.6	Forres. A room in the palace	À Forres
IV.1	A cavern	0
IV.2	Fife. Macduff's castle	Le château de Macduff
IV.3	England. Before the king's palace	En Angleterre
V.1	Dunsinane. A room in the castle	Chez Macbeth
V.2	The country near Dunsinane	Dans la campagne
V.3	Dunsinane. A room in the castle	Chez Macbeth
V.4	Country near Birnam Wood	Près de la forêt
V.5	Dunsinane. Within the castle	Chez Macbeth
V.6	A plain before the castle	Devant le château
V.7	Another part of the plain	Ailleurs dans la plaine

Garneau's translation retains fewer than half of the places that appear in the original text, and these are given a vaguer designation; the characters appear, for example, 'au bord de la forêt' (A park with a road leading to the palace), 'dans la campagne' (The country near Dunsinane), 'chez Macbeth' (Dunsinane. A room in the castle). These neutral settings remove the disquieting nature of the myth. Thus, the cave disappears, while the deserted heath, reminiscent of that in *Wuthering Heights*, reappears in the more domesticated form of a 'brûlé' (slashed and burnt,

TABLE 18
A Comparison of Place-Names: Shakespeare and Garneau

Shakespeare		Garneau	
England	2	Angleterre	2
Scotland	1	Écosse	1
Forres	5	Forres	1
Dunsinane	4		0
Inverness	2	Inverness	1
Birnam	1		0
Fife	1		0
Total of proper nouns	16		5
castle	10	château	5
palace	7		0
room	8	chambre	1
room of state	1	salle à manger	1
		la grande salle	1
court	1	cour	1
park	1		0
heath	3	brûlé	3
country	2	campagne	1
plain	2	plaine	2
wood	1	forêt	2
road	1		0
camp	1		0
cavern	1		0
Total of common nouns	38		17
Overall total	54		22

deforested land). The Québécois audience will inevitably associate this 'brûlé' with its colonial past of land-clearing settlers, defensive works, forts and castles. In his stage directions, Garneau retains none of the numerous occurrences of the word 'palace.' He does, however, translate 'castle,' a more modest type of building, although he reduces its value by using it only half as many times as it appears in the original. It is not surprising, either, that he transforms 'A room of state' into the more familiar 'salle à manger.'

One explanation for this systematic shift to the commonplace[6] might lie in the dialectal nature of the target language, which, it could be argued, limits the possibilities open to the translator. But, surely, the aim of translating a canonical work into 'Québécois' is to dedialectalize Québécois and to prove that it is a language in its own right. One characteristic feature of a language is its ability to express any reality and, if necessary, to create the means of doing so. There is, therefore, no reason why there should not be an equivalent for the 'King's palace' in Québécois. Garneau could have used his own graphic and phonetic code to translate 'the King's palace' by 'el' pala's du roé.' The systematic omission of the word 'palace' indicates that there is a conflict between what the language can say (even in a dialectal form, given that it reproduces characteristics of the French spoken in Quebec during the Ancien Régime) and what the translator makes it say. The omission does not result from a deficiency in the language, but rather from the relationship the translator sets up between the play's content and the 'fait québécois,' a reality the language is clearly supposed to express and promote.

A castle is a means of defence as well as an aristocratic dwelling. It is a protective enclosure surrounded by ramparts, complete with loopholes, crenels, and watchtowers. As a fortification, the castle is, thus, a real part of the history of Quebec – in contrast with the palace. This explains why the attack on Macbeth's castle has historical resonance for a Québécois audience:

Garneau

MACBETH
Fa's accrocher toutes nos banniéres après 'es crénaux!
Ça m'fa't rien d'entende crier qu'y s'en viennent, l'château
Est assez fort pour prende toutes leus attaques; on va 'es laisser
S'évartuer comme des bons jusqu'à temps qu'y creuvent
ed 'faim
Pis qu'les fieuves 'es mangent tout crus. R'marqu', si-z-éta'ent pas
Renforcis en nombe par eune bande de traîtes qui s'r'a'ent s'posés
D'ête d'not' bord, on s'ra't sorti 'es défier face à face
Dans l'corps à corps pour les r'culer jusque cheuz-eux! (p. 140)

[MACBETH
We have to hang our banners out the crenels!
It doesn't faze me to hear them yelling that they're coming,
The castle

is strong enough to withstand their attacks; we are
going to let them try like crazy until they starve to death
And wild beasts eat them alive. You know,
if they weren't
supported by a bunch of traitors
who were supposed to be on our side, we would have gone out
and faced them
in hand-to-hand combat, to drive them back to where they came
from! (our translation)]

This passage is reminiscent of clichéd descriptions of attacks on forts by Indians or by the English, of the sort found in Québécois popular novels or history books. The similarity is further reinforced by the fact that Garneau omitted many of the proper names that appear in the original *Macbeth*. As the preceding tables indicate, two-thirds of the place-names designating the scene of the action have been removed – a large number. Such omissions are made not only in the stage notes but also in the dialogue of the play itself. Witness, for example, the prophecy around which the play revolves:

Macbeth shall never vanquish'd be until
Great Birnam Wood to high *Dunsinane Hill*
Shall come against him. (p. 861)

Macbeth s'ra pas vaincu tant qu'la forêt descendra pas d'la colline (p. 106)

Indeed, these place-names do not appear anywhere in the translation:

PORTIER
J't'a's en train d'guetter, comme vous m'avez dit, si y s'passa't
Queuque chose su' *a colline*, pis t'à coup, m'a semblé, m'a semblé
Qu'*la forêt*, a commença't à bouger, a s'en v'nir vers nous-autes.
...
J'vous jure qu'j'ai cru voér, vra' comme j'vous voés, lâ,
Eune masse d'âbres pis d'buissons d'un gros mille de profond
Qui descendent d'*la colline*!

MACBETH
[...] la sarcière
M'a ben dit, crains rien tant qu'la forêt descendra pas d'*la colline*,

Crains rien. *La forêt* descend d'*la colline*! (p. 143)

Garneau suppresses not only place-names but also their attributes. 'Great Birnam Wood' and 'high Dunsinane Hill,' larger-than-life places, of mythical proportions, are reduced to normal proportions, and acquire the banality of an everyday rural environment. Similarly, echoes of Holinshed's chronicles, the source of the play's plot, are reduced to a whisper. Uprooted from Anglo-Saxon mythology, *Macbeth* is transplanted to a land resembling New France. The spatio-temporal markers of Shakespeare's tragedy are displaced, if only intermittently, in favour of a historically recognizable Quebec.

Another example, from Act I, demonstrates even better how the elimination of certain elements facilitates the spatio-temporal displacement of the dialogue and, as a result, the projection of ideologemes of *québécité*.

Shakespeare

KING
Whence cam'st thou, *worthy thane?*

ROSS
         From *Fife*, great *king*,
Where the *Norweyan* banners flout the sky. (p. 847)

Garneau

DUNCAN
D'où c'est qu'tu r'ssouds comme çâ?

ROSS
Du plein coeur d'*la bataille*
Ousqu'les drapeaux *des étranges* insultent
Not'beau ciel. (p. 16)

In this description of the battle between Scotland and Norway, the translator has removed all references to the original setting and combatants. The latter become 'les étranges' (the foreigners), and later 'c't'es barbares-là' (those barbarians). The erasure of the names of people and places that clearly place the text in a Shakespearian universe makes it possible for Québécois readers or audiences to project onto *Macbeth* their own history and destiny. Conscious or not, the elimination of such references has a very real function. The message may be subliminal, but it nevertheless succeeds in reminding the public of the *battle* of the Plains of Abraham and the British Conquest, henceforth symbolized by the presence of the federal flag (*drapeaux des étranges* – the 'foreign flag' that replaced the British flag) in the skies of 'La Belle Province.'

We have seen that, in Garneau's *Macbeth*, the discourse through which the Québécois condition is defined meshes with the space–time of the original, by suppressing or adding certain markers. These alterations may well be unconscious, as the translator internalizes the discursive conventions of the society of which they are a part or, to be more precise, of the social group with which they identify. Nevertheless, an audience watching a production of the Québécois *Macbeth* is under the impression that it is, literally, a contemporary play, and does not realize that it is the translator's adjustments that have made it so. Garneau did, however, openly admit to eliminating two passages that he considered irrelevant. These omissions are worthy of our attention. Let us examine in detail the two shortened scenes and the differences between the original and the translation.

The King of England in the Trash-Cans of History

'I omitted lines 38 to 47.'

Garneau justifies his omission of these lines from Act III, Sc. 6, as follows: 'J'saute du vers 38 au vers 47 parc'c'est mêlé mêlant' (I omitted lines 38 to 47 because they are a jumble). What is striking about the scene the translator chose to expurgate is its proliferation of characters and patronyms. In the space of sixty lines, no fewer than ten characters are introduced:

- Duncan, the assassinated King of Scotland;
- Macbeth, the usurper of the throne of Scotland;
- Edward, the pious King of England;
- Banquo, Macbeth's rival, assassinated on his orders;
- Malcolm and Donalbain, sons of Duncan, refugees at the English court;
- Fleance, Banquo's son, survivor of an assassination attempt;
- Macduff, leader of the rebellion against Macbeth;

120 A Sociocritique of Translation

- Siward, Count of Northumberland and English general, whose army is supporting the rebels led by Macduff;
- a messenger sent by Macbeth to Macduff.

Garneau untangles this jumble of characters by suppressing a number of names, for example, that of Fleance, whom he replaces with 'l'p'tit à Banquo' (Banquo's little boy) (p. 96) or 'son garçon' (his son) (p. 95). The following passage illustrates the way in which Garneau clarifies the identity of the protagonists:

Shakespeare

LENNOX
But, peace! for from broad words, and 'cause he fail'd
His presence at *the tyrant's* feast, I hear,
Macduff lives in disgrace. Sir, can you tell
Where *he* bestows himself?

LORD
                    The son of Duncan
From whom *this tyrant* holds the due of birth
Lives in the English court and is receiv'd
Of *the most pious Edward* with such grace
That the malevolence of fortune nothing
Takes from his high respect. Thither Macduff
Is gone to pray *the holy king*. (p. 860)

Garneau

LENNOX
[...] Nous-autes, on est mieux d'parler bas pis rester tranquilles.
Macduff a parlé un p'tit peu haut pis y'est allé jusqu'à r'fuser
L'invitâtion du *tyran* pis *Macbeth* y'en veut à mort. Au faite,
As-tu su où c'est qu'y sont rendus *Malcolm pis Macduff*?

ROSS
Eune foés, *son père* défunt, *Malcolm* s'voya't dépossédé par le tyran,
Y s't'en allé rester à cour du roé d'*Angleterre*. Y'a été parfa't'ment
R'çu, aveuc toutes les honneurs, même si y'ava't pardu son héritage.
D'son côté, *Macduff* en profite pour asseyer d'avoér l'appui du *roé*. (p. 96)

Shakespeare, Québécois Nationalist Poet 121

The position of the pronoun ('he'/'Macduff') is reversed ('Macduff'/ 'y') to make the passage clearer. Similarly, Garneau provides the name of the tyrant (Macbeth) and he anticipates Ross's response by including the name of the organizers of the rebellion in Lennox's question ('Can you tell where he bestows himself?' 'où c'est qu'y sont rendus *Malcolm pis Macduff?*'). Clearly, Garneau is trying to help his audience make sense of this jumble of characters. He replaces the periphrase 'The son of Duncan' with the name of the protagonist himself (Malcolm) and repeats the name 'Macduff' to guide the reader and, more important, the audience in the theatre, through a morass of confusing references. Yet, are these substitutions motivated solely by a concern for clarity? Let us look, for example, at his treatment of the following references to the King of England, all taken from the same scene:

The English court
À cour du roé d'Angleterre

The most pious Edward
not translated

The holy king
(du) roé

The omission of the second reference deprives the King of England of his own name and, more important, prevents a Québécois audience from hearing the praise for him contained in the original text. In the third reference, the positive attributes of the King are once again omitted (censored?), an excess of attention for this otherwise secondary character. This suppression is all the more revealing in that it occurs alongside an expansion introduced by the translator to praise an even more secondary character:

Shakespeare
                    Thither Macduff
Is gone to pray *the holy king,* upon his aid
To wake Northumberland and *war-like Siward.* (p. 860)

Garneau

D'son côté, Macduff en profite pour asseyer d'avoér l'appui du *roé*

Ainsi que celui du Northumberland pis d'son *vaillant Siward*
Q'y est toute un guerrier. (p. 96)

Here, Garneau's modelling or reshaping of *Macbeth* operates on two levels. But the reshaping is, above all, ideological, as it removes from the original text attributes which differ from those that Québécois society associates with the British monarch, a central figure in the collective memory of the history of Quebec. Several lines later, we see another example of Garneau's ideological reshaping, conscious or not, of a passage that was somewhat ambiguous in the original:

Shakespeare
                      And this report
Hath so exasperate *the king* that he
Prepares for some attempt at war. (p. 860)

Which king is being referred to here? Is it Edward or Macbeth? A translation by Pierre Leyris, which appeared one year before Garneau's translation, and which was based on extremely thorough textual analysis, identifies the king of the original text as Macbeth:

                      Et ces nouvelles
Ont si furieusement exaspéré *Macbeth*,
Qu'il se prépare à quelque guerre.[7]

Garneau also makes the original text explicit, but he gives this same king, who is preparing for battle, the identity of the King of England, a person held in contempt by the history of Quebec and by Québécois social discourse:

En tout cas, son rapport, à Macduff a si tant touché
El'roé d'Angleterre, qu'y sont là-bas, en train d'fére leu
Préparatifs de guerre. (p. 96)

These lines are immediately followed by: 'I omitted lines 38 to 47, because they are a jumble' (p. 97). Admittedly, the dialogue that follows is somewhat opaque in the original:

LENNOX
Sent he to Macduff?

LORD
He did: and with an absolute, 'Sir, not I,'
The cloudy messenger turns me his back,
And hums, as who should say, 'You'll rue the time
That clogs me with this answer.' (p. 860)

This passage is sufficiently obscure to warrant a number of notes in an annotated edition of the original *Macbeth*. One such note reads: '*Cloudy: unhappy (at having to take such an answer to Macbeth)*.'[8] Here the ambiguity with respect to the identity of the king preparing for war is resolved in favour of Pierre Leyris. Leyris also makes it clear that the person who replies to Macbeth with the line 'Sir, not I' is indeed Macduff himself:

[...] après quoi lesté d'un 'Jamais' péremptoire,
Son courrier rembruni vous[9] a tourné le dos
En grognant comme qui dirait: 'Vous vous repentirez de l'heure
Qui me met sur l'échine une telle réponse.'[10]

In Yves Bonnefoy's translation, the reply is also clearly from Macduff:

Certes, mais en entendant
Un 'Monsieur, non, pas moi' catégorique,
Le soucieux messager s'était retiré,
Marmonnant quelque 'Vous regretterez l'heure
Qui vient de m'accabler de cette réponse.'[11]

By refusing to respond to the summons, Macduff invites vengeance from Macbeth, whose infamy Lennox has just described. The rest of the dialogue follows logically the theme of the discussion and in no way impedes comprehension of the text:

LENNOX
And that well might
Advise him to a caution to hold what distance
His wisdom can provide. Some holy angel
Fly to the court of England and unfold
His message ere he come, *that a swift blessing*
May soon return to this our suffering country
Under a hand accurs'd. (p. 860)

Garneau's translation of Lennox's speech retains only the words 'that a swift blessing,' which he then expands on:

Ça s'ra't eune bénidiction pis *eune sainte justice*
Si not' pays s'ra't libéré d'la main damnée qui l'opprime. (p. 97)

[It would be a benediction and *a blessed justice*
If our country were freed from the cursed hand that oppresses it. (our translation)]

The audience's attention is drawn to this passage, which can now be interpreted at two levels – at one level, the play itself, and at the other, the Québécois context, with discernible echoes of 'Vive le Québec libre!' Removed from its original context, whose possible ambiguity could distract the audience's attention from the plot, the passage now stands out and assumes greater significance – all the more so because it has been expanded to include 'pis eune sainte justice,' an utterance clearly inspired by the prevailing social discourse rather than by the corresponding passage of the original text, in which there is no equivalent. We also note, in particular, the omission of the reference to England, whence liberation would come to a country suffering at the hands of a hated oppressor. Clearly, the narrative of Shakespeare's tragedy disturbed the order of Québécois sovereigntist discourse.

The plot of *Macbeth*, which revolves around tyranny and the usurpation of power, parallels the representation of history in the discourse of Québécois liberation. More than *Othello*, and many other Shakespeare plays, *Macbeth* has clear affinities with the values and ideas that define the Québécois condition. Clearly, the choice of *Macbeth* was not entirely arbitrary. The play was most likely chosen because of its narrative macro-structure; but one of its instantial micro-structures is problematic – the English monarch appears in the role of liberator, and not in the role of oppressor. A major drawback to this otherwise appropriate vehicle for symbolizing the Québécois condition is, thus, the fact that the English are not portrayed as villains. Indeed, quite the opposite is true; the King of England is 'the holy King,' 'the most pious Edward,' or 'gracious England.' Garneau eliminated these modifiers, minimized the role of the King, and omitted a passage that clearly runs counter to the ideological presuppositions of the sovereigntist discourse, a discourse for which *Macbeth* now becomes an indirect mouthpiece. In his role of social subject, relayer of the social discourse, the translator eliminated disruptive passages, invoking a need for clarity to justify this removal of parts of the text: 'I omitted ... because they are a jumble.' The passage referred to above is not one of exemplary clarity, but neither is it incoherent. Indeed, *Macbeth* contains many, much more obvious examples of incoherence, but Garneau did not remove these. Was he afraid that the audience would confuse fiction with reality and that the benevolence of King Edward might conceal the despoiling of Quebec by his successors, who continue, in the mind of the audience, to be their oppressors? Therein lies the problem of censorship. It shelters behind an alleged connection between the real and the symbolic to justify its actions.

Intentional or not, the removal of parts of the original text keeps intact the order of a social discourse whose cohesion and presuppositional coherence were threatened. Validating a King of England would introduce a disturbing dialectical element into this otherwise ideologically homogeneous discourse. Garneau minimizes the liberating function of the King, but he does not do so consistently. The modifiers praising the King were most likely omitted at this precise point in the text because the passage contains a phrase of vivid immediacy, one of exceptional resonance for the Québécois public, a phrase that can be summed up as follows: Oh, that our land were soon freed of foreign domination! The co-presence of two utterances that are compatible on the stage, but contradictory in the space–time of the receiver, would prevent an audience from making the connection between the real and the fictitious. It would weaken the perlocutory force of the message that the 'surdestinateur'[12] of the play, in this case the translator, conveys to the Québécois public. We note in passing that the same passage is also shorn of its Christian references:

Shakespeare

LENNOX
    Some *holy angel*
Fly to the court of England and unfold
His message ere he come, that a swift blessing
May soon return to this our suffering country
Under a hand accurs'd!

LORD
    I'll send my *prayers* with him. (p. 860)

It would not be appropriate, in the Québécois *Macbeth*, to send a heavenly angel to the English court to plead for help and liberation. Removal of the religious elements, despite their limited role in the play, indicates clearly that in post-Quiet Revolution Quebec, when the influence of the Church had already been destroyed, religious references could still obscure a message that the translator obviously wished to express as clearly and as directly as possible. Freed of context, the utterance leaves the space-time of fiction for the space-time of public opinion. Now possessing a coherence that makes it possible for the Québécois receiver to interpret it, the utterance moves from the *aesthetic* to the *perlocutionary*.

The scene is reshaped not only ideologically but also axiologically, as illustrated by the treatment of the passage immediately preceding the lines removed by the translator:

Shakespeare

That, by the help of these – with him above
To ratify the work – we may again
Give to our tables meat, sleep to our nights,
Free from our feasts and banquets bloody knives,
Do *faithful* homage and receive *free* honours;
All which we pine for now. (p. 860)

Garneau

[...] et pis toutes eux-autes ensembe
Ac'l'aide du bon dieu vont p't'ête ben nous ram'ner le bon temps,
Qu'on dorme tranquille, la nuitte, *qu'on mange sans méfiance*
Qu'les pognards pleins d'sang s'éloégnent d'nos banquets,
Qu'on soye capabes d'rende hommage à ceux-là qui l'méritent,
Qu'on soye à même de r'çevoér des honneurs véritabes, *pas des asemblants*,
Pour l'amour que *tout un chacun s'ennuie terriblement d'l'honnêteté*
Icitte asteur. (p. 96)

Garneau's axiological reshaping of *Macbeth* is realized not as much through transposition of reality into fiction, and adaptation to Québécois reality through suppression or introduction of certain values, as through extension and repetition of passages praising values identical to those justifying sovereigntist aspirations in the Québécois social discourse. Hence, once more, we see the exemplary value of *Macbeth*, a play that depicts the overthrow of tyranny by collective action. Of all Shakespeare's plays, *Macbeth* is the most amenable to the expression of Québécois demands and aspirations.

Macbeth, like a fable, contains a moral that the Québécois translation highlights through adjustments to the text. Combat is a virtue: 'war-like Siward' is neither 'martial' (Leyris), nor 'belliqueux' (Bonnefoy), but 'vaillant' and 'toute un guerrier' (p. 96), capable of leading the uprising that will re-establish the values suppressed by the usurper – peace and honesty. It is no longer 'meat,' as in the original play, or, by metonymy, 'food' that is demanded in front of an audience that enjoys one of the highest standards of living in the world, but the right to 'manger sans méfiance' (eat without being on guard). The oft-repeated message is that one must be on guard against the insidious treachery of the dominant power and those who are seduced by it; one must be able to distinguish friend from foe: 'Qu'on soye capabes d'rende hommage à ceux-là qui l'méritent / Qu'on soye à même de r'çevoér des honneurs véritabes, pas des asemblants' (May we be able to pay homage to those that deserve it / May we be able to accept true honours, not fake ones). The original text says much more simply: 'Do faithful homage and receive free honours.' The insistent anaphoric structure of the Québécois translation gives it a resonance that subordinates the aesthetic function to the persuasive function. This is the very process that makes political or advertising slogans effective, as Jakobson demonstrated with the formulaic *I like Ike*.

The perlocutory effectiveness of the Québécois *Macbeth* is also derived from its exploitation of a latent interdiscursivity, which involves highlighting those points where the dialogue of the play and the discourse of the Québécois condition converge. The audience is surreptitiously invited to take part in this play on double meanings, as we shall see even more clearly when we examine the other scene expurgated by Garneau.

'I didn't translate lines 139 to 161.'

This is how Garneau justifies the omission of these lines from Act IV, Sc. 3: 'I didn't translate lines 139–61 (Oxford University Press) because this is the scene with the doctor, where they speak of the King of England's talent as healer – a "scène de ventilation" (breather), as they say in the cinema; it has nothing to do with the dramatic action and it doesn't sound very much like Shakespeare' (p. 121). The reasons he gives for this second omission are similar to those that he gave for the first deletion, but this time the translator is more explicit. He begins with a brief summary of the deleted passage and then indicates its irrelevance to the dramatic action, claiming that he has restored the purity of the original text, which, presumably, was adulterated by these lines. *Macbeth* is recognized as one of the most-debated texts in the Shakespearian canon,[13] but critics long ago identified which parts of the text were, in fact, additions. However, the authorship of the passage omitted by Garneau has not been clearly established. According to Yves Bonnefoy:

... There is also general agreement on two significant additions, the scenes involving the witches in Acts III and IV, which are attributed to Thomas Middleton. It is less certain that lines 140-155 in Act IV, Scene 3 ('Comes the King forth, I pray you? etc.), were added to Shakespeare's text to please James I: although the Folio was undoubtedly published when the play was being performed before the Court.[14]

There is nothing in the passage to justify its omission on grounds of textual purity. Garneau could have omitted any other passage discussed by Bonnefoy; for example, the scene involving Hecate, a character with no relevance to the plot. Clearly, the explanation must lie elsewhere; an omission as glaring as this, to which the translator himself draws attention, must surely arise from a particular discursive logic.

In contrast to the first passage eliminated, this one is not ambiguous and contains nothing irrelevant to what precedes or follows it. Critics question the dramatic relevance of parts of this scene, but their criticism focuses on the meandering dialogue that the doctor interrupts, rather than on his own tirade:

... Act III, Scene 1, in which Macbeth incites the future assassins of Banquo, as well as *Act IV, Scene 3, in which Malcolm probes Macduff at length*, appear, in their persuasive, dramatically effective, but *overblown* rhetoric, to be left over from a more discursive, more loosely constructed first draft. In particular, the long, *reptilian unfolding* of the Malcolm–Macduff scene, however pertinent and important it may be, and whatever choric value it may have, is disconcerting.[15]

Garneau sacrifices nothing in this long 'reptilian' scene! On the contrary, he emphasizes its dramatic intensity. Let us look, however, at the passage he did choose to omit:

ENTER A DOCTOR

MALCOLM
Well; more anon. Comes the king forth, I pray you?

> DOCTOR
> Ay, sir; there are a crew of wretched souls
> That stay his cure; their malady convinces
> The great assay of art; but at his touch,
> Such sanctity hath heaven given his hand,
> They presently amend.
>
> MALCOLM
> I thank you, doctor.
> *EXIT DOCTOR*
> MACDUFF
> What's the disease he means?
>
> MALCOLM
> 'Tis call'd the evil:
> A most miraculous work in this good king,
> Which often, since my here-remain in England,
> I have seen him do. How he solicits heaven,
> Himself best knows; but strangely-visited people,
> All swoln and ulcerous, pitiful to the eye,
> The mere despair of surgery, he cures;
> Hanging a golden stamp about their necks,
> Put on with holy prayers; and 'tis spoken
> To the succeeding royalty he leaves
> The healing benediction. With this strange virtue
> He hath a heavenly gift of prophecy,
> And sundry blessings hang about his throne
> That speak him full of grace.
>
> MACDUFF
> See, who comes here?
>
> MALCOLM
> My countryman; but yet I know him not. (p. 864)

Here, the King of England is not just good, pious, or saintly, or even a prophet. He is a man with supernatural powers, and these powers are truly liberating. The panegyric brings the action in the scene to an abrupt halt and momentarily diverts the attention of the audience to the King of England. This sudden focus on the King is precisely what caused critics to say that the passage had been added to please the monarch before whom the play was to be performed. Garneau is therefore correct in stating that this passage is not relevant to the plot. Despite his concern for coherence, he does not, however, omit other scenes that could be criticized for the same reason. Why, therefore, did he deem it necessary, indeed vital, to omit this particular scene, whose lack of importance he underlines with the expression 'scène de ventilation.'

Let us take him at his word and accept that he omitted the passage because it functions as an interlude, and is thus disruptive of the plot. But why exactly did he think it so important that there should be no interruptions in the scène? Before addressing this question, let us briefly review the action in the scene.

Malcolm, rightful heir to the throne of Scotland, has taken refuge in England after the assassination of King Duncan. He learns from Macduff, a general who has deserted and come to join him, of the servitude into which Scotland has been plunged by the usurper Macbeth. The two men appraise each other and then decide on the forces they will need to launch an uprising with the support of the King of England. Their discussion is interrupted by the doctor's praise for the supernatural gifts of the King, who is due to arrive. At that moment, General Ross arrives, bearing terrible news of recent atrocities committed by Macbeth, in particular, the massacre of the Macduff family. Macduff is devastated by news of the disaster but quickly recovers and vows that he will lead the rebellion to liberate Scotland.

In this scene, the action moves from a national tragedy experienced by a whole people to an individual tragedy that galvanizes the victim into mobilizing all available forces of resistance. In the middle of the scene, we encounter the pleasant chatter of the doctor, who describes the strange talents of a visionary king who has the ability to cure ulcers, swellings, and other scrofula. The interlude clearly has no connection with the dramatic action, and even less with the situation in Quebec. However, one would have to be totally ignorant of the history of New France not to recognize, in the dialogue before and after this interlude, a striking analogy to the Conquest and the Patriote uprising, and not to hear echoes of present-day sovereigntist aspirations. This second scene shortened by Garneau is, thus, an even better illustration of how the translator introduces at the discursive level of the play certain assumptions from the discourse of the society of which he is a member.

By definition, 'territoriality' is a focal point, a *doxological node*, of nationalist discourse. Any reference to territory in the source text is therefore

TABLE 19
References to Scotland (Nouns, Phrases, and Determiners):
Shakespeare and Garneau (*Macbeth,* Act IV, Scene 3)

Shakespeare	Garneau
0	cheuz-nous
our down-fall'n birthdom	not'droit d'exister ram'né à rien
Scotland	not'pau'pays
0	not'pays
poor country	pauv'pays
0	mon pauv'pays
our country	not'pauv'pays
0	c't'un pays
0	c't'un pays
my poor country	mon pauv'pays
poor state	l'pays
Scotland	Écosse
Scotland	pauv'pays
Scotland	pauv'Écosse
nation miserable	nation ben misérabe
Scotland	mon pays
thine and my poor country	l'pauv'pays/l'tien pis l'mien
Scotland	not'Écosse
poor country	not'pauv'pays
our mother	not'mére-patrie
our grave	tombeau
0	fosse commune
0	cheuz-nous
0	cheuz-nous
Scotland	Écosse
Scotland	0

likely to attract the attention of Québécois translators, especially if they are committed to the sovereigntist cause. In the scene under discussion, the territory described as Scotland would have no particular resonance for a Québécois audience if it were not accompanied by a series of predicates similar to those defining 'Quebec' in the discourse of the target society. Let us examine how the translator organized the *doxological relevance* of territorial elements in the source text.

In the original text, the word 'Scotland,' a marker of the dramatic action, occurs frequently in Act IV, Scene 3, and is the main theme of the dialogue. The word alternates with substantives such as 'nation,' 'state,' 'country,' which are accompanied by dysphoric qualifiers such as 'poor,' 'miserable,' 'down-fall'n.' Table 19 lists occurrences of all nouns describ-

TABLE 20
A Comparison of References to Scotland:
Shakespeare and Garneau (*Macbeth,* Act IV, Scene 3)

Shakespeare		Garneau	
Scotland	8	Écosse	4
birthdom	1	droit d'exister	1
country	5	**pays**	13
state	1	(pays)	
nation	1	nation	1
mother	1	mére-patrie	1
grave	1	tombeau	1
		fosse commune	1
		cheuz-nous	3
Total	10		21
down-fall'n	1	ram'né à rien	1
poor	5	**pauv'**	9
miserable	1	ben misérabe	1
Total	7		11
our	4	**not'**	7
thine and my	1	l'tien pis l'mien	1
my	1	mon	3
Total	6		11
General total	31		47

ing the setting of the dramatic action, and their determiners (articles, possessives, demonstratives, and qualifiers). For each occurrence, Garneau's translation equivalent is provided. Table 20 compares references to Scotland in the source text and the target text; figures indicate the number of occurrences of each item.

To illustrate further the differences between Garneau's translation and the original, Table 21 compares references to Scotland in three recent French translations of *Macbeth*: by Pierre Leyris (1977), a year before Michel Garneau's translation; by Yves Bonnefoy (1983); and by Jean-Michel Déprats, staged at the Comédie Française during the 1985 season.[16]

These three translations all contain the same degree of lexico-semantic density in relation to the source text. The similarity of lexical choice

TABLE 21
References to Scotland: Leyris, Bonnefoy, and Déprats (*Macbeth,* Act IV, Scene 3)

Leyris	Bonnefoy	Déprats
notre mère patrie à bas	la patrie jetée si bas	notre pays natal terrassé
Écosse	Écosse	Écosse
pauvre pays	pauvre pays	pauvre pays
notre pays	notre pays	notre pays
mon malheureux pays	mon malheureux pays	mon malheureux pays
la très misérable Écosse	le malheureux royaume	le pauvre royaume
Écosse	Écosse	Écosse
Écosse	Écosse	Écosse
Écosse	pauvre Écosse	Écosse
ô malheureux pays	ô nation malheureuse	ô nation misérable
Écosse	Écosse	Écosse
mon infortuné pays	ma pauvre terre	mon pauvre pays
	notre pays	mon pays
Écosse	Écosse	Écosse
pauvre patrie	malheureux pays	pauvre pays
notre mère	notre mère	notre mère
notre tombe	notre tombe	notre tombe
Écosse	Écosse	Écosse
Écosse	Écosse	Écosse

shown in table 21, as well as in table 22, indicates that when there is no word-for-word equivalent, the three French translators all make rigorous use of compensation.

Garneau's translation favours certain terms at the expense of others, and the terms he does retain are used more extensively than are their equivalents in the original. In Shakespeare's text, the term 'Scotland' occurs more frequently than all the common nouns with the same referent. Garneau, however, makes sparing use of the word 'Scotland,' employing it only half as often as Shakespeare, and shows a preference for items which form the syntagm 'not'pauv'pays' (our poor country); whereas in the original, the syntagm '*my*' / '*poor*' / '*country*' occurs only twice, and there is no occurrence of 'our poor country,' in the translation there are altogether six occurrences of the two syntagms. In the Québécois version, the phrase 'our poor country' and its variants take on a resonance for the reader or for the audience, a resonance it did not have in the original.

A comparison of (common) nouns referring to Scotland (table 23) reveals other interesting changes made by Garneau to the original. The list of terms from the original play is organized hierarchically. It starts

134 A Sociocritique of Translation

TABLE 22
A Comparison of References to Scotland: Shakespeare, Leyris, Bonnefoy, and Déprats (*Macbeth,* Act IV, Scene 3)

Shakespeare		Leyris		Bonnefoy		Déprats	
Scotland	**8**	**Écosse**	**9**	**Écosse**	**8**	**Écosse**	**8**
country	5	pays	5	pays	5	pays	5
state	1	(Écosse)		royaume	1	royaume	1
nation	1	(pays)		nation	1	nation	1
birthdom	1	patrie	2	patrie	1	pays natal	1
mother	1	mère	2	mère	1	mère	1
grave	1	tombe	1	tombe	1	tombe	1
Total	10		10		10		10
poor	5	pauvre	2	pauvre	3	pauvre	4
miserable	1	misérable	1	(malheureux)		misérable	1
		malheureux	2	malheureux	4	malheureux	1
		infortuné	1				
down-fall'n	1	à bas	1	jetée si bas	1	terrassé	1
Total	7		7		8		7
our	4	notre	4	notre	4	notre	4
thine & my	1		0		0		0
my	1	mon	2	mon/ma	2	mon	3
Total	6		6		6		7
General total	31		32		32		32

with 'birthdom' and ends with 'grave,' two axiologically marked words, as compared with 'country,' which is a neutral designation. In Garneau's translation, the same list begins and ends with 'cheuz-nous' (homeland), an expression added to the text by the translator and for which there is no equivalent in the original.

> Let us seek out some desolate shade, and there
> Weep our sad bosoms empty. (p. 863)

> Quand j'pense à *cheuz-nous,* j'ai jusse envie d'me trouver un coin
> Tranquille à l'ombe pour m'laisser fére pis brailler tout mon soûl. (p. 116)

TABLE 23
Common Nouns Referring to Scotland
(in order of occurrence): Shakespeare
and Garneau

Shakespeare	Garneau
	cheuz-nous
birthdom	droit d'exister
	pays
	pays
country	pays
	pays
country	pays
	pays
	pays
country	pays
state	pays
	pays
nation	nation
	pays
country	pays
country	pays
mother	mère patrie
grave	tombeau
	fosse commune
	cheuz-nous
	cheuz-nous

In discursive terms, this first occurrence of 'cheuz-nous' is strategic, as the two lines quoted above open the scene. The introduction at this early stage, of the catch phrase 'Quand j'pense à cheuz-nous' immediately captures the attention of the audience and leads it to interpret the ensuing dialogue in terms of Québécois reality. We must bear in mind, and the particular spelling attests to this, that the Québécois phonetics of this introductory clause function as an actualizer. The fact that this was the first time a Shakespearian play had been heard in Franco-Québécois served all the more to reinforce the effect of the language as an actualizer. The language used is, thus, highly effective in what Jakobson terms the 'phatic function,' a function that ensures communication is occurring. This spatial and discursive re-actualisation through language makes it possible for the Québécois audience to claim ownership of the expression 'Quand j'pense à cheuz-nous' with its follow-up, 'j'ai jusse envie d'...

brailler tout mon soûl,' an expression that falls in line with the social discourse. After the tone is set in these introductory lines, the translation introduces the expression 'défendre not'droét d'exister' (defend our right to exist), a shift that further strengthens the projection of Québécois reality onto the original scene:

> Let us rather ...
> Bestride our down-fall'n *birthdom* (p. 863).
>
> Moé, j'pense qu'on f'ra't mieux d'... défende
> Not' *droét d'exister* qui s'trouve ram'né quasiment à rien (p. 116).

P. Leyris and Y. Bonnefoy use 'patrie' (fatherland) or 'mère patrie' (motherland) as equivalents of 'birthdom.' We do not know if Garneau avoided these terms because of their ambiguity: today these words would refer (problematically) to Quebec, while, in days gone by, they would have referred only to France. Such terms could thus introduce discursive incompatibility between the audience's space–time and that of historical Quebec. In the latter chronotope, the words 'patrie' and 'mère patrie' would conflict with the underlying predicate 'despoiled nation.' But one thing is sure, the use of the syntagm 'défende not'droét d'exister' makes it much easier for the audience to recognize the ideologeme 'Quebec is a despoiled nation.' From this point of view, 'not'droét d'exister' is more radical than J.-M. Déprats's translation: 'pays natal' (native land). The expression 'pays natal' might almost represent a mistranslation in a discursive space in which the search for identity is explicitly based on the fact that the 'pays natal' has never really existed. For, as leitmotifs of Québécois literature, especially poetry, tell us, the Québécois no more have a 'native land' than they have a 'native language.'

In the original text, 'birthdom' is immediately followed by a reference to Scotland, a juxtapositon that makes the passage incompatible with the Québécois social discourse. The term 'Scotland' is eliminated by the translator:

> ... new sorrows
> Strike heaven on the face, that it resounds
> As if it felt with *Scotland* and yell'd out
> Like syllable of dolour. (p. 863)
>
> ... des nouveaux malheurs éclatent

Shakespeare, Québécois Nationalist Poet 137

Comme des orages dans l'ciel, si tant qu'tout' *not' pau 'pays* l'ressent
Si tant qu'on peut quasiment l'entende crier sa douleur. (p. 116)

Not only does Scotland disappear, but heaven is prosaically reduced to its meteorological reality and given a less metaphysical and less poetic role. The religious symbolism of heaven, a negative value in Québécois society, is de-emphasized. This shift falls in line with the translator's elimination of the term 'heavenly angel' and of the reference to praying in the earlier scene. But the original scene is highly compatible with the discourse on the Québécois condition. This would explain the high density of axio-ideological shifts the scene undergoes in translation. These changes frequently involve neutralization, or sometimes outright substitution, of determiners:

... I think withal,
There would be hands uplifted in *my right.* (p. 863)

[...] j'pense que ben des bras sont parés à se l'ver
Pour défende *nos droéts.* (p. 117)

In the original text, the rightful heir to the Kingdom of Scotland appraises the support he would *personally* receive to overthrow the usurper. In the Québécois version, we find a hero of the 1837–8 uprisings, a Patriote who is fighting for the common cause, to free the country 'd'la main damnée qui l'opprime' (from the cursed hand that oppresses it), a slogan that would not have been unappealing to Front de Libération du Québec (FLQ) militants during the October Crisis of 1970. And wouldn't a Québécois audience be prompted to interpret an extract such as the following against the background of the period between the October Crisis and the 1980 referendum:

Not'cause peut pas ête plus jusse! La victoére nous attend
Au boutte d'la route!
[...]
Bon yeu qu'j'ai hâte qu'les temps changent!
C'tes temps-citte sont en train d'nous *virer en étranges!* (pp. 120–1)

[Our cause could not be more just! Victory is waiting for us
At the end of the road!
...

Dear God! I can't wait for times to change!
These times are *turning us into foreigners*! (our translation)]

With the omission of the interlude with the doctor, the two passages quoted above were conveniently brought together. We note that, this time, the translator considers it relevant to include the religious references: 'J'dis un gros amen à ta prière' (p. 121).

The translation displays a distinct ideological shift when compared with the original:

ENTER ROSS

MACDUFF
My ever-gentle cousin, welcome hither.

MALCOLM
I know him now. Good God, betimes remove
The means that makes us *strangers*. (p. 864)

There is no ambiguity in this passage. Malcolm does not immediately recognize General Ross, whom he has not seen since his exile in England. Events in Scotland have kept them apart and they have become strangers:

MACDUFF
Voyez qui vient là.

MALCOLM
Un homme de mon pays; pourtant je ne le connais pas.

MACDUFF
Mon très noble cousin, soyez le bienvenu ici.

MALCOLM
Je le reconnais maintenant, Grand Dieu, écarte vite
Ce qui nous rend *étrangers l'un à l'autre*.[17]

Leyris and Bonnefoy do not make this scene as explicit as Déprats does, but they conclude with the same expression, 'étrangers l'un à l'autre' (strangers to each other).[18] However, the anaphoric expansion in Garneau's translation leads the Québécois public, threatened by assimilation and preoccupied with being 'Maîtres chez nous' (Masters in our own house), to interpret the word 'strangers' as also meaning, or meaning only, 'foreigner': 'j'ai hâte qu'les temps changent / C'tes temps-citte sont en train d'nous virer en étranges!' (I can't wait for times to change / these times are turning us into foreigners!). That is to say, *foreigners in our own country*. And the implicit message in this is: Independence Now! Guarantee Our Survival!

At times, differences between the English text and the Québécois translation are much more subtle than those in the examples cited above. Changes introduced by the translation are concealed by the fact that they seem natural in the new context. However, if you listen closely, you will note throughout the scene a network of minute alterations that clearly bring the text into the sphere of Québécois social discourse. Listen, for example, to Macduff's reaction when he learns that his home has been destroyed and his wife and children massacred:

> I cannot but remember such things were,
> That were most precious to me. Did heaven look on,
> And would not take their part! (p. 865)

The French translations discussed above replace the object 'things' with personal pronouns (ils, eux) that refer back to the preceding lines:

> Eh quoi, tous *mes précieux poussins avec leur mère,*
> Ravis d'un coup? [...]
> Comment ne pas me rappeler qu'*ils* ont été,
> *Eux* qui m'étaient si précieux? Comment le Ciel
> A-t-il pu voir cela sans prendre *leur* défense?[19]

Garneau retains the impersonal character of the object of the first clause, but let us listen carefully to what follows:

> C'que j'ava's d'plus précieux dans l'monde, chu t'obligé d'commencer
> A *m'en souv'nir.* Comment c'est que l'bon dieu peut laisser fére
> Des afféres pareilles? Sans prende la part *des faibes*? (p. 125)

Although Garneau's translation retains the semantic neutrality of the object, in the form of 'C(e) que' (what), he changes the personal determiner 'their' into a much broader collective noun, 'des faibes' (the weak). This noun, which possesses a referential flexibility, will be readily interpreted by a Québécois audience, who will then see the entire passage as a variant of the Québécois motto, 'Je me souviens' (I remember). These words, which appear on Quebec licence plates, are a daily reminder of the British Conquest and of the loss of what was most precious to the Québécois, their freedom, a key word in Québécois social discourse. The presence in the source text of the two words 'I'/'remember' no doubt prompted the projection of the motto 'Je me souviens' onto the target text. This appears to be confirmed when we compare the Québécois version with any of the recent French translations. These translations could not permit any reading of *québécité* into them, since they do not contain the bundle of relevant changes:

Y. Bonnefoy

Je ne puis pas ne pas me souvenir
Qu'*ils* existaient, qu'*ils* furent tout mon bien.
Le Ciel regarda-t-il, sans *les* défendre?[20]

The considerable difference between the semantics of Garneau's translation and those of the original text is a function of the discursive coherence imposed on the translation by the target milieu. In the original, the utterance expresses an emotional state (this deadly grief) that must be overcome (Dispute it like a man). In Garneau's translation, the utterance is realized in a first-person-singular imperative form – I must from now on remember that I have lost that which was most precious to me. This first-person imperative is of the same order as the social injunction 'Je me souviens,' in which the 'I' is used to address *all* Québécois. This type of injunction, which links word and act, is referred to as a 'performative' in speech-act theory. Here, the effectiveness of the performative flows directly from Garneau's subjectivization of the utterance. Compare, for example, 'Souviens-toi' (remember) and 'Je me souviens' (I remember). In the latter case, *to say* is *to do*.

Subjectivization, or the use of the first-person singular, is a common feature of the discourse of persuasion and of advertising in Quebec. The following examples are taken at random: 'As-tu fait ta part? *Moi, je* fais ma part,' 'Voyageur. *Moi, j*'embarque,' 'Grossesse secours. *Je* suis enceinte, *j*'en parle,' 'MacDonald. *J*'M,' 'La Croix-Rouge, moi *j*'y crois,' '*J*'embellis

Montréal' ... '*Je* me souviens.' It is thus not surprising to find this cultural trait in Garneau's translation, in passages in which the original text makes no use whatsoever of the first person:

O nation misérable, ...
When shalt thou see thy wholesome days again. (p. 864)

J'appartiens à une nation ben misérabe
[...] *J'me d'mande* si on va
Jama's r'voér les beaux jours d'avant. (p. 119)

The introduction of the first-person singular into the text of *Macbeth* brings the Shakespearian play clearly in line with Québécois social discourse. The process is reinforced by the elimination of the linguistic difference between the protagonist, or rather, the actor who speaks the lines, and the member of the audience who hears them. The language employed in this translation, which is not the code used in Québécois translations of works from the classical repertoire, abolishes the difference between fiction and reality. Garneau's translation uses a *lect* that is distinctly rooted in the reality of Quebec and of no other francophone region. The fact that this is the first time Franco-Québécois has been used to translate Shakespeare has a captive, cathartic effect on the Québécois audience. The use of the *lect* in the dialogue fuses fiction and reality, allowing the audience to find in the text their subjective reality, their individual and collective life experience: 'J'appartiens à eune nation ben misérabe.'

At the same time, the use of the *lect* grafts reality onto the symbolic. For the Québécois audience, the language in Garneau's *Macbeth* is as marked as regional French would be for an audience in France. Michel Garneau's 'langue québécoise' is archaic, and therefore markedly different from the standard language spoken in Quebec. It is an *Edenic language*, the language of a pre-Conquest Quebec, of a Quebec that was once free. Thus, this language, which is never actually spoken by a single theatre-goer, nor by Garneau for that matter, acquires a symbolic value and, in the context of the reception, becomes a kind of plea: omnipresent but none the less concealed, since the audience, whose attention is focused on the dialogue, hears the language without actually listening to it, the 'langue québécoise' becomes a mode of persuasion in itself. It constitutes, in other words, the perlocutory base of the dialogue.

Shakespeare Bemoans the Québécois Paradise Lost

Not only does Garneau's translation reshape the text ideologically, it also introduces aesthetic transformations; these are, however, difficult to isolate from the ideological. Links between the ideological and the aesthetic are present in any literary text, in so far as literature exploits the same paradigm of ideas and values as other discursive formations through which a social group defines itself. Without going so far as to say that 'society and literature share this common function, in that they attempt to realize ideologies,'[21] it is clear that, during the period under examination, literature was closely tied to politics, a fact attested to by 'professions of faith' from writers: 'La littérature est un combat' (Literature is a struggle), proclaims the title of an article by André Belleau in the literary magazine with the evocative name *Liberté*.[22] Writer Paul Chamberland is even more explicit: 'The poetic process parallels the political process (of national liberation) exactly.'[23] The emerging Québécois literature is indeed dominated by the theme of individual and collective dispossession, a theme that is reiterated again and again, with little variation in form, in Québécois poetry:

Jacques Brault
Il n'a pas de nom ce pays que j'affirme et renie au long de mes jours.[24]
[It has no name this land that I reaffirm and deny throughout all my days.]

Gaston Miron
Je vais mourir vivant dans notre empois de mort.[25]
[It will be a living death for me in our pitch of death.]

Gérald Godin
J'ai mal à mon pays.[26]
[My country pains me.]

Paul Chamberland
Je souffre d'une terre à naître.[27]
[I am suffering from a country waiting to be born.]

These utterances take their meaning partially from the underlying ideologeme: 'Québécois are not masters in their own house.' The use of the words 'j'appartiens à eune nation ben misérabe' to translate Macduff's invocation to the despoiled nation (*O nation miserable!*) is thus not fortuitous. It follows a pre-established model for content as well as for form, a model provided by Québécois poetry.

We could say then, that *for the semantic content of the original utterance, there is in the target discourse, a corresponding ideologeme,*[28] *for which there is also, in the receiving literature, a codified expression.* It is codified in the sense that the subject of the utterance is represented as belonging to a collective characterized as a 'nation misérabe.' Hence, the *discursive equivalent* in the space–time under discussion, 'J'appartiens à eune nation ben misérabe.'

The characteristic 'je' (I) of lyrical poetry is omnipresent in Québécois poetry, where it is inexorably linked to the theme of the lost nation. Thus, the poetic 'I' becomes an engagé 'I,' in works ranging from Gaston Miron's to those of Denis Vanier, whose first collection of poems was, in fact, entitled *Je*:

> La nuit dont mon peuple est
>
> [...] peuple foetus criant à l'écloison d'un verbe
> dans la langue des 'interdits-de-parole.'[29]
>
> [The night of which my people are part
>
> ... a foetal people calling out for the birth of a verb
> in the language of the 'forbidden-to-speak.' (our translation)]

The individual in search of an identity who expresses himself as part of a collective fate (*nous*) is alienated from himself because he is dispossessed of a nation:

> je refuse un salut personnel et transfuge
> je m'identifie depuis ma condition d'humilié
> je le jure sur l'obscure respiration commune
> [...]
> à tous je me lie [...]
> dans la résistance
> à l'amère décompositon viscérale et ethnique
> de la mort des peuples drainés [...]
> je suis sur la place publique avec les miens
> [...]
> je vois nos êtres en détresse dans le siècle
> je vois notre infériorité et j'ai mal en chacun de nous.[30]

[I reject a personal salvation that is treacherous
I derive my identity from my condition of humiliation
I swear on the obscure collective breath
...
I join with everyone ...
in resistance
to the bitter visceral ethnic decomposition
of the death of drenched peoples
I am on the public square with my own
...
I see our being in distress in the century
I see our inferiority
And I hurt for each of us. (our translation)]

We need look no further for what lies behind a category of transformations such as those in the following example, considered earlier:

Let us ...
Weep our sad bosoms empty. (p. 863)

Quand j'pense à cheuz nous, j'ai jusse envie d'[...] brailler tout mon soûl. (p. 116)

Here, translation conforms to the poetic conventions of the target society. With the introduction of the first-person singular (*'J'appartiens* à [...]'/ 'Quand *j'pense* à cheuz-nous'), Shakespeare's lines fit into the paradigm of the 'common places' of the discourse of *québécité* and assume significance in the Québécois field of discourse. As such, they can be ideologically interpreted by the receiver in the space–time of reading and listening. This chronotopic shift in the decoding of signs results from echoes of these common places, or *topoi*, in the receiver's perception of the Shakespearian text:

Jacques Brault

Ainsi donc encore une fois j'écoute la rumeur du fleuve et
je me souviens que cette eau saigne d'une très ancienne blessure.[31]

[And therefore once again I listen to the sound of the river and

I remember that this water bleeds from a very
ancient wound. (our translation)]

Shakespeare

I *cannot but remember* such things were,
That were most precious to me. (p. 865)

When Garneau uses the word 'brûlé' as the equivalent of 'heath,' he reactivates a line from Gaston Miron's *L'Homme rapaillé*, a beacon of Québécois literature. 'Homme aux labours des brûlés de l'exil [...] / en vue de villes et d'une terre qui te soient natales'³² (Man labouring on the scorched earth of exile ... / for towns and a land that are truly native to you). The word 'brûlé' appears at an important point in the play, at the very beginning. It places the dramatic action in a specific setting and thus takes on a number of axio-ideological interpretations. For the translator and for the receiver immersed in social discourse, the 'brûlé' becomes the metaphor *par excellence* for the condition of the Québécois people, a people described by the social discourse as being marginalized, cut off from the political and economic power exercised by the anglophone hegemony.

Even though there is no obvious link between Shakespeare and the new generation of Québécois poets, between *Macbeth* and the emerging Québécois literature, there is a 'commonality' of axiological and ideological *topoi* that revolve around the theme of the despoiled nation. *Macbeth* is an appropriate vehicle for this theme, because the play contains metaphorically, and almost mythically, the archetypical expression of the notion of despoiled nation, so central to the emerging Québécois literature. Do we not hear echoes of the Weird Sisters in the following poem by Roland Giguère, 'La grande main finit toujours par pourrir,' written during the authoritarian regime of Maurice Duplessis:

Grande main qui pèse sur nous
grande main qui nous aplatit contre terre
grande main [...]
grands ongles qui nous cousent les lèvres
grands ongles d'étain rouillé
grands ongles d'émail brûlé [...]
la grande main pourrira.³³

[Big hand that weighs on us
big hand that flattens us to the earth
big hand ...
big nails that sew up our lips
big rusty pewter nails
big burnt enamel nails ...
the big hand will rot. (our translation)]

Apart from the theme of *Macbeth*, there is no obvious connection between Hexagone or Parti pris writers and Shakespeare. However, *Macbeth* abounds with images identical to the obsessive and almost clichéd images found in Québécois works of these two literary movements. The most frequent image is one of injury, wounds and blood:

Mon Québec ma terre amère [...]
avec une large blessure d'espace au front
[...]
Je marche avec un coeur de patte saignante.[34]

L'entendez-vous sous ses blessures
gémir, ce pays [...]
et moi, dans cette souffrance.[35]

J'étais prisonnier de ses pores
prisonnier de ses blessures
plaie quotidienne
d'un espoir.[36]

Une plaie au coeur même des blessures
[...]
Québec [...]
en ciel bas sur la terre de sang.[37]

[My Québec my bitter land ...
with a large wound of space on its forehead
...
I walk with the heart of my bleeding legs.

Do you hear it groaning underneath its wounds
this land ...

and I, in this suffering

I was prisoner of its pores
prisoner of its wounds
daily wound
of a hope

A wound in the very heart of wounds
...
Québec ...
under a low sky on the land of blood. (our translation)]

In the original *Macbeth*, the same images describe the state of the country oppressed by Macbeth:

Bleed, bleed poor country!
... our country sinks beneath the yoke;
It weeps, it bleeds, and each day a gash
Is added to her wounds (p. 863)

The metaphors and themes of *Macbeth* seem to echo Québécois poetry, which in turn echoes *Macbeth*:

le sang failli s'annule en tous miroirs aveugles nos cris
ne peuvent se joindre et tresser l'entrelacs d'une fronde
à tendre contre le roc ouranien du Maître

    nommer la terreur du sang
        la foudre du sang
qui nous rende aux plages finies d'une terre qui flambe
nôtre dans nos bras armés.[38]

[the dishonoured blood disappears in blind mirrors our cries
cannot reach each other and braid the interlacing of a
revolt against the Uranian rock of the Master

name the terror of the blood
    the thunder of the blood
that takes us to the delimited beaches of a land that burns
ours in our arms raised in revolt. (our translation)]

This particular scene of *Macbeth* (IV, 3) develops a twofold theme of national and individual tragedy, themes very similar to those of Québécois poetry, as seen, for example, in the expression of pain:

> Let us seek out some desolate shade, and there
> *Weep* our sad bosoms empty. (p. 863)

> [...] les larmes
> poussent comme de l'herbe dans mes yeux [...]
> je voudrais m'étendre avec tous et comme eux [...]
> *me morfondre* pour un sort meilleur.[39]

Or the metaphorical expression of despair:

> *Alas! poor country;*
> ... It cannot
> Be call'd our mother, but *our grave*. (p. 864)

> ce continent me trahissait *ce pays*
> *ce cercueil.*[40]

> Nous vivons encore [...]
> *fossoyés* mais drus [...]
> cet âge scellera notre aurore ou *notre tombeau*.[41]

Then there is the resignation of the innocent:

> where nothing,
> But who knows nothing, is once seen to *smile*; (p. 864)

> il a toujours *le sourire* échoué du pauvre avenir avili.[42]

Or bitterness expressed ironically:

> ... the dead man's *knell*
> Is there scarce ask'd for who; and good men's lives
> Expire before the *flowers* in their cap. (p. 864)

> Le *glas* y sonne perpétuel et jaune à la façon des *tournesols*.[43]

Shakespeare, Québécois Nationalist Poet 149

Muets hébétés nous rendons l'âme comme d'autres rendent la monnaie
nos *cadavres* paisibles et proprets font de *jolies bornes* sur la route de l'histoire.[44]

The images in this Shakespearian elegy correspond word for word to images in Québécois poetry of the 1960s and 1970s, as if they were literal translations of each other. There is really nothing more than a simple affinity between them, but they have sufficient mutuality of theme to suggest that the choice of foreign works to be translated in a given society at a given time is by no means fortuitous.

Anaphora, like the lyrical *I*, is a dominant characteristic of the poetic genre. It is also one of Shakespeare's preferred structures. Garneau's translation overexploits this device, introducing it even when the original in no way justifies it:

Macduff, this noble passion,
Child of integrity, hath from my soul
Wip'd the black scruples, reconcil'd my thoughts
To thy good truth and honour. (p. 864)

Ah, mon Macduff, la belle colère, la belle tristesse, qui sont
Les enfants d'ton honnêt'té! Ah, mon homme intègre! Ta colère
M'allège de toutes mes grands scrupules, m'réconcilie ac'toute
Ton honneur, ta colère m'allie toute ta belle franchise! (p. 120)

This profusion of interwoven anaphoric structures, which is not present in the original text, accentuates a value that (along with that of freedom) is a common theme in Québécois discourse – the theme of integrity, read: 'fidelity' to the Québécois 'nation.'[45] Thus, the aesthetic choice of the translator reinforces an axiological given in Québécois discourse.

If we look at the scene as a whole, we observe that, while there is some degree of anaphora in the original text, the profusion of anaphoric structures in the translation, which accentuate certain passages, is primarily dictated by a pattern within Québécois poetry. We can say, then, that anaphora is the surface expression of a specific axiologeme or ideologeme.

The reader will recall the substitution of the syntagms 'pauv'pays,' 'mon pauv'pays,' or 'not'pauv'pays' for the word 'Scotland.' This substitution produces an anaphoric structure that dominates the whole scene. This particular anaphora is, in fact, fundamental to, or even stereotypical of, Québécois poetry. Consider the following extract from Jacques Brault's *Mémoire*:

Il n'a pas de nom ce pays que j'affirme et renie au long de mes jours
mon pays scalpé de sa jeunesse
mon pays né dans l'orphelinat de la neige
mon pays sans maisons ni légendes où bercer ses enfançons.[46]

[This country that I reaffirm and deny all through
my days has no name
my country scalped of its youth
my country born in the orphanage of snow
my country without homes or legends to nurture
its little children. (our translation)]

The lyrical *I* speaks for the despoiled collectivity, thereby equating 'my country' and 'our country.' What is more, in Québécois poetry the political objective is so strongly marked that the use of anaphora has a strong perlocutory effect. The constant repetition of utterances gives them an apparent ring of truth, just as it does in political discourse. The matching of ideologeme (underlying the surface utterance) and its linguistic realization (such as anaphora or subjectivization) provides a *translation matrix*, a template that cuts out new contours for the original text, a mould in which the original text is reshaped. We could say, then, that in the preconstructed discourse of the target society there is a 'ready to translate,' element. This order of discourse gives a character of *necessity* to the form in which the translation is realized.

What we have just demonstrated at the micro level can be verified at the level of the text as a whole. Shakespeare's plays belong to both the dramatic and poetic genres. With its use of the vernacular, the Québécois translation of *Macbeth* has affinities with the new Québécois theatre; while in its images, its subjectivizing and anaphoric form, it has affinities with Québécois *poetry*, in which dialogue figures prominently.[47] If we switch our focus from the mode of expression, the language itself, whose choice is dictated by the conventions of the new Québécois theatre, and concentrate on the discursive structures produced by the translation, we see that the scene under discussion conforms so closely to Québécois poetic conventions that it seems to be a literal calque of a poem by Paul Chamberland, a leader of the Parti pris movement. The poem, 'L'afficheur hurle', written in the form of a political manifesto, is a seminal text of the emerging Québécois literature. It contains the same apocalyptic vision of a humiliated society; the same indictment of the dominant power; the same discourse of despair, exile, and dispossession; the same subjectivization of

Shakespeare, Québécois Nationalist Poet 151

collective fate; the same elegiac tone; the same images of wounds and blood; and the same anaphoric, incantory structure – in other words, all the conventions of Québécois poetry of the 1960s and 1970s:

P. Chamberland

> je vis d'une *blessure* inguérissable [...]
> je vis je meurs d'un *pays poignardé* dans le plein coeur
>   de ses moissons de ses passions [...]
> j'habite en une terre de crachats de matins hâves et de
>   rousseurs malsaines les poètes s'y suicident et les
>   femmes s'y anémient les paysages s'y lézardent et la
> rancoeur purule aux lèvres de ses habitants [...]
> *la douleur est mon pays* [...]
> *mon pays* [...]
> *étrange terre* qui te lamentes doucement sous mes pieds
> *lointaine terre*
> *étrange terre perdue* pour ses habitants expropriés
>   expropriés du monde et de la joie
>   expropriés de leur présent de leur futur
>   expropriés de leur vivre et de leur mourir
>   expropriés de la colère et de l'amour [...]
> *terre captive* par *le sang* et par les os
> dans *le sang* et dans les os [...]
> *étrange terre perdue* [...]
> terre maîtresse
> terre matrice [...]
> *étrange terre perdue* sous la mêlée des chemins voués à
>   la folle aiguille des errances de l'exil et
>   de la déraison
> petit à petit le monde s'effrite les horizons se bousculent
>   dans la déroute les paysages *blessés à mort*
>   découvrent en *saignant* l'os nu de la malédiction
> et cela de toujours et cela de toujours
> *l'ordre l'abondance la quiétude mensonges mensonge*
>   [...]
> parce que seule est vraie depuis toujours la haine et la
>   *dépossession* [...]
> la *mort* est la forme de mon corps de mon destin de mon
>   histoire de *mon pays* [...]

je souffre d'une terre à naître
d'une *terre occupée*
nous n'aurons même pas *l'épitaphe* des décapités des
morts de faim des *massacrés* nous n'aurons été qu'une
page blanche de l'histoire.[48]

[I live with an incurable *wound* ...
I live I die with a *land knifed* through the very heart of its
    harvest of its passions ...
I live in a land of spittle of haggard mornings of
    unhealthy blemishes where poets commit suicide and
    women go anemic the countryside basks in the sun and
resentment is purulent on the lips of its people ...
pain is my country ...
my country ...
foreign land that laments for you softly under my feet
distant land
foreign land lost for its people expropriated
    expropriated from the world and from joy
    expropriated from their present, from their future
    expropriated from their living and from their dying
    expropriated from anger and from love ...
    a land *captive* of *blood* and of bones
    in *blood* and in bones ...
foreign land lost ...
mistress land
matrix land ...
foreign land lost in the mêlée of roads doomed to
    the misdirected wanderings of exile and
    madness
little by little the world breaks down horizons jostle
    in flight the countryside *fatally wounded*
    reveals *bleeding* the naked bone of the curse
since forever, since forever
order abundance quiescence lies lie
    ...
because only hatred and *dispossession* ...
    are true since forever
death is the form of my body, of my fate of the
    history of *my country* ...

I suffer from a land waiting to be born
from a *land occupied*
> we will not even have the *epitaph* of the beheaded
> of the dead of hunger the *massacred* we will only have been a
> white page in history. (our translation)]

Garneau's translation of *Macbeth* differs from French translations more in its discursive structures, which are governed by the Québécois literary norm, than in its choice of language. There is indeed a gulf between Garneau's translation and those of Pierre Leyris, Yves Bonnefoy, and Jean-Michel Déprats. In contrast, the similarity between the three French translations is as great as that which allows us to superimpose Garneau's translation onto Chamberland's poem:

Garneau

Quand j'pense à cheuz nous, j'ai jusse envie d'me
> trouver un coin
Tranquille à l'ombe pour m'laisser fére pis *brailler*
> tout mon soûl

[...]
Not'droét d'exister... s'trouve ram'né quasiment
> à rien;
Chaque matin qui vient, y'a eune nouvelle veuve
> qui *hurle sa peine*,
Des nouveaux *orphelins qui pleurent*, des *nouveaux
malheurs* éclatent
Comme des orages dans l'ciel, si tant
> qu'tout' *not'pau'pays* l'ressent,
Si tant qu'on peut quasiment l'entende *crier sa douleur*

[...]
Pauv'pays, mon pauv'pays, tu vas *saigner*
> jusqu'au boutte de ton *sang.*
La grande tyrannie peut s'accoter su un maudit
> bon solage
Quand' la bonté d'*l'honnêteté a pus son mot à dire*
> dans rien;
[...] Pour toutes les terres que l'tyran

A *volées* au monde [...] *not'pauv'pays s'trouve pogné*
   dans un carcan terrible.
C't'un pays qui pleure, qui geint, qui grince,
   c't'un pays
Qui sent son mal, *qui saigne*, chaque jour, y'a eune
   plaie neuve
Dans ses *blessures* [...]
J'appartiens à eune nation ben misérabe [...]
   J'me d'mande si on va
Jama's r'voér les beaux jours d'avant [...]
J'ai pas l'coeur de t'dire combien *mon espérance*
   est morte.

[...]
Not'pauv'pays a quasiment d'la misére à se r'connaîte
   lui-même.
Not'mére-patrie, on peut quasiment pus la nommer
   mére, faudra't
Ben proche dire *tombeau, fosse commune.* Y'a ben
   jusse les innocents
Qui savent arien su rien qu'y'ont l'coeur d'sourire
   cheuz nous.
On entend tell'ment d'soupirs, d'grognes pis d'cris
   qu'on en a
Quasiment l'habitude. La seule extase que l'rêgne
   nous parmet
C'est d'avoér *toute la peine du monde.* (pp. 116–21)

[When I think about our homeland. I just want to
find myself a quiet corner
In the shade to let myself go and *cry*
   my heart out

...

Our right to exist ... has been reduced to almost
   nothing;
Every morning, there is a new widow
   who cries out her grief,
New *orphans crying* new
   misfortunes erupt

Like storms in the sky, so much
    that *our whole poor country* feels it
So much that you can almost hear it *shouting out its pain*

...

Poor country, my poor country, you are going to *bleed*
    to the last drop of your *blood*.
The great tyranny really has something to lean on
When the goodness of *honesty no longer has anything to say*
    about anything,
... For all the *lands* the tyrant
Stole from people ... our poor country is caught
    in a terrible yoke
A country that cries, moans, gnashes
    a country
That feels its pain, *that bleeds*, every day, there is
    a new *injury*
In its *wounds* ...
I belong to such a miserable nation ...
    I wonder if we will
Ever retrieve the beautiful days of yesteryear ...
I don't have the heart to say how *dead my hope*
is.

...

Our poor country can hardly recognize
    itself.
Our mother-country, we can hardly call it
    mother anymore, we will
before long be saying *tomb, common grave*. It's
    just the innocent
Who don't know anything about anything who have the heart
    to smile in our country.
We hear so much sighing, groaning, and crying
    that we are
Almost used to it. The only pleasure the tyrant
    allows us
Is to have *all the pain in the world*. (our translation)]

Although Garneau's *Macbeth* and Chamberland's 'L'afficheur hurle' use different linguistic codes – a function of the gap separating the two generations of Québécois poets – they display a striking rhetorical and ideological resemblance.[49] Indeed, in some passages, there is a surprising, if not exact, resemblance:

Chamberland

>oui je suis foncièrement méchant caduc pervers je suis
>ignare mesquin je suis ce que vous voudrez je suis le
>mal je suis le mal que vous m'avez fait je suis ce que
>vous avez fait de moi Dorchester Colborne Durham
>je suis la négraille dans la galère Amérique je suis le
>butin de Sa Gracieuse Majesté.[50]

>[yes I am basically nasty obsolete perverse I am
>ignorant mean I am what you want I am the
>evil I am the evil you made me I am what
>you did to me Dorchester Colborne Durham
>I am the nigger on the American slave ship I am the
>booty of Her Gracious Majesty. (our translation)]

Shakespeare/Garneau

>[...] mon pauv'pays va-t-ête encôre pogné
>Aveuc plusse de méchanc'tées qu'y'en' a connues, plusse
>   de souffrance
>Encôre, ac'el'successeur du tyran. [...]
>C't'à moé-même que j'pense; j'conna's toutes les vices
>Qu'j'ai dans l'corps, [...]
>Les vartus, quelles vartus, j'en ai aucune. Aucune d'celles
>Qui font les grands roés, comme la justice, la franchise,
>   la tempérance,
>El'jug'ment, la générosité, la persévérance,
>   la compâssion, l'humilité,
>La dévotion, la patience, l'courage, la grandeur!
>   J'possède aucune
>D'ses vartus-là mé j'conna's toutes les maniéres d'fére
>el'mal! (pp. 117–19)

> [... my poor country is going to be trapped again
> with more cruelty that it ever knew, more
> suffering
> Again, with the successor of the tyrant ...
> I'm thinking about myself; I know all the vices
> That I have in my body ...
> Virtues, what virtues, I have none at all. None of those
> That make great kings, like justice, honesty
> temperance,
> And judgement, generosity, perseverance
> compassion, humility
> Devotion, patience, courage, greatness!
> I don't have any of them
> Of those virtues I know all the ways of being
> evil! (our translation)]

Chamberland's poem is a good example of Québécois hostility towards the British monarchy. It underlines why Garneau obviously decided that, in a scene from *Macbeth* whose theme is so close to that of Québécois social discourse, praise for the King of England would clearly sound a false note, as out of place as such praise would be in 'L'afficheur hurle.' A comparison of the two texts thus further clarifies the motivation for, or at least the effect of, Garneau's decision to expurgate the original *Macbeth* in his translation; nothing should interfere with the projection of the scene onto Québécois reality nor with its ideological intelligibility in the Québécois field of reception.

There are, however, some notable differences between the two excerpts. In Chamberland's poem, the denigration of self is a form of revolt against history. In the scene from *Macbeth*, the protagonist uses self-denigration to test the integrity of his interlocutor. That said, the protagonist is the rightful heir to the usurped kingdom and, as such, symbolizes the Québécois condition as represented in the social discourse: the Québécois is split, caught between two languages and two cultures, in a divided land. The frequent use of the double as a theme, 'double' being one of the key words in Québécois discourse, leads *axio-logically* to the themes of duplicity and treason. To betray is to reject Quebec and the ideal of autonomy, to ally oneself with anglophone hegemony and risk assimilation or to play the game of double identity, which amounts to the same thing.

Even though they are from works as disparate as *Macbeth* and

158 A Sociocritique of Translation

'L'afficheur hurle,' the two passages we have just compared contain the same thematic and axiological structure. Each exploits the theme of lost innocence, the degeneration that results from an external act of aggression and betrayal. The similarity between the two works, which is not as accidental as it might first appear, demonstrates the degree to which the original scene from *Macbeth*, subsequently expurgated by the translator, was in tune with the discourse of the translator's society.

The Translating Subject

Comparison of an original text with its translation benefits from an examination of the textual and discursive ensemble of which the translation will become a part. Consideration of the target discourse makes it possible to explain differences between the target and source texts in terms of a coherent system and reveals the literary and, more generally, discursive codes that are characteristic of the contemporary target milieu.[51] It is a well-established fact that the translation process involves more than language. Equally, however, it is not simply a question of a vast abstract notion of culture. Translation operates within social discourse, a preformed material whose presuppositional articulation lends coherence and intelligibility to surface utterances. In other words, this presuppositional articulation determines 'the ideological intercomprehension field' of these utterances, a field coextensive with social practices.[52]

Translation, like any writing, reflects the institutional norms of a given society. This explains why foreign works selected for translation are those that already contain discursive structures in harmony with codes governing what is thinkable, sayable, and writable within the target society. Thus, translation theory should concern itself as much, if not more, with contrastive analysis of social discourse as with contrastive linguistics or comparative stylistics.

In a Québécois society still unsure of its identity, translation has a primarily mirroring function; it must legitimize the discourse of social representation by bringing in, from the outside, support that will reinforce social identity. This is indeed the goal of the explicitly 'Québécois' translation of the Shakespearian classic *Macbeth*. In Quebec, where literature closely parallels politics, and where it is proclaimed that the very existence of a Québécois nation is dependent on the existence of a national literature,[53] translation and writing overlap, in that they both consolidate ideologemes of social representation, particularly in its historical and political dimensions. This explains why, in the translation process, the basic alterity of the foreign text is marginalized, as the main function of the text is now to promote a representation of *québécité*.

The audience at a performance of Michel Garneau's *Macbeth* may well get the impression that Shakespeare's tragedy is a perfect symbolic representation of the Québécois condition. Conversely, the destiny of Quebec, using as its vehicle a Shakespearian classic transformed through translation into an equally powerful but different text, can take on a certain universality, and acquire a timeless legitimacy that recognizes no borders. Under these conditions, the Québécois problem is raised to the level of myth.

The perlocutory effect of translation can thus be described as the effect on the consciousness of the audience that is brought about through transformation of the presuppositions of the original text and through manipulation of point of view. Here, the reshaping of the foreign text is perlocutory, a mode of argumentation and persuasion.[54] Through a sort of 'stencil effect,' the translation cuts and pastes the original text, using a grid imposed by the discursive institution of the target milieu. Sometimes the translator omits part of the text; other times he adds to it. But it is not sufficient to conclude, as is so often done, that the target text simply says something different from the source text. In fact, the omissions and additions introduced by the translator manipulate the receiver's perspective of the text. The translator sets up a point of view around which a new coherence and a new intelligibility are organized. One is reminded of anamorphosis, an artistic technique in which the distorted contours of an image can be reconstituted only from a single viewpoint. Faced with an original text in a language they do not understand, readers are in a comparable situation to someone looking at an anamorphosis from the wrong angle. Anamorphosis is a coded distortion of the image. Translators, like artists, employ master-coded transformational rules, even though they do not always do so consciously. They construct an intelligible representation of the original text from a particular discursive position. The transformation of the text is constructed or deconstructed in terms of a particular point of view. In forcing the audience to see the text from this viewpoint only, translation becomes a mode of persuasion.

Thus, in the given society that is the focus of our analysis, translation turns the aesthetic text into a persuasive text. The themes and images of the original text are given a new motivation, in the Saussurian sense of the word; they assume an ideological content designed to bring about a particular response. Garneau's translation is the product of a society and of its history. It is anchored in a discourse underpinned by *québécité*, a

Québécois vision of the world. This ideology both opens and closes the perspective from which the translation of the Shakespearian play will be read. It filters and normalizes the heterogeneous elements of the original text, that is, elements that are heterogeneous vis-à-vis the discourse produced by the target society. Through manipulation of point of view, a translator can ensure the ideological relevance of the foreign text within the target society. The persuasive function of Garneau's translation is derived from this process; it leads the audience to project an ideologically determined content onto the reshaped source text. Specific passages of *Macbeth* are reinforced or suppressed to make the representation of a fictitious Scotland coincide with the spatio-temporal entity known as Quebec, or, more specifically, 'Québec libre.' For here, we are dealing with a construct of the social discourse, around which crystallize a number of ideologemes, ideologemes that define and characterize Quebec in terms of its historicity.

The schema introduced at the beginning of our analysis presented three space–times corresponding to levels of reading constructed by Garneau's translation. However, these levels do not always completely overlap. Taken individually, many passages or scenes of Shakespeare's *Macbeth* do not lend themselves to dual interpretation. They acquire meaning only in the space–time of Shakespearian fiction. But, in the translation, there is intermittent interplay among space–times and it is this that produces its perlocutory effect. The audience would never take Garneau's *Macbeth* for a doctrinaire work on Quebec; their idealization of literature reinforces their assumption that texts are 'innocent,' especially in the case of a literary classic such as *Macbeth*. Moreover, the ideological substratum introduced in the translation gains validity from the status of the original text. Literary criticism, a variant of social discourse at its most institutional, also allowed itself to be taken in by Garneau's *Macbeth*:

Garneau's translation of *Macbeth* into Québécois is faithful both to the Shakespearian plot and to its tragic writing. The break with the tone of the original, stemming from the use of decidedly popular speech, whose phonetic, lexical, and syntactical structures are reproduced, does not preclude rigorous respect for sequence of events, development of discourse, and even repetition of ideas ... all are changes that are faithful to the meaning of the original, changing only the tone of it; the translation is accurate. It is the work of a poet who substitutes the familiar rhythms of his vernacular language for those that the foreign poet had written in his language.[55]

Shakespeare, Québécois Nationalist Poet 161

This seal of approval conferred on Michel Garneau, the translator, reflects and reinforces the position he occupies as author in the Québécois literary system. Thus, the inventor of what could be a national language for Quebec becomes the Québécois counterpart of Shakespeare. Although critics recognize that all translators are 'part of a given socio-historic system,' they justify Garneau's translation by stressing the importance of restoring the true 'Shakespearian speech,' which, they hasten to add, is a 'popular' speech, a speech that has been 'tampered with' by classical or romantic translations:

Garneau translated Shakespeare in reaction to those translations that diminished Shakespeare, and cut him off from his roots ... He reorganized the text in his own language, omitting or slightly modifying that which had no resonance in Québécois or which could cause confusion. This approach tightened up the text; by being, above all, faithful to the plot and to the poetry, the translator, in fact, stayed close to the essence of the authentic text.[56]

Given the assumptions in this quotation, we may well ask if Garneau's aesthetic reshaping of the text, which is based mainly on choice of language of translation (a language that, contrary to what is said, in no way corresponds to the language in Garneau's other writings) is more respectful of the original text than similar superstructures so criticized in French translations. We have attempted to demonstrate that Garneau's translation is equally a function of the literary stereotypes of its period and of its place of production. Clearly, we see here evidence of an axio-ideological symbiosis between translation and literary criticism: Québécois criticism implicitly validates works that participate in the search for 'Québécois' identity. Translation and translation criticism display what Deleuze would call the same 'coefficient of territorialization.'[57]

4

The Search for a Native Language: Translation and Cultural Identity

... we need more than a mother tongue to come into our own, we also need a native language.

Gaston Miron, *L'Homme rapaillé*

Issues of Language in the Theory of Translation

Language is an indispensable element in the realization of the verbal act. It is a necessary precondition for communication. As Jakobson observes, 'the message requires ... a Code fully, or at least partially, common to the addresser and addressee (or in other words, to the encoder and the decoder of the message).'[1] Translation is a dual act of communication. It presupposes the existence, not of a single code, but of two distinct codes, the 'source language' and the 'target language.' The fact that the two codes are not isomorphic creates obstacles for the translative operation. This explains why linguistic questions are the starting-point for all thinking about translation. A basic premise of translation theory is the famous 'prejudicial objection' dismantled by Mounin, piece by piece, in one of the first works to elevate translation to the status of a quasi-scientific area of scholarship.[2] Translation is a unidirectional operation between two given languages. The target language is thus, every bit as much as the source language, a *sine qua non* of the translative operation. If the target language remains elusive, the act of translation becomes impossible. This is true even in the hypothetical case in which a text must be translated into a language that has no writing system. Throughout history, translators have had to contend with the fact that the target language is deficient when it comes to translating the source text into that language. Such deficiencies can be clearly identified as, for example, lexical or morpho-syntactic deficiencies or as problems of polysemy. More often, however, the deficiency in the receiving code has to do with the relation between signs and their users, a relation that reflects such things as individuality, social position, and geographical origin of the speakers: 'thus the relatively simple question arises, should one translate or not translate argot by argot, a patois by a patois, etc. ...'[3] Here, the difficulty of translation does not arise from the lack of a specific translation language. It arises, rather, from the absence in the target language of a subcode equivalent to the one used by the source text in its reproduction of the source language. How should the cockney dialogue in *Pygmalion* be translated? What French-language dialect equivalent should be used to render the lunfardo of Buenos Aires in translations of Roberto Arlt's novels? What variety of French would correspond to the Roman dialect of the Via Merulana in a translation of Carlo Emilio Gadda's *Quer pasticciaccio brutto de via Merulana*? What is the French equivalent of the English of the American South in Faulkner's novels? Such are the questions ritually posed by the translator, torn between the source text and the target language. These problems become more complex when historical time is factored in. Should the translator re-create the feeling of the time period of the text for the contemporary reader? Or, conversely, should the archaic form of the language be modernized to make the text more accessible to the contemporary reader? Should Dante, Shakespeare, Cervantes, or Chaucer be translated into archaic language? Should Cicero's style be rendered by the style of a well-known politician of modern times?[4] The choice of a target language becomes even more difficult when the text to be translated is a parody of a variety of the source language. *Gawęda*, a 'museum language' of Great Poland, reproduced and parodied by Gombrowicz in his *Trans-Atlantyk*,[5] is a case in point. Translation problems can arise not only from deficiencies in the receiving society but also from a surfeit of linguistic options. For example, in certain societies, the language of men is different from that of women, and these differences are governed by particularly strict constraints. Charles Taber and Eugene Nida have discussed the problem of whether the Scriptures should be translated into the language of men or of women.[6] Writings on the translative operation abound with such questions. Translators address these issues in prefaces to their work, outlining the deficiencies of the target language, deficiencies arising from sociological, geographical, or historical variation in the source language.

Although the target language cannot always provide equivalents of the source language, the absence of a target language, the language into which one translates, is not usually cited as a formal translation problem. One could object that there have been instances in which translation has indeed created languages. But then there would have to be some agreement on the meaning of the word 'create,' because it would be wrong to assume that these languages had no prior existence and that translation created them from whole cloth. A case in point is the translation of the Bible by Luther, a translation that gave rise to the German language. In this case, the difficulty of translation arose from the fact that the target language was not a single unified language but a number of dialects:

> Good German is the German of the people. But the people speak an infinite number of Germans. One must then translate into a German that somehow rises above the multiplicity of *Mundarten* without rejecting them or suppressing them. Thus Luther attempted to do two things: translate into a German that a priori can only be local, his own German, *Hochdeutch*, but at the same time elevate, by the very process of translation, this local German to the status of a common German, a *lingua franca*. So that the German he used did not become itself a language cut off from the people, he had to preserve in it something of the *Mundarten*, of the general modes of expression and of the popular dialects. Thus, we find at the same time a consistent and deliberate use of a very oral language, full of images, expressions, turns of phrase, together with a subtle purification, de-dialectalization of this language ... Luther's translation constitutes a first decisive self-affirmation of literary German. Luther, the great 'reformer,' was henceforth considered as a writer and as a creator of a language ...[7]

Another example is the replacement of Latin by French after the edict of Villers-Cotterêts in the sixteenth century. By requiring that all civil acts be 'pronounced, registered and delivered to the parties in the French mother tongue,'[8] François I set into motion a translation movement that helped 'elevate our vulgar [tongue] to the equal of and as a model for the other more famous languages.'[9] As a result of this and ensuing decrees, vernacular French was to become the language of law, science, and literature. It acquired the status of national language, the founding language of the French state.

Strictly speaking, translation does not fill a linguistic void, no more so in the France of Du Bellay than in the Germany of Luther. Translation can, however, change the relation of linguistic forces, at the institutional and symbolic levels, by making it possible for the *vernacular language* to take the place of the *referential language,* to use distinctions from Henri Gobard's tetraglossic analysis. According to his analysis, a cultural field, or a linguistic community, has at its disposal four types of language or subcode:

I. A *vernacular language,* which is local, spoken spontaneously, less appropriate for communicating than for *communing,* and the only language that can be considered to be the mother tongue (or native language).

II. A *vehicular language,* which is national or regional, learned out of necessity, to be used for communication in the city.

III. A *referential language,* which is tied to cultural, oral, and written traditions and ensures continuity in values by systematic reference to classic works of the past.

IV. A *mythical language,* which functions as the ultimate recourse, verbal magic, whose incomprehensibility is considered to be irrefutable proof of the sacred ...[10]

In 'renascent' France as well as in 'reformist' Germany, the referential language was a *foreign* language. In the corpus under review, the goal of translation is to supplant such foreign forms of expression, which are viewed as alienating, literally dispossessing. The task of translation is thus to replace the language of the Other by a native language. Not surprisingly, the native language chosen is usually the vernacular, 'the linguistic birthright, the indelible mark of belonging.'[11] Translation becomes an act of reclaiming, of recentring of the identity, a re-territorializing operation. It does not create a new language, but it elevates a dialect to the status of a national and cultural language.

'Translated into Québécois'

The inclusion of the annotation 'traduit en québécois' (translated into Québécois) on the cover of Michel Garneau's translation of *Macbeth* can be explained by the translation's role as a re-territorializing operation. This reference to the language of translation is a reversal of usual procedure, which is to inform the reader of the language from which the work has been translated. Normally, the language of translation is a given; for readers, it is implicit, understood, that the language of translation will be the language of their own literature. A French publisher would never preface a book by Claude Simon, Marguerite Duras, or Michel Tournier with the annotation 'written in French.' The reader of a translation does not need to be told what language has been used to translate the foreign text. However, in cases where the reader is unlikely to be aware of the language of the original text, information about the language of origin is normally provided with the expression 'Translated from.' But when, against all normal usage, there is a perceived need to indicate that the translation is 'into Québécois,' it is precisely because it cannot be taken for granted that a work will be translated into Québécois. Similarly, would one not write the annotation 'translated into Occitan' on a literary work in France? The annotation underscores the marginality of the language. But there is a considerable difference between the linguistic status of Occitan and that of Québécois. Occitan is a different sign system from French, as Catalan is from Spanish. Québécois is not a different sign system from French: '*Phenomenology of the Mind* would never be translated into Québécois.'[12] Thus, the expression 'traduit en québécois' forms part of the ideological construction of the presumed difference between 'Québécois' and French. Clearly, this annotation heralds the birth of a language that translation will have to bring to the fore, or at least, *expose*, in the photographic sense of the word. This function of translation, to give more exposure to the language, is reinforced by the proliferation of lexicographical studies of Québécois. New dictionaries of Québécois appear almost yearly. Of these, Léandre Bergeron's was the best-known during the period under study.[13] The dictionary aims less to codify usage than to demonstrate, if not to construct, the difference between Québécois and the French of France. The following examples, taken from the *Practical Handbook of Canadian French – Manuel pratique du français canadien* by Sinclair Robinson and Donald Smith are a good illustration of such a lexicographical endeavour. The handbook, whose very title is a serious misnomer, sets out to prove to anglophone students that Canadian French is a separate language. 'It has the same capacity to express the whole range of human concerns as any other tongue.'[14] Using a more ideologically motivated than naïve categorization, the authors divide French and Québécois lexical items into three pseudo-contrastive groups:

Canada	**France**	**Translation**
beurre d'arachides	pâté de cacahouètes	peanut butter
lait écrémé	–	skim milk
colline parlementaire	emplacement en pente du gouvernement canadien	Parliament Hill

électorat	corps électoral	electorate
relevé de notes	copie des notes au niveau universitaire	transcript[15]

Mystified by the alleged difference between the two types of French, the reader of the handbook will be left with the impression that the French of France is a limited language, and that it is fundamentally incapable of expressing 'Québécois reality.' On the other hand, Léandre Bergeron defines 'Québécois,' as opposed to French, as 'a sign system, mainly spoken but sometimes written by the Québécois people.'[16] The existence of a Québécois language is also tangible proof of the existence of a 'Québécois people,' in the restrictive sense of the expression 'a people' as compared with 'a population.' Bergeron's Québécois is a language 'rich with all the tension of a small people who are still wet from their birth on the eve of the twenty-first century, still shy in the presence of grown-ups, reluctant to walk among all those big people.'[17] This explains why so much importance is placed on translation, because it proves irrefutably that the Québécois language exists. 'We have even started to be translated into other languages for those who want to hear our distinctness, to talk about Melville to the Americans, make the "matantes" heard in Tokyo, and make the citizens of Berlin dream of our forests.'[18] Conversely, translating canonical works or literary masterpieces such as *Macbeth* into Québécois is an attempt to legitimize Québécois by elevating it from its status as a dialect. It proves that it is the language of a people and that it can replace French as the language of literature for its people. Here, the roles are reversed: the goal of a translation is not to provide an introduction to the Other or to mediate the foreign work. It is the foreign work that is given a mission – to vouch for the existence of the language of translation and, by so doing, vouch for the existence of a Québécois 'people.' Thus, when Shakespeare, Chekhov, and Brecht are given the task of establishing Québécois as a literary language in its own right, and ultimately as a national language, they are also given the task of reflecting the reality of the society that speaks that language, of literally speaking for it, or of being its mirror. Thus, when a foreign text is adapted or 'culturally translated,' it stands to reason that it will be translated into 'Québécois.'[19]

The annotation 'traduit en québécois' and, at a different level, the proliferation of lexicographical works are both signs of institutional conflict in Quebec. The battle has begun against the language that hitherto served as a referential vehicle. This language is, of course, French. French is not a foreign language in Quebec, as Latin or Italian were in Du Bellay's time; yet it has suddenly been rejected as foreign, that is, incomprehensible. Consider, for example, this extract from *Défense et illustration de la langue québécoise* by Michèle Lalonde:

> Thus, even for the most educated people in the country, there is still a wide gap between spoken and written language and a kind of conflict that could cause great anguish and terrible feelings of dichotomy when a whole chagrin tries to express itself. And it is true that, in that light, the French language of France is like a second language to us, an almost foreign language because it does not have a strong emotional content and immediate allusions to our affects and experiences.[20]

Rejecting French is tantamount to eliminating internal bilingualism, a bilingualism that puts the vernacular language in conflict with the referential; a language without constraints is set against a highly regulated, 'polished' language from overseas, a language thus not suitable for translating local experience. The 'chagrin' that is inexpressible in the French of France is the 'Conquest,' the 'colonization,' the socio-economic 'oppression,' the very foundation of the nationalist interpretation of history, both real and ideologically constructed.[21] The language conflict was one expression of nationalist aspirations at the time. Another, in the political arena, was the nationalist movement that led to the birth of the Parti Québécois and the emergence of the Front de Libération du Québec. The demand for territorial and political autonomy was logically extended to a demand for a distinct native language. Suddenly, the French of France became unsuitable for communication among Québécois. The nationalist *doxa* used a solipsistic concept of language to explain why French was suddenly incapable of expressing the 'affects and experiences' of the Québécois people, who, it would appear, do not share the affects and experiences of other peoples and other nations. After being in contact with a new reality, French had undergone a transformation, with the following result: 'even when the words are the same, they express another reality, another experience.'[22] It may appear to be the same language, but this is deceptive – Quebec French is no longer the same language as the French of France. This argument is generally supported by allegedly irrefutable proof – a vocabulary list. The manuals and dictionaries mentioned above are a development of this trend. They also lend 'scientific' support[23] to the argument for the difference between the two languages. A case in point being the list of Québécois words produced by

Michèle Lalonde, which includes such un-French words as 'savane,' 'raquette,' and 'feu-follet'![24]

The year 1968 marked the beginning of changes in Quebec's relation to the French of France. To satisfy the needs of the nationalist cause, French was held up as an ideological fiction – a socially and geographically homogeneous language, homogeneous to the point of being totalitarian. Was it not continuously subjected to normalization by a small group of academicians, and to censorship by a handful of intellectuals in Paris? This portrayal of the French language as a frigid and withered language, as opposed to a vigorous, natural Québécois, has been widely debated and denounced by many.[25] We will, thus, not pursue the matter here. Suffice it to say that the language conflict that developed around 1968 is clearly symptomatic of a change in relations with the Foreigner.

Québécois in the Market of Symbolic Commodities

A linguistic community is a market. Its vernacular and referential languages are its symbolic commodities, each with its own use value and its own exchange value. The circulation of these commodities is governed by power relations.

A linguistic community appears to be a sort of *huge market in which words, expressions and messages circulate as commodities.* We may ask ourselves what rules govern the circulation of words, expressions and messages, beginning with the values according to which they are *consumed* and *exchanged.*[26]

As nationalist Quebec began asserting itself at the end of the 1960s, its vernacular and referential languages suddenly started competing with each other. Thus, in the market economy of symbolic commodities, there was competition between the exchange values of the two languages. On the cultural level, the Québécois product had to take precedence over the imported product. This gave rise to a form of protectionism, the aim of which was to limit importation and circulation of non-Québécois symbolic commodities in cultural institutions such as theatrical publishing and production, criticism, and literary awards and grants. The language conflict mirrored the newly engaged battle to conquer the symbolic-commodities market, that is, the battle to become institutionally dominant.

In the theatre, foreign symbolic commodities were dominant, but they remained so by default. Statistics quoted in chapter 1 reveal, however, that as the number of Québécois productions increased, the exchange value of artistic creations such as foreign translations was more and more seriously eroded. If they were to replace French productions, which were clearly dominant, and if they were to appropriate the symbolic capital held by these productions, Québécois productions had to be different. This was the first condition for the emergence of a distinctly Québécois theatrical institution. Here is how Jacques Dubois explains the 'law of distinctness' as it applies to the literary institution:

> ... at the time when an institution is being founded, we see the development of legitimacy within the literary sphere, and this legitimacy defines the activity of this sphere as autonomous and distinctive ... Thus, writers find themselves engaged in the logic of distinctness. If distinctness becomes the issue for them, and that is indeed how one gains the recognition of one's peers and competitors, the only way to achieve recognition is to make one's writing culturally marked in a way that is pertinent in a given literary field.[27]

In the dramatic arts, language would fulfil the distinctive function that was needed for Québécois productions to become institutionally recognized and autonomous vis-à-vis French and French-Canadian productions.

The Distinctive Function of Québécois

This breaking away into a separate aesthetic particularity closely paralleled contemporary political demands, with all their ramifications. We have seen that, in Quebec, the quest for a native language is tied to the need to be different, not to be mixed in with the others in the North American melting pot:

> nous distincts
> différents
> à ne point confondre
>
> [we [are]
> distinct
> different
> not to be confused with anyone].[28]

'*Québécité*' (Quebecness) defines itself as the search for absolute distinctness, a distinctness that will counteract the danger of assimilation.

The threat of assimilation looms on a number of fronts. First, a battle must be waged against the assimilation inherent in the position of a francophone community hemmed in by anglophones. But, of course, the danger of anglicization comes not only from the geopolitical structures of Quebec within the Canadian federation; it also comes from the proximity of the United States, which exerts a strong sociocultural fascination. Economically and politically all-powerful, the United States provides Quebec with its new cultural models and can be viewed, therefore, as a second assimilating front. A third threatening front is immigration. The foreigner, who is called 'immigrant,' 'ethnic,' and 'allophone' or 'neo-Québécois,' is seen as the enemy within:

Mais au contraire, à peine peuvent-ils [les Québécois] s'aventurer hors de leur demeure sans être cernés de toutes parts par des puissances estrangières tantôt Anglaise, tantôt Américaine, voire, récemment, Italienne, qui les repoussent à leur bon plaisir & les soumettent à leurs lois, privilèges ou droits acquis de plus ou moins longue date sur ce territoire...

[But on the contrary, they (the Québécois) can hardly step outside their doors without being surrounded on all sides by foreign powers, sometimes English, sometimes American, and more recently, Italian, who feel free to push them aside and subject them to their laws, privileges, or rights that were acquired a more or less long time ago on this land ...][29]

This way of thinking attributes to the Italian, the symbol of all immigrants, the assimilating characteristics of the anglophone. The assimilation of francophones is an undeniable threat, if only by virtue of the law of numbers. Moreover, immigrants were quick enough to decide which group to model themselves after, the minority group or the dominant prestigious group. Imbued with the American dream, immigrants had not left everything behind only to end up in the camp of a group that insists on depicting itself as the colonized, the loser, and the victim. It is easy to understand why their allegiances go spontaneously to the anglophones, who, in fact, have traditionally extended a warm welcome to immigrants, excluded, as they themselves were, from francophone institutions on linguistic or religious grounds. The immigrant thus becomes an agent of assimilation. But this negative portrayal of the immigrant goes even further. It characterizes the newly arrived as the conqueror, the usurper, who receives special treatment. We know how the English got where they are; they have history on their side. But where does an Italian (a Portuguese, a Greek, a Pole, a Haitian, a Vietnamese, a Chilean, a Turk), that bare-foot peasant who just arrived yesterday on 'our' soil, get such rights? There is an interesting transfer of blame in this depiction of the immigrant, for it is clear that, in reality, the immigrant does not exactly occupy the upper social, economic, cultural, and political echelons of Quebec society. Is this depiction not, in fact, an indictment specifically designed to justify keeping immigrants on the margin of society, outside all spheres of authority in Quebec? In a province 'under siege,' the Italian symbolizes internal alterity, a sort of fifth column, a true incarnation of the fear of the Other. No one has been more forthright than Jean Éthier-Blais in expressing the idea of the 'foreign peril,' a peril that had only become more threatening with the arrival of the Vietnamese, the Chileans, and the Tamils:

[...] le Québec est déjà divisé contre lui-même. D'une part, Montréal, qui se veut *multiculturel, donc objectivement anti-québécois, viscéralement, dans ses néocomposantes*; d'autre part le grand Québec, qui joue la politique de l'autruche et sombre dans l'optimisme tactique. [...] Nos gouvernements sonts prêts à sacrifier tout ce qui nous est cher, langue, histoire, pour ne pas décevoir *ces « réfugiés politiques »*.

[... Quebec is already divided against itself. On the one hand, Montreal, which likes to see itself as *multicultural, thus objectively anti-Québécois, viscerally, in its neo-composition*; on the other, Quebec as a whole, which plays the politics of the ostrich, drowning in tactical optimism ... Our governments are ready to sacrifice everything we hold dear, language, history, so as not to disappoint these 'political refugees.'][30]

Clearly, here, group membership is not fortuitous or a natural state of affairs. It is guided by nationalist interests, and by definition does not allow for inclusion of neo-Québécois. They have the misfortune of being what they are: foreigners. This argument, which is designed to prevent the dissolution of the Québécois identity, tacitly reproduces the dominant/subordinate schema that is so vigorously denounced when the group is speaking of itself. Any relationship with the Other seems inconceivable outside this framework of domination. This is because the Other is at fault and wears a mask, as insinuated by Éthier-Blais's use of quotation marks, which make the official status of 'political refugee' suspect – no doubt, illegitimate. Only the Québécois are tragic figures, exiles in their own country. Foreigners use a false identity to pass themselves off as victims and abuse the generosity of an overly hospitable country. The

The Search for a Native Language 173

poetry of Michel Garneau opposes the fascist undertones of such rhetoric. His apologia for cross-breeding uses poetic language to reveal and acclaim the mixed background of the Québécois identity: 'J'ai toutt le sang mêlé / les ancêtres sont mes étrangers / un peu d'hurabénaquois / un peu d'irlancossais [...]' ['My blood is all mixed up / my ancestors are foreigners / Hurabénaquois / a little Irishscotch .:.'] In another poem, 'L'avenir câllé' (Calling to the Future) he even writes:

> qu'on réalise québécois combien nous sommes
> écœuremment racistes
> baie-james-réserves-rythme de nègres-
> maudits-anglais-français-italiens-juifs
> poloks-chicken flied lice-sauvages
> pis qu'on arrête ça tout d'suite.

> [that we realize Québécois how sickeningly racist
> we are
> James-Bay-reservations-nigger rhythm-
> cursed-English-French-Italians-Jews
> Polaks-chicken flied lice-savages
> now let's stop that right now.]³¹

The foreigner poses a problem precisely because he introduces heterogeneity, impurity into the Québécois community.

> Nous autres
> dit couramment ce peuple
> à propos de lui-même
> marquant ainsi d'un mot
> l'intime ambiguïté
> de son identité.

> ['Nous autres'
> says frequently this people
> about itself
> underlining thus with a single word
> the intimate ambiguity
> of its identity.]³²

Ideally, no foreign presence should ever stain the Québécois identity.

Doing away with any 'ambiguity' of identity means getting rid of the Other. In the name of distinctness, the salvation of the Québécois identity, all forms of alterity must be automatically ejected from the group, confined to their own differences. The first-person plural, 'nous,' is used to justify various kinds of difference – ethnicity, language, identity, and separation. Close association between 'nous' and 'les autres' is dangerous, harmful, and therefore to be deplored. The 'Québécois language' is entrusted with establishing this separation and constitutes, in effect, the *differentia specifica* of the Québécois. If the French language is no longer sufficient, it is because the stakes are no longer simply linguistic; they have become topological. Language must be coextensive with a territory. There can be no sharing of language or territory.

The Enigmatic Québécois Language[33]

Gaston Miron makes a distinction between 'mother tongue' and 'native language,' a distinction, he says, the Québécois need to make.[34] How does he explain the relevance of this distinction between two concepts that, in actual usage, are one and the same? He does not define what he means by 'native language,' but he holds it up as the symbol of political liberation. Miron's native language is still French, but it is not spoken in the same cultural and sociopolitical circumstances as French. In fact, Miron uses the notion of a native language as an antithesis to a series of axioms on which his whole argument is built: if a native language is to emerge, Quebec must rid itself of its colonial status; once Quebec is freed of its colonial socio-economic constraints, its newly emerged native language can be used to justify the rejection of French culture. The existence of a native language presupposes that its speakers are 'in the world according to a culture, that is according to an ontology' which is *unique* to that language, and to that language only. In other words, the emergence of a native language implies the elimination of alterity.[35] To acquire a native language is to be reborn in a free country, to have a country entirely to oneself. Reclaiming one's native language naturally leads to the idea of a pure nation that exists in 'the consciousness of the world.'[36] Their own native language or national language is a sign of the unity and purity of the Québécois 'people.' It is the distinctive feature of what Gaston Miron calls the '*Québécanthrope*,' the *homo quebecensis*, who sees himself, to use Weinmann's rejoinder, 'as a new man' who comes from a *separate* branch of the development of humanity.[37] Miron's native language does not exist. It is a political postulate founded on an identity fetish and on the

The Search for a Native Language   175

rejection of the Other: 'only political action can restore him [the Québécois] to his homogeneity, the basis for exchange between cultures.'[38] The call for a return to homogeneity is not exactly a subtle one. There seems to be no awareness of the fact that there is no such thing as a homogeneous culture, no more than there is homogeneous literature. Indeed, the ideology of homogeneity rejects all dialogism and is, thus, a form of totalitarianism.[39]

Creating a distinction between a native language and a mother tongue entails more than the reappropriation of the native language, a language deformed and alienated by interference from English. The distinction also implies rejection of the mother tongue, which, in this case, is the language of a 'foreign' culture, the French culture. Pierre Gobin points out what this distinction specifically means to the playwright 'living in a society that bears the marks of colonial experience.' The author 'experiences even more profoundly the distance between "indigenous" language and "foreign" writing, especially if both have the same linguistic heritage, that is to say, if there is *diglossia* rather than *bilingualism*.'[40] Furthermore, sharing a language with French does not sit well with a solipsistic and ontological concept of culture. According to this line of thinking, the mother tongue of the Québécois is someone else's language, in the same way that their native country, which has been despoiled by the English, has become someone else's country. Therefore, claiming one's native language means rejecting one's mother, severing a tie that, in any case, was never nourishing:

Y a-t-il doncques une Langue Québecquoyse, ou Québécouayse, ou kébékouaze distincte de la Françaement puisse m'exprimer? D'aucuns aussi prompts à trancher cette question que lents à trancher le cordon ombilical qui les relie à la Mère-patrie, soutiennent péremptoirement que *non* et qualifient de barbare & impure la Parlure de nostre « vulgaire » qu'il faudrait châtier sans pitié comme une façon tout au plus de parler ineptement français.

[Is there indeed a Québecquoyse, or Québecouayse or kébékouaze language distinct from French, in the way French used to be distinct from Latin, in which I can express myself? Some are as quick to answer this question as they are slow to cut the umbilical cord that connects them to the Mother Country; they maintain that the answer is simply no, and say that the language of our 'vulgar' is a barbarous and impure way of speaking that should be punished mercilessly for being an inept way of speaking French.][41]

Mother tongue is not the same notion for Michèle Lalonde as it is for Gaston Miron. Lalonde's concept of mother tongue corresponds more to what Miron terms a 'native' language. For Lalonde, the mother tongue is not the language of the mother country, a borrowed language, with 'a French superior lineage, devoid of all our turpitude, thus of a less vulgar Culture.'[42] The mother tongue is truly the language-of-my-mother [la langue-à-ma-mére]. It is the language of one's roots, full of 'lovely words ... invented to describe, for example, *les bordages* (in-shore ice), *les bordillons* (piles of in-shore ice), *les fardoches* (undergrowth), and *les cédrières* (cedar groves), and other common things in our wild surroundings.'[43] The mother tongue is an Edenic, native, natural language, dating from the idyllic era of colonization (when 'we' were the colonizers). In those days, it was a free language, a language in perfect harmony with the territory of the Québécois, a language nothing could resist, 'neither the blue spruce, nor the white cedar, nor the plains, nor the hemlock spruce, that so awed our ancestors but did not leave them speechless and unable to name them.'[44] Lalonde's definition of mother tongue is full of nostalgia for a paradise lost, a time when the Québécois could invent their own names for things, when the Québécois language was 'Cratylean' and in complete harmony with nature. The deterioration of the language followed the loss of the country to the venal hands of a foreign power:

À la claire fontaine du Toronto Stock Exchange il en
coule des dollars sous nos doigts comme billets
d'amour pour la belle dame des maîtres

brrrou goudourou xouliminimini crrah vrrah khmè strix
j'attendais un vrai langage là où il n'y avait que des
pieuvres pour me bouffer tout cru tout vivant

crisse de câlice de tabarnaque
le jour où j'ai pensé hors des fantômes admis pensé de
ce qu'est vivre ici je n'ai su que sacrer profaner.

[In the clear fountain of the Toronto Stock Exchange
dollars flow through our fingers like love
notes for the beautiful lady of the masters

brrrrou goudourou xouliminimini crrah vrrah khmè strix
I was expecting a real language in the place where there was
only octopus to eat me completely raw and totally alive

The Search for a Native Language 177

crisse de câlice de tabarnaque
the day I thought outside of the acceptable ghosts thought about what it is to live here I could only swear profanities.]⁴⁵

In a lyrical, humorous register, Paul Chamberland's poem 'L'afficheur hurle' also takes up the theme of nostalgia for a pure language unspoiled by the Other. He expresses his anguish that a 'true language' is impossible and sings the praises of a paradise lost:

l'amour m'a mis entre les dents les clés de la vengeance
[...]
pourtant j'aurais pu être tendre comme de la dentelle
mais il aurait fallu depuis toujours voler rouler sur
le muscle d'une terre forte cascader sur les hanches
d'une mère ouverte aux razzias du plaisir   Mère
Liberté Mère Amour Mère debout dans le création du
monde.

[love put the keys of vengeance in my mouth
...
but I could have been tender like lace
but it would have been necessary to fly roll
over the muscle of a strong land cascade onto the hips
of a mother open to the plunders of pleasure. Mother
Liberty Mother Love Mother standing in the creation of
the world.]⁴⁶

It would be possible to return to the mother on two conditions: she must be a lover and she must incarnate liberty. The metaphor of incest sits well with the metaphor of the family that is often used to describe Québécois society ('this little society that comes together like a family').⁴⁷ Implicit in the metaphor of incest is a longing for an unreal past, a past that can be re-created by staying among one's own people. Thus, we see the formation of a vicious circle of nostalgia which, exclusive and inward-turning, rejects the Other and its culture. In this nostalgia for a return to nature, there is also a call for a return to a language which, if not lost, has yet to re-emerge.

How does one choose between the language of a paradise lost and the futile search for a native language; futile because the language is contaminated by the 'contemporary landscape in which *le Workshop*, *le Warehouse* and *le Shopping-centre* already have a name before they even sprout and there are many more of them than the *blé d'Inde* [corn on the cob] and the *arbre à sucre* [maple tree]'?[48] This is the very dilemma that led Michèle Lalonde, in her defence of the Québécois language, to adopt the sixteenth-century French of Joachim Du Bellay just as Du Bellay had vindicated French by using an Italian text as a model. And we know how highly he thought of Italy! Returning to this archaic form of French represents an attempt to pay 'homage to the very rich and original Langue Québécoyse, to the time when it was spoken freely and without so many unhappy complications on the free Canadian soil.'[49] In other words, the Québécois language is a nostalgic language, a myth, a fiction, a fantasy of a lost object. Justification for its existence is found in nationalist rhetoric, which equates a language with a people and with a specific territory. None the less, when Michèle Lalonde is not writing manifestos, she switches to standard contemporary educated French to explain what the relationship between the Québécois writer and the language of Québécois society should be:

The role of writers is simply to take as much interest as possible in the Québécois collectivity and to ADDRESS THIS COLLECTIVITY IN ITS LANGUAGE. By this I mean: we must regenerate the language, rediscover it, reinvent it, we must give it new significance, fill in the gaps with the help of international French, shake it up, refine it, make love to it with abandon, and do with it what we will but adopt it as the language of the six million who speak Québécois.[50]

Here, once again, we encounter the view that language must be homogeneous and unified, as should the people who speak it in their daily lives. But these people have never used this language in their literature. Oh, Guilty Literature! You must be removed from your place at the centre of the institution! The Québécois writer who is deserving of the title should 'renounce literary egocentrism' and 'for the time being pull out of the Prix Goncourt,' and adopt the language of the Québécois, the true speech of 'real people.' The duty of writers is in fact to 'give the power of speech back to the collectivity from which they come ... to the point where they should try to have more contact with students, workers, in other words, with ordinary Québécois, even if it means going to write among them.'[51] And, of course, Québécois workers, like their French counterparts, are avid readers of *Change*, the avant-garde journal in which this exhortation appeared! But the contradiction is even more profound: Québécois writers, who themselves do not speak the language of the collectivity, are asked to return to their linguistic roots. What is truly paradoxical here is that writers are expected to use the language of the people while playing the role of demiurge. Are they not expected to restore the language, consolidate it, give it back the vigour it had at the time of its origins, the time of liberty? To rediscover freedom of language is to regain liberty itself. To give the power of speech back to a people is, in both senses of the word, to allow them to speak and to provide them with a language. More to the point, it is, in fact, to give them what the Other took away with the injunction 'Speak White!'[52] But does this not constitute a change in ideological direction? The nationalist goal, anchored in the notion of 'difference,' does, in fact, need to be reinforced by distinctive characteristics, and language is the most important of these. Yet, this form of Québécois distinctness really exists only in the lower classes. In other words, the desire to give a language back to the 'people,' a conveniently ambiguous term, masks the ideological reappropriation of the language by the élite, as they attempt to prove the absoluteness of the Québécois 'difference,' and thereby justify the demand for political autonomy. Perhaps more than anything else, such a difference guarantees recognition to a new group of writers and sets them apart institutionally from other writers. This, of course, ensures that they have no competition from those who continue to compete for the 'Prix Goncourt.'

Michèle Lalonde's suggestion that writers should live and write among the working class – which V.L. Beaulieu does for several months of the year – brings to mind Luther's dilemma as he pondered the state of the German language at a time when it was not yet unified. What variety of German would be appropriate for translation? Luther proposed the following:

... We must seek out the mother in her home, the children in the streets, the common man in the market-place and examine what they are saying to discover how they speak; so that we may translate according to that. Then they will understand and notice that we speak German just like them.[53]

In pre-referendum nationalist Quebec as well as in reformist Germany, the success or failure of an ideology depended on a willingness to communicate with the people. To achieve hegemony, a group needs grassroots support. This was the case in the creation of a new religious institution in Germany and remains so for the creation of a literary institution in Quebec. The emergence of a truly Québécois literary institution is dependent upon the existence of a public. The Québécois language, which has been entrusted with this mission, is to 'international French' what the dialects of Germany were to Latin. But there is a difference. Whereas Latin was truly a foreign language to the 'mother in her home' and to 'the common man in the market-place,' international French in Quebec is found on the radio, in the newspapers, on television, and in the theatre. Nationalist ideology rejects the notion of Quebec French being 'international.' In this context, the word 'international' has a negative connotation and reveals a desire to exclude; the 'multicultural' and the 'transcultural' are negative values, to be fought at all costs. Suddenly characterized as 'international,' French has been defined as, and deliberately made into, a foreign language. Such an ideology emphasizes the illegitimacy of French, claiming that it is neither heard nor understood in Quebec. And proof of this assertion is to be found in the speech of ordinary Québécois.

More than any other literary genre, the theatre lends itself to the differentiating role entrusted to language. More than any other, the theatre, which gives primacy to the oral, makes it possible to hear the difference between referential French and vernacular French, a difference that is mainly a phonetic one.

The Myths of 'Québécois' as a Language of Translation

The phrase 'traduit en québécois' contains a paradox. It indicates, in French, that the language in which the work will be read is not French. This contradiction clearly illustrates the confusion surrounding the meaning of 'Québécois.' Native language? Mother tongue? Lost language or the true speech of the Québécois? But which Québécois, and under which circumstances? Characterizations of Québécois range from the myth of its Edenic origins via the standard French of Gaston Miron or Michèle Lalonde, all the way to the sociolectal reality of a 'decimated' language called 'joual.' What does 'traduit en québécois' then mean? Theatre translation illustrates the elusive nature of the Québécois language. Inconsistencies in the target language from one translator to another reflect the paradoxes and the incoherence of definitions of Québécois, as well as the diglossia of those who speak it. As definitions of Québécois itself fluctuate, so translations assume various forms.

Michel Garneau, the translator of *Macbeth*, appears to have given himself the task of rebuilding the original language of Quebec, the language of a distant past when Quebec was still free. With this goal, translation becomes a philological endeavour. To return to the birth of the spoken tongue in Quebec, Garneau undertook a veritable archaeological exploration of the language: 'I dug deep (as if digging a well) into the Québé-

The Search for a Native Language 181

cois language until I reached its ancestral source, I rummaged through the glossaries like crazy.'[54] Garneau also states that he reproduced the phonetics of the Gaspésie dialect. But why not the dialect of the Beauce or the Saguenay? His choice was apparently based on a concern for greater authenticity: 'Beginning with lexical and syntactic archaisms, from the rural poetry of old laments and Gaspésien pronunciation (that Garneau, like Jacques Ferron, finds more authentic), he creates a sort of ideal Quebec language.'[55]

The primacy Garneau accords to the speech of the Gaspé Peninsula clearly smacks of ideology. It so happens that the Gaspésie was the original site of Quebec, since it was here that Jacques Cartier landed in 1534 and planted a cross to claim the new land. The motivation for choosing the Gaspésie dialect is perhaps unconscious. The choice, none the less, is a functional one, since its purpose is to restore the Quebec language to its original truth and purity. The resulting language is an 'ideal' language – in other words, a perfect, nostalgic, mythical language. It is, indeed, the same language as the native tongue called for by Miron; it represents, literally, the language of the country at its birth. It is the language of the 'savage that I was,' according to Garneau, 'in the infancy of the tall grass.'[56] Moreover, nostalgia for this lost innocence suffuses the whole of the 'naïve' poetry of the author of *Petits chevals amoureux* (Little Amorous Horses) or *L'Élégie au massacre des nasopodes* (Elegy for the Massacre of the Nasopodes). The language in Garneau's *Macbeth* allows us to hear the words of the mother tongue that Michele Lalonde calls the 'language-of-my-mother,' in a world inhabited by *chats sovages, engoul'vents, éparviers*, where people *criaillent, s'époétrinent, rôdaillent*, and *s'acagnardissent*. Listen to Lady Macbeth convince her husband of the necessity of the crime:

> Toute est organisé pis tu sais pus d'quel côté avoér peur?
> Écoute, j'ai déjà nourri à mon lait, j'sais c'que c'est
> D'aimer le p'tit qui tète après toé, ben si j'ava's juré
> De l'fére comme t'as juré, même pendant qu'y m'ara't gazouillé
> Su'a falle, j'y a'ra's arraché l'teton des gencives
> Pis j'y'a'ra's craqué 'a tête en deux![57]

The language in Michel Garneau's *Macbeth* harks back to the early days of Quebec. It is a language both innocent and ancestral, a 'natural' language imbued with a primitive force. It is the language of the pioneers who had to hold their own against a hostile nature. It ties the search for identity to the myth of origins, a myth that the language itself helps to create. The Shakespearian world, and, in particular, that of *Macbeth*, a sacrificial tragedy of primitive violence, provides a perfect backdrop for a prehistorical exploration of the Quebec language. It is a perfect vehicle for reconstructing a past and for bringing to light a time when the language and those who spoke it owed nothing to anybody. The archaeology of the Quebec language reduces 'alienation' to degree zero and returns the language to its point of origin, where all forms of dependence on the Other are abolished.

Literary classics such as *Macbeth* are chosen as vehicles for the Quebec language in an attempt to remove the language from its dialect status and to prove that it is capable of fulfilling a referential function. At least, this is the view of critics: 'Shakespeare, through his work, gave poetic status to a language which hitherto had none; Garneau wants to demonstrate the richness of the Quebec language and to place it on an equal footing with other languages.'[58] Based on an inaccurate idea of the state of the English language in pre-Elizabethan times, this view makes Garneau the equal of Shakespeare and elevates Québécois to the status of a language at the height of its poetic maturity. The Québécois in Garneau's *Macbeth* is an anachronistic language, just as Shakespeare's language is today. In this sense, we can say that Michel Garneau's translation aims to provide contemporary Quebec speakers, not with a language they can actually speak, but rather with a feeling for their history and their ancestral ties. In any case, the creation of this ancestral language, 'native language' according to Miron, or 'mother tongue' according to Michèle Lalonde, brings to a successful conclusion the search for a language of one's own, a necessary condition for establishing the Québécois identity.

Michel Garneau's philological endeavours are unique. Generally speaking, what is termed 'Québécois' translation attempts to establish a difference between the contemporary French of Quebec and the 'French of France.' In this way, it falls in line with the programme of the new Quebec theatre, which, according to Jean-Claude Germain, must 'restore our national language to the full vigour of its true expression.'[59] But this language, which is theoretically the language of the Québécois 'nation,' displays astonishing diversity when used as a language of translation. Let us look, for example, at several extracts from the stage directions of Québécois translations:

The Search for a Native Language 183

Chekhov, *Les Trois Soeurs (The Three Sisters)*, translated by Robert Lalonde

LA MAISON DES COTÉ. UN SALON MODESTE; BEAUCOUP DE MEUBLES ET DE BIBELOTS. ATMO-SPHERE TRES « FAMILIALE » ET ORDINAIRE. LA SALLE À MANGER EST CONTIGUË AU SALON. C'EST UN DIMANCHE ENSOLEILLÉ DE PRINTEMPS.

GISÈLE EST EN UNIFORME D'INSTITUTRICE POUR JEUNES FILLES ET CORRIGE SES DEVOIRS. ANGÈLE EST ASSISE, SON CHÂLE SUR LES GENOUX ET LIT. ISABELLE EST OCCUPÉE À METTRE LA TABLE. ON VA DÎNER.

GISÈLE *(EN CORRIGEANT SES DEVOIRS)* – Ça fait un an aujourd'hui que papa est mort. Le jour de ta fête Isabelle. On gelait. J'pensais virer folle. Toi Isabelle, t'étais étendue sur le divan, blanche comme une morte... Ça fait rien qu'un an pis on peut déjà en parler comme de n'importe quoi d'autre... Tu vois, t'es-t-en robe blanche Isabelle, pis t'as l'air tellement en santé! T'es si belle dans c'te robe là. C'est avec la robe de maman que tu l'as faite?[60]

Theoretically, the translator has reproduced authentic North American rural French. The dialogue uses oral contractions such as 'j'pensais,' 'pis,' 't'as,' and 'c'te robe là.' Expressions like 'virer folle' and 'être en santé' immediately identify the speaker as French Canadian. She is a teacher and a doctor's daughter, but her speech, full of expressions like 't'es-t-en robe,' is not the speech of a cultivated person and is in marked contrast to the 'Québécois' used by the translator in his stage directions. These language choices can be explained by the fact that translators of plays into Québécois always begin by transposing the original setting into a lower register. Brigadier-General Prosorov's house becomes the house of a village notable. The 'salon' (complete with columns) 'behind which there is a large room'[61] is transformed into 'a modest living-room' with a 'very domestic and ordinary' atmosphere. We have already noted that Garneau has a tendency to remove from the original text any indicators that place the characters in a dominant social position. It could be said that, in the interests of representing *québécité* on the stage, the characters of the original work undergo a social lowering in the translation. We may well ask, then, to what extent the choice of foreign plays translated in Quebec is a function of the social position of their characters. This social lowering has a direct effect on the language used by the characters in the translation, allowing them to speak a type of language marked by phonetic, lexical, and syntactic features characteristic of speech in Quebec, and particularly characteristic of the lower classes. And it is the lower classes who must be portrayed, since portrayal of the lower classes reinforces the sovereigntist credo, based, as it is, on the concept of the alienation of the people. This ideology of difference does not allow for the neutrality of the French spoken by the educated classes in Quebec. The difference between Quebec French and the French of France is, in point of fact, a sociolectal one. This is evident in written stage directions, which carry no specific linguistic markers of Québécois speech.

Brecht, *La Bonne Âme de Se-Tchouan (The Good Person of Sechuan),* **translated by Gilbert Turp**

LE SOIR – LE VENDEUR D'EAU S'ADRESSE AU PUBLIC

WANG – *Chu vendeur d'eau* dans capitale du Setchouan: ici.
mon travail? c'est pénible
pendant les sécheresses – faut que je cours à l'autre bout du monde
pour trouver de l'eau
pis pendant les pluies ben... j'en vends pas
ce qui règne surtout dans notre belle province c'est la misère
en fin de compte – ya à peu près rien que sués Dieux
qu'on peut compter pour se faire aider
ben à ma plus grande... grande joie
j'ai appris par un marchand de bétail comme yen passe souvent dans le coin que des Dieux – pis des hauts placés – sont en route pour icite pis qu'on serait en droit de s'attendre à les recevoir
je suppose que le ciel s'est tanné de nous entendre nous plaindre vers lui dins airs.[62]

The central ideological matrix of the discourse on Québécois alienation mirrors the theme of Brecht's *Good Person of Sechuan,* a fable set in the province of Sechuan, 'which represented all those places where men exploit other men.'[63] And Quebec is one of those places where men ... By sheer chance, the first line of the play sets the tone for the theme of Québécois identity. Wang is the very symbol of the Québécois. The 'marchand d'eau' (water merchant) of the French version becomes in Quebec the 'vendeur d'eau' (water-seller). This change may appear insignificant, but the phonetic significance of the expressions chosen by the Québécois translator should not be overlooked. The 'vendeur d'eau' captures much better the sense of the 'porteur d'eau,' a term traditionally employed by Québécois to describe the inferiority of their social condition and their exploitation since the English Conquest. Elsewhere in the play, the expression 'notre province' acquires a modifier, becoming 'notre belle province,' thereby changing the referent of the discourse: Sechuan becomes an allegory for Quebec, just as Scotland does in the Québécois translation of *Macbeth:* ('les drapeaux des étranges insultent not' beau ciel' – 'foreign flags are an insult to our beautiful sky'). This new referent echoes one of the main themes of the discourse of Québécois alienation: 'Quebec is a despoiled nation,' a theme that clearly informs Garneau's idiosyncratic translation: 'O nation miserable' / 'J'appartiens à eune nation ben misérabe' and corresponds exactly to 'Chu vendeur d'eau' (I'm a water-seller). We now begin to see why translation into Québécois almost always involves proletarization of the language.[64] The pauperization of the signifier reflects the alienation of the Québécois public for whom the text is intended. The procedure used to achieve this is graphemization. By graphemization we mean the graphic realization of the difference between the phonetics of the Québécois language and those of an unmarked French: 'chu' / je suis,' 'sués' / 'sur les,' 'dins airs' / 'dans les airs.' But this transcription is not always functional. Consider, for example, Jean-Claude Germain's retranslation of Brecht's *A Respectable Wedding*:

LA MARIÉE – Ah oui... çé lui qu'y a eu l'idée pour toute han?... Y a tiré les plans, y a achté le bois, y l'a scié, y l'a sablé pis y l'a collé... parsque toute est embouffeté pis collé han... a parre les pantures, y a pas un clou... çé faitte rustique![65]

Here, the written form is tampered with to give the illusion that there is an irreconcilable difference between 'Québécois' and French. But how does the French pronunciation of words such as 'acheter,' 'embouveté,' 'parce que,' or 'à part' differ from the Québécois pronunciation, a pronunciation that is supposedly reflected in Germain's spelling? On the same page and in the mouth of the same character we find the following: 'votre oncque Hubert' and 'votte oncque Huberre.'[66] There are similar inconsistencies throughout the text. As we mentioned earlier, these inconsistencies form part of an ideological pattern: the deformed spelling, invented by Germain and presented as what he calls 'our national language,' is in fact an 'in' code that functions primarily as a form of differentiation and, consequently, a form of exclusion.

In many cases, the language used for translation resembles that used in dramatic writing, in which an alienated speech variety is realistically transposed and takes on a cathartic function. This is what Michel Tremblay set out to achieve. His plays paved the way for implementation of Michèle Lalonde's program for the Québécois language:

... the subject of *joual* as a language for the theatre has received a great deal of attention ... Many accepted it immediately, while others categorically rejected it; however, both groups spent too much time and effort on the subject, in my opinion, to the detriment of its intended use in the theatre ... As I have often said ... it is all well and good to speak of my audacity in writing in 'true' *joual*, but we must not forget what lies behind this outcast of a language, this ugly, poor, anaemic 'disgraceful' etc., etc., etc. ... It is not only the élite who have 'profoundly human problems' and it is possible to say 'I am unhappy' without a glass of Martini in one's hand ... Rose Ouimet's 'Maudit cul!' is the strongest expression of despair that a Québécoise can utter. Did the audience understand this in *Les Belles-Soeurs* or was it enough for them to be shocked because it was vulgar?[67]

The sociolect chosen by Tremblay is functional. It plays a role in the renewal of the theatrical aesthetic by modifying those norms that produce the effect of reality. The naturalistic reproduction of the language jolts people into a new awareness. But Tremblay does not claim to be supplanting what previously functioned as a referential language. *Joual* is for him simply one of those registers available in the written language:

My role is to continue to describe the working-class world, while from time to time allowing myself the luxury of a 'Lysistrata' and a 'Cité dans l'Oeuf.' But those whose role is to continue to produce such plays as 'Lysistrata' and 'Cité dans l'Oeuf,' they, too, ought to allow themselves the luxury of a 'Belles-Soeurs' occasionally ... I cannot accept people looking down their noses at *Les Belles-Soeurs* just because it is vulgar ... they should read Edward Albee, Tennessee Williams, and John Arden in English! Were the Americans and the English ashamed of coming to grips with *their 'joual'*?[68]

Michel Tremblay's *joual* plays created an opening in the literary system in Quebec. No such opening existed in the literary system of France. This new theatrical form had an important consequence; it broadened the translatability of the sociolects of Anglo-American plays, which now had a 'natural equivalent' in Quebec culture, though not in French culture: 'It is time for us to begin translating American plays ourselves! The French, whom I much admire incidentally, have the gift of "disfiguring" American theatre.'[69] The inadequacy Tremblay addresses here is systemic and was a feature of French theatre of the time, as opposed to Québécois theatre, where the translation of works by Tennessee Williams, Edward Albee, or Eugene O'Neill was no longer faced with a linguistic void. Let us look at two Québécois translations of the following extract from *Desire under the Elms*:

CABOT – I couldn't work today. I couldn't take no interest. T'hell with the farm! I'm leavin' it! I've turned the cows an' other stock loose! I've druv 'em into the woods whar they kin be free! By freein' 'em, I'm freein' myself! I'm quittin' here today! I'll set fire t'house an' barn an' watch 'em burn, an' I'll leave Yer Maw t'haunt the ashes, an' I'll will the fields back t'God, so that nothin' human kin never touch 'em! I'll be a-goin' to Californi-a.[70]

Translation by Robert Ripps and Yves Sauvageau

CABOT – J'pourrais pas travailler aujourd'hui... m'y sens pas l'coeur. Au diabe la terre! J'la lâche là! J'viens d'lâcher les vaches pis l'reste du bétail! J'les ai poussés de par le bois où c'est qu'y vont ête libes! Leu rendant la liberté, j'me la donne aussi. C't'aujourd'hui que j'pars d'ici. J'vas sacrer l'feu à maison pis à grange, m'a r'garder brûler les bâtiments... m'a laisser ta mére s'promener dins cendres... pis m'a r'mette mes champs au bon yeu comme ça y aura jamais rien d'un humain qui y toucheront. M'a m'embarquer pour la California.[71]

Translation by Michel Dumont and Marc Grégoire

CABOT – J'ai pas été capable de m'mette à l'ouvrage aujourd'hui. Ça m'tentà pas. Au yâbe la farme! J'en veux pus. Les vaches, j'les ai lâchées lousses, pis toute le resse du bétail itou! J'les ai amenées dans l'bois pour qu'y soyent libes! J'les ai libérées pis en faisant ça, J'me sus libéré moé-même! J'm'en va d'icitte pas plus tard qu'aujourd'hui! J'va sacrer l'feu à maison pis aux bâtiments; j'va les r'gârder brûler, pis toute c'que j'va laisser au fantôme de ta mére, c'est des cendres; c'est l'bon Yeu qui m'a denné la térre, j'va y r'denner à mon tour, pis y arra pus jamà rien d'humain qui va pouvouère y toucher! J'va partir pour la Califournie.[72]

The diversity of social and regional lects of vernacular French in Quebec provides the translator with a broad range of language possibilities. This 'co-linguism' exists to the same extent in France. There is no reason why a French translator should not translate O'Neill into the sociolect of farmers of any region in the country. Such a translation, however, would be considered as artificial as a translation into 'neutral' French, as Michel Tremblay is all too well aware. The target text would not meet the criteria of acceptability set by the literary institution.

To translate sociolects into French, the translator has to contend, not with an intrinsic deficiency in the linguistic system of France, but rather with *a linguistic void in the normative system of its literature*. Ideology can be detected behind the void, as Renée Balibar has shown in her study of language use and its social effect in the nineteenth-century French novel.[73] A Québécois writer managed to use language to establish a new and distinctive dramatic form. No French writer has ever managed to defy the normalizing linguistic ideology of the Republic to this end. Two social currents in Quebec made this possible – the glorification of difference and the recognition of an American component in the affirmation of the Québécois identity. Since Michel Tremblay began writing in *joual*, abundant use has been made of all the social registers of spoken French in Quebec, both on the stage and on television. Yet, it would not be unreasonable to suggest that *joualization* of the French-Canadian theatre has been influenced by the sociolectal character of the Anglo-American theatre, the most popular foreign-language theatre in Quebec. One thing is clear, the use of the vernacular, an innovation in Quebec, has led to the emergence and institutionalization of a national theatre that does not use French models. Use of the vernacular has also reinforced sovereigntist aspirations by turning the theatre into an ideological springboard. The vernacular is thus an effective vehicle for the central theme of the sovereigntist discourse – the alienation of Quebec society.

Why Translate into Québécois?

The search for a language of one's own offers one explanation for the phenomenon of retranslation. The rejection of the French of France, deemed inadequate for translating foreign plays into Québécois reality, provides another. The search for a native language also explains the phenomenon of retranslation. The 'repatriation' to Quebec of the translation of foreign works hitherto available only in French translation is seen as essential. Quebec is able to provide its own translations of foreign plays, but they will be retranslations. Retranslation is a particularly interesting phenomenon from the point of view of comments that are made in relation to it.

As it is deemed important to avoid using imported translations, Québécois translators have been known to translate from languages they are not familiar with. In such cases, the translator has to work from intermediate translations. For example, Gilles Marsolais translated Strindberg and Chekhov without knowing Swedish or Russian. The same is true of Michel Tremblay's translation of *Uncle Vanya*. Both used word-for-word transla-

The Search for a Native Language 189

tions provided by speakers familiar with the language of the original text. They then produced the definitive version by working with existing French or English translations. On occasion, the influence of these earlier translations is so pronounced that the origins of the Québécois version are hardly in doubt. A comparison of two translations of *Uncle Vanya* speaks for itself:

Michel Tremblay

SÉRÉBRIAKOV
Donner toute sa vie
    à la science,
s'habituer à son cabinet
    de travail,
à son auditoire, à des camarades
    vénérés
et, tout d'un coup,
    de but en blanc,
se retrouver dans ce sépulcre
côtoyer tous les jours
    des gens stupides
écouter des propos insignifiants...

je veux vivre, j'aime le succès

j'aime la célébrité, le bruit
    et, ici,
j'ai l'impression d'être en exil.
Pleurer sans arrêt le passé,
épier le succès des autres,
craindre la mort...
Je n'en peux plus!
Je n'en ai pas la force!
    Et là, en plus,
on ne veut pas me pardonner
ma vieillesse!

Elsa Triolet

SÉRÉBRIAKOV
Donner toute sa vie
    à la science,
être habitué à son cabinet
    de travail,
à son auditoire, à des camarades
    vénérables
et, soudain,
    on ne sait pourquoi,
se retrouver dans ce caveau,
voir tous les jours
    des gens idiots,
écouter des conversations
    qui ne présentent pas
    le moindre intérêt...
je veux vivre, j'aime le
    succès
j'aime la célébrité, le bruit,
    et, ici,
c'est l'exil.
Pleurer sans arrêt le passé
épier le succès des autres,
craindre la mort...
Je n'en peux plus
Je n'en ai pas la force!
    Et si avec ça,
on ne veut pas me pardonner
ma vieillesse![74]

The two extracts are remarkably similar. Compared with Elsa Triolet's translation, Michel Tremblay's translation contains occasional paradigmatic differences (caveau/sépulcre), but his syntax follows Triolet's almost exactly. The similarity makes one wonder what the real role of retranslation is in Quebec. In some countries, intermediate translations play an essential role. They provide access to foreign works that would remain otherwise unknown for want of a translator capable not only of reading them in the original but of translating them directly into the language of the country.[75] There are a number of explanations for the phenomenon of indirect translation in Quebec, that is to say, translation based on earlier translations. Works translated in this manner *already* exist in the target language. There can even be several contemporary translations of a single work. A number of French translations of classics from other languages have achieved canonical status – translations of Strindberg by Boris Vian, Pirandello by Benjamin Crémieux, or Chekhov by Elsa Triolet. Given the similarity between Québécois translations and their French 'models,' it is difficult to sustain the notion that a Québécois audience would find the French version hard to understand. Moreover, when the translations are by Adamov, Pitoeff, or Vitez, one can hardly claim that they do not measure up because they were not translated by theatre specialists. We may therefore conclude that, in the Quebec theatre, translations imported from France are seen to play an anti-mediating role. This is Gilbert Turp's argument: 'When I read the French translation of *Mother Courage*, no image came immediately to mind ... what was lacking in the French translation was not reflection or emotion; rather, it was evocation. The French translation of *Mother Courage* said nothing to me.'[76] This same argument is used by Michel Tremblay and Gilles Marsolais to justify their own translations, which were mediated, paradoxically, through the very French translations they wished to replace:

When he read Elsa Triolet's translation, Tremblay was struck by its relatively rigid, literary character ... He therefore invited Kim Yaroshevskaya, whose native language is Russian, to translate for him, word by word, the language of Chekhov. The result was significant and revealing. Tremblay noticed that Chekhov's language is *more natural than literary* and that Chekhovian dialogue is full of understatement. It was in this spirit that he produced his translation ... The result, and you will be able to judge for yourself, is a *direct idiom*. It is certainly closer to Chekhov than Elsa Triolet's translation, precise but not *too literary*.[77]

Director Gilles Marsolais used the same procedure in his translation of *Miss Julie*:

The Search for a Native Language 191

As I didn't know Swedish, I would not have dared to produce a French translation of *Miss Julie* except that I was fortunate to meet Ulla Ryghe, a Swedish cinematographer living in Quebec ... I was then able, thanks to her collaboration (and to her dictionaries!), to go directly to the Swedish text and to correct certain mistakes which had been carried over from translation to translation ... I compared this text to existing translations and was then able to produce the first draft of the present translation.[78]

After reworking the first translation, which he felt to be too literal, Gilles Marsolais arrived at the same conclusion as Michel Tremblay:

The result was a second, more direct, more 'spoken' translation, a translation more immediately accessible to the public and, finally, I believe, closer to the spirit of Strindberg.[79]

The similarity of argumentation is striking. Paradoxically, ignorance of the source language led the two translators to discover the 'truth' of the original text that previous translations, and especially French translations, had concealed. According to Tremblay, the two English translations of *Uncle Vanya* are more 'natural, simpler and closer to us.'[80] The literariness, or artificiality that the Québécois translator criticizes in French translations can be seen as proof that the distance between the vernacular and the literary language is no longer the same in France as it is in Quebec. This is especially true for the theatre. The new Québécois theatre has achieved its own singularity, by doing away with this linguistic distinction. It has given the *koine*, the language of the home and the street, its status as a literary language. To conform to the criteria of acceptability in the new Québécois theatre system, the translation of a work like *Mademoiselle Julie* by Boris Vian must be shorn of its French literariness. This is precisely what G. Marsolais did in his translation:

Boris Vian

JEAN – Je rêve d'ordinaire
que je suis couché sous un
grand arbre dans une forêt
obscure. Je veux monter,
monter au sommet, pour voir
le clair paysage tout brillant
de soleil, et dénicher le nid

Gilles Marsolais

JEAN – Moi, Je rêve
d'ordinaire que je suis
couché sous un grand arbre
dans une forêt sombre. Et
j'ai envie de monter,
monter jusqu'au sommet,
pour regarder le clair pay-

où dorment les oeufs d'or.[81]   sage où brille le
soleil et dérober les oeufs
d'or de cette nichée.[82]

Marsolais's retranslation has removed the poetic scansion that reinforces the expression of the dream, but, aside from that, in what other ways is his translation particularly Québécois? We are dangerously close to the ideology of 'the language of one's own' and of solipsism when a work written in or translated into the French of France is rejected on the grounds that it would be inaccessible to the Québécois public. Monique Mercure, who played Mother Courage in Gilbert Turp's Québécois translation, has this to say:

In the French translation there are occasional expressions that I didn't understand and a different syntax; these have become patently clear in this translation. If, for example, I had had to act in the French translation of the play, I would have had to read the English translation to grasp all the subtleties and all the nuances. This is often the case for French translations of foreign writers.[83]

The French translation, understood by the Québécois public for decades, suddenly becomes opaque and inaccessible to this very same public. To understand the French text, the francophone reader in Quebec must henceforth make a detour by way of English, that is to say, via a foreign language. Granted, what the actress is really objecting to in French translations is the 'polished' language that detracts from the original text.

According to Gilles Marsolais, it would be abnormal if a foreign-language play were not 'translated or adapted by a Québécois before being staged.'[84] Given the desire to reterritorialize, the nationality of the translator becomes, apparently, a major criterion for legitimizing translations of plays staged in Quebec and for ensuring their acceptance. Yet Marsolais echoes Boris Vian, who himself foresaw the necessity for a 'new Francicization of *Julie* ... as part of the evolution of the language of the French theatre.'[85] In 1968, the language of the theatre in Quebec underwent a revolution of truly Copernican proportions. Québécois translators had good reason for trying to bridge the gap between the language of the French theatre and the language of the new theatre. For Tremblay and for many others, Québécois translations are more effective on the stage than French translations because they make use of an oralcy that echoes everyday speech. And indeed, parts of the dialogue in Michel Tremblay's translation of *Uncle Vanya* are markedly different from those of Elsa Triolet's version:

Tremblay

MARINA – On est touttes des pique-assiette chez le bon Dieu. Toi, comme Sonia, comme Ivan Pétrovitch, personne reste à rien faire, on travaille toutes! Toutes... Ousqu'est Sonia

TÉLÉGUINE – Au jardin. Avec le docteur, ils cherchent Ivan Pétrovitch partout. Ils ont peur qu'il se fasse du mal.

MARINA – Pis ousqu'i est son fusil?

Elsa Triolet

MARINA – Nous sommes tous des parasites chez le bon Dieu. Toi, comme Sonia, comme Ivan Pétrovitch, personne ici ne reste à ne rien faire, tous nous travaillons! Tous... Où est Sonia?

TÉLÉGUINE – Au jardin. Elle est avec le docteur, ils cherchent partout Ivan Pétrovich. Ils ont peur qu'il n'attente à sa vie.

MARINA – Et où est son pistolet?

The difference between these two translations reflects the difference between French and Québécois literary codes for the theatre. In the Québécois theatre, the 'naturalist' code is the equivalent of the French literary code. This is clearly exemplified in Tremblay's plays. But in his translation of *Uncle Vanya*, the naturalist code is found only in the language employed by Marina. If we compare Tremblay's and Triolet's translations of the play, it becomes clear that there is only a fine line between the theatrical language of the two countries. It is even finer in Gilles Marsolais's translation of *Mademoiselle Julie*. His Québécois translation of the play belies what, as a translator, he says of his work: 'our approach to international French is far removed from that of our French cousins. We have a vocabulary, a spirit, which are all our own.' He has hidden this irreconcilable difference extremely well:

JULIE – Assez pour commencer! Viens avec moi! Je ne puis voyager seule aujourd'hui, le jour de la Saint-Jean, entassée dans un train étouffant, au milieu d'une foule de gens qui vous dévisagent! Et le train qui s'arrête à chaque station, quand on voudrait voler! Non, je ne peux pas. Je ne peux pas![86]

Is this not the language of an aristocrat? The cook expresses herself in an international Québécois as refined as that of her mistress, even if occasionally she uses a local turn of phrase emphasizing her status as a woman of the 'people':

CHRISTINE – Écoutez Jean, voulez-vous venir danser avec moi quand j'aurai fini? [...]

Oh, ses mauvais jours approchent et elle est toujours à l'envers *dans ce temps-là*. Venez-vous danser avec moi maintenant?[87]

There is, however, a difference between the language used to translate and the language used by translators to discuss their translations, especially when the translators are playwrights or directors, and therefore belong to the theatre. Quite clearly, they are trying to dissociate themselves from their French cultural and linguistic heritage. They are trying to place a *cordon sanitaire* around their burgeoning theatre, but they have failed to create a distinctive language for the theatre, a language that could be used as a systematic and coherent language of translation. When the chosen target language is a sociolect that is distinctively Québécois, we are immediately struck by the diglossia between the translation, on the one hand, and the preface and instructions to the directors or actors, on the other. The justification for the 'Quebecization' of foreign texts is written in a language that no longer bears any trace of its *québécité*. We have already observed that the language translators use to translate is not the same as the language they use to explain to their Québécois readers that the play was translated for the express purpose of putting it within their reach. Gilles Marsolais and Jean-Claude Germain are, each in his own way, the most obvious examples of this tendency. Québécois translators are inconsistent, in that they employ both the vernacular and the referential language. However, the role of the languages is reversed: the vernacular is used to translate the foreign text, while the referential language is used to comment on the text. Translations into Québécois therefore play an ideological rather than a mediating role. The diglossia between the dialogue and the commentary or stage directions in these translations demonstrates to what extent the audience is being manipulated. The discourse on language used by translators, who often double as playwrights, enables them to introduce an ideology of *québécité* to the public, a public from which they exclude themselves.

Conclusion

Our analysis has demonstrated that, during the period under study, theatre translation in Quebec was regulated by phenomena that ultimately revolve around the concealment of alterity. In a country where the hegemony of the Other, the English, is all powerful and all consuming, the Self must be 'invented.' The translator therefore assumes the task of *inventing the Self* in the foreign text; and this *invention of the Self* extends all the way to the invention of a language of one's own, the *invention of a native language.*

This contradiction in terms, in which the *foreign* text is used to invent the *Self*, may appear to be paradoxical. However, our analysis has revealed that the search for an identity, a focus of theatre translation throughout these two decades, was indeed deeply rooted in a *doxa*, or collective viewpoint, that created a totally fictitious Other. At issue then is the invention of the Other, or as Derrida puts it: '... is the invention of the Other, an absolute initiative for which the Other is responsible and which is its prerogative? Or is it what I imagine *of the Other* still retained in my *psyche*, my soul or the me of my mirror image?'[1]

The discourse of liberation transforms the Other into an entity devoid of interest. The Other is either directly identified with the English, who are considered too familiar to be worthy of attention, or seen as absolutely too unfamiliar, and deemed incapable of producing a recognizable reflection of the Self. Quite simply, the Other must respond to a need for identity. At best, the Other is given an instrumental role, that of a mirror in which one tries to find the image of oneself. However, this image is a preconstruct: the sought-after identity is already present in all domains of social discourse. Thus, the paradox of inventing the Self in the foreign text is not a true paradox; the Self does not need to be invented. Initially, the search for an identity in Quebec was a defence mechanism. Then, creating an identity became an ideological imperative and took a new direction – a search for *legitimization*. Clearly, the identity created by the nationalist discourse can be legitimized only through some form of invention: invention of the Other, which makes it possible to *forget* the Other.

In this context, translation both obfuscates and assimilates the Foreigner. Naturalization of foreign plays is a prerequisite for their *acceptance* into the literary institution, as well as for their *relevance* in a wider field of the discourse permeated by the nationalist doxa. To give a text from outside Quebec a profile that conforms to the symbolic representations of the Québécois collectivity in social discourse, the translator 'forgets' markers of alterity, obliterating them through transference of the context of the utterance. In other words, the translator reverses the normal direction of communication in a translation. The translator's task is no longer to introduce the receiver to that which is unusual or original in the foreign work, but rather to turn the foreign work into a vehicle for representing the 'Québécois fact.' Driven by this preoccupation with identity, the translation fulfils, above all, a doxological function. Its objective is no longer to transmit the discourse of the Foreigner; rather, it is to use the Foreigner as a vehicle for its own discourse, the discourse of national liberation. The doxological function reinforces the aesthetic function, and vice versa. During the period under discussion, especially in the 1970s, these two functions were mutually supportive. On the one hand, a national theatre had to be created, a process which made liberal use of deforming and iconoclastic translation practices. On the other hand, the emerging theatre had to be seen as a specifically 'Québécois' theatre; in other words, it had to make the Québécois aware of their identity. This imperative directly influenced the selection and transformation of foreign texts, which were chosen according to the capacity of their plot and dialogue to echo Québécois social discourse; a discourse constructed around a set of ideologemes whose nodal points were colonization, alienation, exploitation, marginalization, and (the positive side of this doxa) independence.

The relation to the Foreigner that emerged in translative practices during this period closely paralleled political events of the time which were paving the way for national affirmation and formation of a Québécois state. The 1980 referendum marked a turning-point in this process. From then on, the number of Québécois translations increased rapidly, replacing translations from France. A large proportion of the plays produced during this period were Québécois works, rather than foreign works, giving the lie to those critics who suggest that the converse was true. Our analysis has shown that, during periods dominated by the nationalist question, the major theatres kept the Foreigner at bay, as if to give more voice to the sovereigntist doxa. Furthermore, the productions put on by these major theatres contributed to the institutionalization of Québécois theatre, to its emergence and consecration. Translation, which during this period was annexing in nature, and even *agonic* in its use of adaptation and parody, helped Québécois theatre take over the dominant institutional position hitherto held by foreign theatre.

Language is at the heart of the doxa of identity. Language 'distinguishes' the Québécois from the English and from the French. It marks in a tangible way the Québécois 'difference' and is thus the very symbol of the legitimacy of sovereigntist aspirations. The main aim of Québécois social discourse is to dislodge the foreigner's hegemony incarnated in official bilingualism. Official bilingualism makes translation omnipresent and creates a situation in which the French language tends to melt into English. Québécois social discourse expresses the fear that Quebec is a society in danger of losing its voice for ever. In the name of 'difference,' this discourse also rejects French, classifying it as a foreign tongue so as to facilitate the emergence of the 'Québécois language.' Sometimes, as we have seen, this Québécois language assumes an Edenic form, a language invented out of nostalgia for a pre-Conquest Quebec. On other occasions, it 'scrambles' the French language to create its own difference. Sometimes, it even reproduces a sociolect and proposes it as a native or national language. But the translator speaks two languages: the language of the 'Québécois text' is often different from the language of commentary on the text. We can say, then, that the Québécois language is an ideological fiction serving the nationalist doxa, a fact clearly demonstrated by the diglossia of the translator and the linguistic instability of translated works. Moreover, when works are translated into Québécois, there is a reversal of roles; the foreign work helps the language of translation to emerge in the receiving society, and not the reverse. This treatment of the foreign text can be seen as a form of subjection, a subjection contained in the phrase 'traduit en québécois.' The phrase underlines the marginality of the Québécois language, a language that, paradoxically, translation must 'put to the test' as a literary language. Such manipulation of language is an expression of the search for a distinctive, self-sufficient code. It is one of a number of practices that use the pretext of 'decolonization' to keep Québécois society isolated and to construct a void around its imaginary.

At the same time, during this period, translation was charged with the task of responding to the need of people to be heard and to be recognized outside Quebec, for recognition would prove that they *existed*. Today, this has been achieved. Quebec has made its mark on the political landscape. After the 'death' of the Meech Lake Accord, it remains only to work out the modalities of a sovereignty, which has been more or less gained in principle. Thus, translation has paid its patriotic dues, and today, the translator need no longer wonder whether *Romeo and Juliet* must be set on the banks of the St Lawrence. There is a return to an international repertoire and renewed interest in foreign works. The way is now open for these works, as the existence and originality of Québécois plays are no longer in question. Québécois works, in the words of Dominique Lafon, 'initially played on parodic reference, until they started conquering textuality. We could say that they went all the way from memory to theatrical independence ...'[2] Now that Québécois plays have achieved textual autonomy, they have even begun to be exported. The plays of Michel Tremblay, Marie Laberge, Gilles Maheu, Robert Lepage, René-Daniel Dubois, and Michel Marc Bouchard have been performed in cities such as Paris, London, Brussels, Milan, Barcelona, and Caracas. A discourse of *universality* in the theatre has replaced a discourse of national specificity. The new theatre is seeking to be part of a global cultural heritage. The Québécois theatre has freed itself from immediate political imperatives, including the obligation to use a 'shattered' language. The main focus of the new Québécois theatre is aesthetic experimentation. Directors like Gilles Maheu and Denis Marleau, who worked on the fringe during the period of nationalist theatre, are today receiving official recognition. Their openness to a new aesthetic is clearly evident in their choice of repertoire (Heiner Müller, Kurt Schwitters, Botho Strauss, Raymond Queneau, Alfred Jarry, etc.), as well as in their productions, which are based on theatricality in the true sense of the word. Their highly original, avant-garde theatre has been internationally recognized.

Experimental theatre has, of course, always existed, but it did not form part of our study, whose focus was the *dominant* theatrical institution, an institution that, by definition, best reflects the *dominant* social discourse. Experimental theatre is not popular with the public and has had a precarious existence in Quebec. Theatre groups like Eskabel, which refused to make any concessions to the prevailing nationalism, disappeared. However, in more recent years, in its pursuit of international cultural recognition, the theatrical institution has promoted experimental theatre.

Confinement to regionalism is now seen as a trap – this awareness, which had influenced the novel in the 1960s, was a long time coming to the theatre. Moreover, the way Quebec sees itself has changed – its entrepreneurial prowess and its economic successes are now being given prominence. It is no longer acceptable to portray Quebec as a society in decline, through a language itself in decline. The theatre is participating in this new image of Quebec with a renewed focus on the aesthetic. This probably explains the success of experimental theatre, which has become Quebec's window on the outside world; witness, for example, the critical praise heaped upon productions by Robert Lepage, Gilles Maheu, and Denis Marleau in the European and Latin American press. This new context has inevitably introduced new translation practices, practices which coexist, however, with older ones. What better example than translations of Shakespeare such as the rhymed 'textual' translation of *A Midsummer Night's Dream* by Michelle Allen,[3] alongside *Squat: As you like it* by La Compagnie Béton Blues, in which R. Villeneuve transforms Elizabethan courtiers into Montreal financiers, and shepherds into department-store clerks; and finally, in between, an adaptation of *The Tempest* by Michel Garneau, in which one finds not a single trace of the regional language used in the Québécois version of *Macbeth*.

Our case-study of the socio-discursive framework of the translative operation allows us to draw the following conclusions regarding literary theory and translation theory. Our study has provided a better understanding of how and why the literary system of a society absorbs certain foreign works rather than others. In a society preoccupied with national identity, such works have both a literary and a doxological function. They contribute to the emergence of a national literature. Quebec's experience is no different from that of many other societies in history, for example, sixteenth-century France, where the emerging state apparatus was reinforced by a national language, and where translation, which was also ethnocentrically driven, provided basic materials for the construction of a distinctly French literature. Thus, when translation becomes an active participant in the development of a literary genre, as it did in the theatre in Quebec, an examination of translation practices can reveal how works emerge and become legitimized within the literary institution. Analysis of these practices sheds light on the tensions in the system, and thereby on the conditions governing literary exchanges and, more generally, cultural exchanges, in a given society. The methodology employed in our case-study of Quebec can also be applied, relatively speaking, to other *emerging literatures* (African, Caribbean, or North American regional and minority literatures), whose emergence and development are linked to a new awareness or redefinition of collective identity.

Of primary interest to translation theory in this study of the Québécois theatrical institution is the role of the translating subject, who is rarely considered in the literature on translation. Yet the translator hardly meets the ideal of transparency, with its objective of faithfulness, ever presented as an inherent part of the translative operation. Analysis of translation as a form of discourse reveals the unconscious and ideological symbols at play in the act of translating. Psychoanalysis has examined the role of the unconscious in the translation process. However, very little has been written on how the translating subject is constrained by the order of discourse in the society for which he or she acts as spokesperson.

Our analysis forms part of those writings on translation that are attempting to break with the prescriptive nature of the vast majority of the literature in the field. Traditionally, such writings attempt to show how one 'should' translate, the prescriptiveness being a function of the speculative nature of their approach. By basing our analysis on an actual case-study, we have extended the field of translation theory. Instead of basing analysis on an isolated text, the traditional practice, our research focused on a number of texts belonging to the same discourse category and sharing the same spatio-temporal coordinates. By thus enlarging the field of analysis, we were able to integrate parameters whose covariations never reveal themselves in a simple comparison of a text and its translation. This approach makes it possible to assess disparities between source texts and target texts by criteria that are not based simply on value judgments ('well translated' or 'badly translated'). These disparities form a system and derive their meaning from the discursive framework of the whole society from which translations emanate.

This approach has enabled us to broaden traditional description of the links between discourse and translation. For translation theorists such as those of the interpretative school, discourse is concerned with the context of an utterance, in the immediate and, hence, narrow sense of the term. We have shown that, in the translation process, the utterance is subject to other constraints, constraints that are less apparent but just as powerful. These constraints derive from a network of presuppositions that maintain the coherence and acceptability of social discourse in all its manifestations.

Notes

Foreword

1 In fact, the two pitfalls of the ethical discourse on translation are moralizing dogmatism and naïvety.

Introduction

1 See the critical inventory of these contradictory rules drawn up by A.P. Frank (1983, 203). These contradictions are also found in the false debate between 'sourciers et ciblistes' (source and target-oriented theoreticians), categories proposed by J.R. Ladmiral (1986).
2 Delisle, 1980, 29–32
3 Foucault, 1972, 117
4 Robin, 1973, 21; our translation
5 Ibid
6 Even-Zohar, 1979; see also 1978. For an overview of works on polysystem theory, see Dimic and Garstin, 1988. Among works on systemic changes and the evolution of a literary genre in a given synchrony, see D'Hulst, 1987. Polysystem theory as specifically applied to translation is developed in Toury, 1980; the theory is similarly explored in Hermans, 1985.
7 On the theory of interdiscourse – in particular, the relation between literature and other discourses – see Link and Link-Heer, 1980; see also Moser, 1985.
8 Belleau, 1981, 16
9 Ibid
10 Meschonnic, 1973, 321

11 Belleau, 1981, 16; our translation
12 Ibid, 15
13 Lefebvre, 1978, 34; our translation
14 For 'systemic' investigation procedures for a corpus of translations, see Toury, 1980, in particular 51–62. See also Lambert, 1980; Lambert and Van Gorp, 1985; and Van Den Broeck, 1985. For the specificity of theatre translation see, among recent works, Bassnett-McGuire, 1985, and Pavis, 1990, in particular 135–70. On the same subject, see the following practitioners: Vitez, Déprats, Schwarzinger, and Jourdheuil; cf. *Theatre/Public* (1982) and the *Assises de la traduction littéraire (Arles, 1989)*.
15 Belleau, 1981, 17; our translation
16 Cf. Graham, 1985
17 Belleau, 1981, 16
18 J. Delisle (1980, 29–31) provides the best summary of this position, a common viewpoint in works on translation.
19 Belleau, 1981, 15
20 Bakhtin, 1973, 93
21 Angenot, 1979
22 Cf. Angenot, 1989
23 Châtelet, 1979, 89; our translation
24 Ibid, 89–90
25 Angenot, 1977, 24; our translation
26 Ibid
27 Foucault, 1972, 72
28 Angenot, 1977, 26
29 Châtelet, 1979, 90
30 Lévesque, 1982, 222
31 Belleau, 1981, 17
32 However, we see more publication of translations of novels and essays. Cf. Simon, 1989, 77–100
33 E. Nardocchio (1986) analyses the role of the socio-political context in the creation and evolution of a truly Québécois French theatre from its beginnings, particularly from the 1930s, or the beginning of the Duplessis era, a period known as 'La Grande Noirceur' (the Great Darkness), up to the end of the 1970s. See also Englebertz, 1989.
34 Szanto, 1978, 6

1: The Foreigner in the Theatrical Institution

1 Dubois, 1978, 16; our translation

2 For a precise definition of these terms, see Pavis, 1987, 32–3 and 419–22. We will use the term 'adaptation' here in the generic sense given to it by directors and theatre publishers.
3 R. Dionne, *Le Devoir*, 15 Feb. 1986; quoted by J. Delisle in 'Faits, dits et chiffres,' in *Circuit* 19. (Dec. 1987), 35; our translation
4 In this 'foreign' series, we note the presence of three Anglo-Canadian plays, one of which is Anglo-Québécois.
5 Dagenais, 1981, 10
6 Ibid, 3; our translation
7 Ibid, 10
8 Ibid
9 Stratford, 1977, 42
10 Simon (1987) points out that 'the tradition of literary translation has been weak, compared, for example, with that of English Canada, where there has been a clear interest in Québécois literature since the end of the nineteenth century.' On the other hand, she adds, 'few literary works were translated in Quebec before 1970 ... The context of national identity in which Québécois publishing evolved after 1960 explains the clear priority given by publishers to local production' (5–6; our translation). Similarly, the case of Mavis Gallant is symptomatic of the lack of interest shown by the Québécois (French-speaking) publishing industry in Quebec writers writing in English. M. Gallant published 'eight collections of short stories, two novels, and one play between 1955 and 1980. Yet she remained unknown to francophones in Quebec until 1980, when her first collection of short stories was published in French, as if it was the work of a foreigner': N. Zandes, 'Mavis Gallant, Québécoise de langue anglaise', in *Le Monde*, 13 Nov. 1987, 24; our translation
11 'Bibliography. Quebec Plays Available in English Translation,' in *Théâtre Québec*, May 1987
12 Herbert, 1971, 11; our translation
13 Bélair, 'Aux yeux des hommes: Une exaspérante vision,' in Herbert, 1971, 97; our translation
14 This is a dominant theme in M. Bélair's *Le Nouveau Théâtre québécois* (1973).
15 Brassard and Tremblay, 1969, back cover; our translation
16 J. Éthier-Blais expresses this idea in a striking turn of phrase, 'l'être national' or 'the national being': 'For a Soviet, an Albanian, or a Québécois, literature is inseparable from politics. The national being is moulded by it. Nature itself is there to serve the collective future. The concept of literature is different from that in countries like France or Italy, which are no longer troubled by problems of historical survival' (in *Le Devoir*, 5 Dec. 1987, D10; our translation). The concept of a national being faced with a precarious future enables us to under-

stand better the parallel between Greece and Quebec contained in the analogy presented in *Lysistrata*.
17 Cardinal, 1986, 9
18 Ibid, 125
19 Ibid, 116
20 Ibid, 125
21 Les Éditions VLB recently changed this practice. In translations of *The Tempest* (1989) and *Coriolanus* (1989) by Michel Garneau, the words 'translated by' appear.
22 Now that Québécois theatre has broadened its foreign repertoire, directors like Gilles Maheu can successfully produce foreign works such as H. Müller's *Depraved Shore*, in which the myth of Medea is used to create a theatrical aesthetic, with no concessions to popular taste.
23 Cardinal, 1986, 122–3
24 Ibid, 25
25 M. Tremblay, from an interview with the magazine *Nord*, reproduced in the *Cahiers de la NCT* 1 (Oct. 1974), 10; our translation
26 Zindel, 1970, 7; our translation
27 Gruslin and Lamoureux, 1983. 102; our translation
28 Germain, 'L'Honnête Monsieur Marchand' (1977, 169–76); our translation
29 Simon, 1987, 7
30 Ibid, 7
31 'How Yvon Deschamps and Jean-Louis Roux came to put on *L'Ouvre-boîte* and how the author discovered a totally new play when he arrived in Montreal, in an unbelievable snowstorm,' in Lanoux, 1976, 8–9; our translation
32 Théâtre du Rideau Vert, Théâtre du Nouveau Monde, Théâtre de Quat'Sous, Nouvelle Compagnie Théâtrale, Théâtre d'Aujourd'hui, Compagnie Jean-Duceppe, and Théâtre du Trident
33 According to A. Gruslin, 'the expression "Institutional Theatre" first appeared in a document from the Ministère des Affaires culturelles, in which it defined its policy on financial assistance to the best-known theatre in Quebec, a group that it described as the "most dynamic." This was in 1977.' Gruslin does not go along with this definition: 'The MAC is wrong in its choice of words. The most popular, the best-known, and the most lucrative is not necessarily the most dynamic. Because it is so established, it could even become pigeonholed in a particular genre from which it can't escape. In the end, it is much more static than dynamic': Gruslin, 1981, 30; our translation
34 See in particular Gruslin, 1981, 27–72.
35 Colbert, 1979, 29
36 Gruslin, 1981, 29, note 2

37 Ibid, 32
38 The catalogue of plays in translation provides an example of this: *Les Cloches d'enfer* (*The Bells of Hell*) by the *Anglo-Québécois* writer Mordecai Richler. The term 'Anglo-Quebécois' may seem inappropriate, but it is typical of the restrictions, implicit or explicit, commonly found in the social discourse: the meaning of the word 'Québécois' assumes different configurations whose semantic shape expands in election debates and contracts in letters to daily newspapers.
39 Bélair, 1973, 13, 24
40 Béraud, 1958, 7
41 Bélair, 1973, 12; our translation
42 Ibid, 25
43 To the question: 'What do you think of Michel Tremblay?' René Richard Cyr, director of *Bonjour, là, bonjour* at Le TNM, replied: 'One of our own writers has succeeded in being both popular and profound.' Note that the most important thing about a Québécois writer is that he is 'one of our own writers.' The writer's origin then becomes a factor when comparisons are made. In A. Ducharme's interview with R.R. Cyr in the program for *Bonjour, là, Bonjour*, TNM, 17 Nov.–12 Dec. 1987, 9
44 Bélair, 1973, 25
45 For the origins and consequences of this ideology of difference, see Taguieff, 1985.
46 Bélair, 1973, 62
47 Ibid, 60
48 For federal, provincial, and municipal grants received by each of these institutional companies, see Gruslin, 1981, 131–54.
49 The proportion of francophones among neo-Québécois and their socio-professional status is yet to be established. However, it would be useful to examine the real status of neo-Québécois in Quebec culture and the place they are allowed to occupy within the literary institution, and under what conditions they may do so. For example, it would be interesting to compare the reaction of the media to neo-Québécois productions and to native Québécois productions. The reaction to *La Petite Noirceur* by Jean Larose and *Du Canada au Québec* by Heinz Weinmann, two works that appeared at the same time, is a case in point. The Québécois writer was immediately given star treatment and put forward for a literary award. In contrast, the *legitimacy* of the neo-Québécois author's discourse, which, it is true, rubs nationalist orthodoxy up the wrong way, was the main theme of one of those rare Québécois examinations of his work.

Another example: the nature of the attacks against the *transcultural* orientation (revealingly called 'confusionist') of *Vice Versa*, 'a glossy magazine controlled by *Canadian* intellectuals of Italian origin, living in Quebec, which is *generously funded* by the two levels of government' (Piotte, 1988, 55; our translation, emphasis added). With respect to the Foreigner's right to speak out, the sequence and contents of the articles in the journal *Conjonctures* 10–11 [Fall 1988]) whose theme is 'Quebec and the Other' are of considerable interest.

50 Bélair, 1973, 44–5. The play referred to was performed in 1969 at Le Quat'Sous.
51 *The Lower Depths* was produced at Le TNM during the 1993–4 season, directed by Claude Poissant. *The Suicide*, written in 1929, was published for the first time in 1973 in a Russian-language journal published in New York; it was performed in Canada in 1986 at the Theatre School of the University of Ottawa, under the direction of William Weiss.
52 Bélair, 1973, 60
53 R. Tessier, from a review in *Photo Journal*, 16 Apr. 1966. Reproduced in the postscript of G. Gélinas, *Hier, les enfants dansaient*, 151–2
54 J. Basile, *Le Devoir*, 13 Mar. 1966; quoted by M. Bélair (1973, 41), who echoes Basile's observations.
55 Bélair, 1973, 41–2
56 'For a situation is tragic, not because it involves suffering, sacrifice, and death, but because every possible course of action leads to an inextricable tangle of right and wrong, guilt and innocence, compulsion and freedom of choice ... Nothing is so characteristic of modern tragedy as the factor of alienation': 'The Birth of Modern Tragedy,' in Hauser, 1968, 137. See also A. Miller, 'Tragedy and the Common Man,' in Martin, 1978, 3.
57 Gruslin, 1981, 37
58 Bélair, 1973, 66
59 Ibid, 43
60 Ibid, 66
61 J. Morisset, 'Cent ans après sa mort, c'est la nationalisation de Louis Riel,' in *Le Devoir*, 30 Nov. 1985, 11; our translation. In another context, M. Rioux (1974, 20–1) observes: 'Towards the end of the French régime in Quebec, the "Canadiens," that is to say, the francophone natives, were inclined to oppose the metropolitan French and emphasized their Americanness because it was this that best distinguished them from the French ... After the English Conquest, religious and political élites emphasized other differences to distinguish Québécois from the English and the Americans: the French language and the Catholic religion. Americanness was concealed ... As the rest of North America was English and Protestant, and as they wished to differentiate themselves from these groups, the Americanness of the Québécois was minimized and suppressed' (our translation).

62 Taken to its logical conclusion, this argument makes it possible to invoke the right of first occupancy, and at the same time effaces memories of a conquest before *the* Conquest, which places the 'French' (but never the 'Québécois') in the role of aggressor. The Québécois, who are American, that is to say, natives, have been here forever. M. Rioux defines 'Canadiens' as 'francophone natives.' The term 'native' usually refers to someone belonging to an ethnic group already living in a land *before* its colonization. In this context, employing 'native' to describe the Québécois is tantamount to eradicating memories of the conquest and the colonization of the indigenous native inhabitants.

This 'loss of memory' returned with a vengeance when Elijah Harper, a First Nations member of the Manitoba legislature, prevented ratification of the Meech Lake Accord and, as a result, Quebec's inclusion in the Canadian constitution. The reaction of writer Claude Jasmin is instructive: 'A squatter who takes possession of Crown land, works it, develops it, and constructs his home there, becomes the owner of that land ... The Native people ... were nomads. They lived by fishing and hunting and the very idea of developing the land left them cold': *Le Devoir*, 28 June 1990, 12; our translation. Thus, there was no violence involved in the appropration of these 'wastelands.' In a reference to what was supposed to have been a harmonious fusion of the two groups, the violence of the 'squatter' is similarly denied: 'What can we say except that Québécois culture became an indigenous culture just like aboriginal cultures?' (P. Constantineau, 'Le Multiculturalisme du malentendu. Une Orientation qui sape le Canada en niant le Québec,' in *Le Devoir*, 13 July 1990, 13; our translation). A rhetorical question, to be sure. A similar question, equating Native struggles and sovereigntist demands in Quebec – 'Québécois and Natives, the same struggle?' – appears as a headline on the opinion page of the same newspaper. The following answer is provided: 'The fact that your struggle echoes the most vital interests of Québécois, themselves ridiculed and scorned, is a just meeting of our two peoples in history' (*Le Devoir*, 9 July 1990, 11; our translation). Several days later, making a mockery of metaphorical references to the 'same struggle,' Mohawks in Quebec made territorial claims, bringing home to the Québécois the brutal truth of the 'conquest' of the ancestral lands of the First Nations.

63 Berman, 1985, 48

64 At the time, the movement was becoming normative. A good example is the production of a Jean Tardieu show by Le Grenier du Carré, in November 1985, at the Salle Calixa-Lavallée, directed by Liliane Knight. The director, who was born in France, replaced two or three Paris Métro station names with Montreal subway-station names, out of respect for the Québécois public, but this could also be interpreted as an act of self-censorship. This was the only substitution

made, and it was incongruous in a text in which it was clearly out of place. However, this change had been considered appropriate. It represented a sort of cultural 'Finlandization,' subtly prompted by the prevailing *doxa*.

2: At the Other's Expense: Iconoclastic Translation

1 This unpublished version of the play was produced by Le Théâtre du Nouveau Monde during the 1968–9 season.
2 A. Pontaut, '*Les Belles-Soeurs* de Michel Tremblay cinq ans après,' in Tremblay, 1972, vi
3 For an analysis of this phenomenon, see Léonard and Siguret, 1972.
4 Darbelnet, 1984, 20; our translation
5 Germain, 1983, 91; our translation
6 *Lord Durham's Report*, vol. 2 (New York: Augustus M. Kelley, 1970), 294
7 Germain, 1983, 52; our translation, emphasis added. In cases where the language of the original text is of particular pertinence or of *linguistic* interest to the reader, we have cited it along with its English translation.
8 Ibid, 134
9 Ibid, 26
10 Ibid, 89
11 Ibid, 88–90
12 Ibid, 98
13 This theme is found in many works on Quebec. One of the best known is *Le Canadien français et son double* by J. Bouthillette, whose influence is clear in Germain's play. The main themes of *A Canadian Play* appear in the first chapter, entitled 'Dépersonnalisation': 'Still an open wound, our past, even if we remember just a certain aspect of it, seems to snatch us as if to pull us down into the abyss forever. We flee the image that the mirror of collective interiorization shows us ... The French Canadian is a man with two shadows. We pretend to escape from this, but in vain: the English shadow is always with us, everywhere. And in this shadow we become a shadow' (1972, 13–15; our translation).
14 Germain, 1983, 93
15 Ibid, 19
16 Ibid, 20
17 Miron, 1970, 127
18 The play opened at Le Théâtre d'Aujourd'hui in April 1979, but it was not published until 1983. In the interim, there was the referendum on sovereignty-association, whose result, as we know, was negative. The play, which makes a case for anti-federalism, begins with a preface in which Germain places his

work in historical perspective and attempts to explain the underlying causes of the defeat of the sovereigntists. The text of the play is followed by biographies on each of the four main protagonists – Lord Durham, W. Laurier, L. Saint-Laurent, and P.E. Trudeau, who was prime minister of Canada at the time. The biographies, in the 'man and his work' style, emphasize the double power base (francophone and anglophone) of the three Canadian politicians; they also link the political beliefs of the three men with the spirit of the Durham Report, from which Germain includes long extracts.

19 Germain, 1983, 23
20 Ibid, 43
21 Bouthillette, 1972, 14
22 A good illustration of this is the fact that foreign names, whatever their origin, are always pronounced with an English accent. The impact of this phenomenon, which is particularly striking on French-Canadian radio and television, was analyzed by A. Belleau in an essay entitled 'L'Effet Derome': 'The real question is the following: What is the *Téléjournal* supposed to say and what does it really say when [anchorman] Bernard Derome speaks English through French? ... For years, through the Derome effect, Radio-Canada has been telling its listeners that their language is only good enough for familiar things and for their immediate milieu, that these sounds, which have a very special status should be muffled and should withdraw as soon as the ELSEWHERE appears on the scene, in short, that French is incapable of PRONOUNCING the world, of saying it, in the strictly physical sense of the term. Worse – and perhaps more serious – certain variations of the Derome effect ... tend to give the public the impression that *alterity* is solely English and that is all there is on the horizon. But this alterity defines the horizon and, in doing so, closes it off ... This is the model imposed by Radio-Canada: language cannot absorb plurality, it must be subjected to the sound system of the one and only language: English. In fact, this plurality does not exist anymore because Max Ernst and Oswald Spengler are Americans and Dunkirk is a town in Texas ...' (1984, 83–5; our translation, emphasis in the original).
23 Germain, 1983, 23
24 Miron, 1970, 'Notes sur le non-poème et le poème,' 122–4; our translation
25 Chamberland, 1969, 67
26 Berman, 1984, 75
27 Germain, 1983, 25
28 Curiously, the memory of alterity goes back no farther than the British conquest. As already indicated, the 'colonized' francophone forgets that he was *originally* a colonizer, himself the perpetrator of a similar trauma inflicted on Native peoples, who were dispossessed of their ancestral lands, their culture,

and their language. This violence is denied. Similarly, the colonization, alienation, and acculturation – indeed, the very existence of the Native peoples – have been expunged. Thus, the notion of alterity is based implicitly on the notion of a hierarchy: there is a superior Other, the English; there is also (at least) one inferior Other, the Native person, a negligible and neglected entity, excluded from the discourse and marginalized in Québécois society.

29 Duval, 1983, ix; our translation
30 Weinmann, 1977, 275
31 On the modalities and consequences of *phonetic translation*, also referred to as *mimetic* or *iconic*, see Lefevere, 1975, and Valesio, 1976.
32 The distinction between 'grand discours' and 'petit discours' was proposed by O. Ducrot during a seminar on pragmatic semantics at the Université de Montréal in 1983.
33 The unpublished manuscript by Roland Lepage was produced by Le Théâtre du Trident in 1976. For a comparison of the two plays, see Lefebvre and Ostiguy, 1978, 41.
34 Tremblay, 1985
35 R. Lalonde applies the same temporal actualization to Chekhov's *Three Sisters* (Chekhov, n.d.).
36 Tremblay, 1985, 168; our translation
37 'Spešu uvedomit' tebja, duša Trjapičkin, kakie so mnoj čudesa. Na doroge občistil menja pexotnyj kapitan, tak čto traktirščik xotel uže bylo posadit' menja v tjurmu; kak vdrug, po moej peterburgskoj fizionomii i po kostjumu, ves' gorod prinjal menja za general-gubernatora. I ja teper' živu u gorodničego, žuiruju, voločus' na propaluju za ego ženoj i dočkoj; ne rešilsja tol'ko, s kotoroj načat', – dumaju, prežde s matuški, potomu čto, kažetsja, gotova na vse uslugi. Pomniš', kak my s toboj bedstvovali, obedali na šeramyžku i kak odin raz bylo konditer sxvatil menja za vorotnik po povodu s"edennyx pirožkov na sčet doxodov angliskogo korolja? Teper' sovsem drugoj oborot. Vse mne dajut vzajmy skol'ko ugodno. Originaly strašnye. Ot smexu ty by umer. Ty, ja znaju, pišeš' statejki; pomesti ix v svoju literaturu. Vo pervyx: gorodničij glup kak sivyj merin': Gogol, 1968, 448–9.
38 Gogol, 1980, 125
39 Ronfard, 1982
40 Vauthier, 1953. *La Nouvelle Mandragore*, directed by J. Vilar, was produced for the first time in 1952 by Le Théâtre National Populaire, at the Palais de Chaillot.
41 Except for Siro, Callimaco's valet, who is replaced by Lira, a new protagonist, a servant of Lucrezia.
42 Ronfard, 1982, 105

43 Ibid, 33, 29, 118
44 Ibid, 78, 94, 99, 105
45 Ibid, 69
46 Maillet, 1978
47 Ibid, 18; our translation
48 Anglomania has traditionally inspired playwrights in Quebec, as E.-F. Duval points out. In his anthology of themes illustrating 'national history and [that of] Québécois society' in the first half of the twentieth century, he quotes, among other examples, Nathalie Michelet's *Contre le flot*, which received first prize in the Action Française drama competition in 1921. The plot is as follows: Corinne Cantin, the daughter of a rich francophone industrialist from Westmount, decides to marry an English Protestant instead of the young Dr Lamarche, who loves her. Several years later, the Englishman leaves her a widow. In the interval, her father goes bankrupt. In vain, she tries to rekindle Dr Lamarche's love for her. But he marries his faithful secretary. 'The readers will decide for themselves that anglomania is a disease that many Québécois families have caught ... Madame Cantin wants to speak English, she sent her daughter to study in the States to experience American culture ... and, furthermore, Corinne is duty bound to marry an English Protestant lawyer ... this amounts to rejecting your customs, your ancestors, your language, your religion ...' (1983, 164; our translation).
49 Maillet, 1978, 36
50 Ibid, 53
51 Ibid, 86
52 Ibid, 86
53 Ibid, 21
54 Ibid, 134
55 Ibid, 105
56 Ibid, 142. 'Mountain' refers here to Westmount, an upper-class, English-speaking area of Montreal.
57 Ibid, 131
58 Ibid, 58
59 Ibid
60 Ibid, 121. Need we point out that this portrait of the Englishman uses the stereotypes commonly adopted in other discursive forms, particularly in newspaper columns and public-opinion pages in the press?
61 Ibid, 32
62 On this subject, see Sénac, 1983.
63 Maillet, 1978, 170–1
64 Ibid, 88

65 This symbol of usurpation is found in a special feature published by *Humanitas*, which deals with the media representation of cultural communities and of Québécois of foreign extraction. In a short article entitled 'Une Plus Grande Ouverture des médias francophones aux autres communautés culturelles,' reference is made to a working paper of the Commission Nationale du Parti Québécois pour les Communautés Culturelles et les Médias: 'Furthermore, analysis of the content of articles [in the Québécois press] would undoubtedly demonstrate that Québécois of other origins are often represented as foreigners by the media (take, for example, an article on the remarkable growth of a Québécois company, Provigo, that had managed to push out Steinberg's, the leading supermarket, within ten years, as if Steinberg's were not also a Québécois company!)': *Humanitas*, 1987, 49; our translation.
66 Maillet, 1978, 85
67 Ibid, 178
68 Ibid, 179
69 Produced by La Nouvelle Compagnie Théâtrale in 1967. The unpublished text is in the library of the National Theatre School.
70 Corneille, 1961, 37
71 Ducharme, 1967, 27
72 Ibid, 14; our translation
73 'O rage, ô désespoir! Ô perruque ma mie! / N'as-tu donc tant duré que pour tant d'infâmie? / N'as-tu trompé l'espoir de tant de perruquiers / Que pour voir en un jour flétrir tant de lauriers?': quoted in Genette, 1987, 26.
74 Ducharme, 1967, 30; italics in original. The author indicates that the italicized lines are to be pronounced with a French accent.
75 Mailhot, 'Le Théâtre "maghané" de Réjean Ducharme,' in Godin and Mailhot, 1981, 214, our translation. For a comparison of Québécois parody and its model, see also Bérubé, 1975.
76 Quoted by Mailhot, ibid, 213
77 Hutcheon, 1985, 55
78 Andrès, 1986, 148–50
79 Written response to one of the questions sent to him by L. Gauvin and O. Guimond, quoted in *Cahiers de la NCT* 1 (Oct. 1976), 22; our translation
80 Ducharme, 1967, 25
81 Ibid, 32
82 Ibid, 13
83 Ibid, 56
84 Ibid, 34
85 Ibid, 59
86 Müller, 1984, 56–7

87 Ronfard, 1977
88 Ibid, 5; our translation
89 Ibid
90 A television interview with D. Pinard and N. Petrowski on the show 'La Grande Visite,' Radio-Canada, 11 Oct. 1987
91 Ronfard, 1977, 24
92 The role of Lear was played by J.-P. Ronfard himself, and Corneille was played by Monique Mercure, who received Best Actress award in Cannes for her role in *J.A. Martin photographe.*
93 Ronfard, 1977, 21
94 Ibid, 57. Constructivism, a movement derived from Russian futurism, first appeared on the Soviet literary scene in 1924. Its manifesto states that constructivism is a 'motivated art,' a 'step towards socialist art,' and a 'reflection of the collectivist movement of the toiling masses.' Constructivists are against literary groups who, claiming that they are fighting for artistic freedom, 'obscure the meaning of the times' and 'disrupt the cultural effort of the proletariat.' Cf. Struve, 1971, 85.
95 Ronfard, 1977, 28
96 Weiss, 1966, 143
97 Bakhtin, 1984, 254; italics in the original.
98 Ibid, 256; italics in the original
99 Godin and Mailhot, 1981, 212; italics in the original; our translation.
100 Marchand, 1899, reproduced in Germain, 1977, 177–295
101 Germain's adaptation of the play bears the subtitle 'Paraphrase.'
102 Marchand, 1899, in Germain, 1977, 274
103 Germain, 1977, 117; our translation
104 Ibid, 169–76
105 Ibid, 175
106 Ibid, 172
107 From the preface, entitled 'Du décor et des costumes,' in which Germain explains his production and his transformation of Marchand's *Les Faux Brillants* ... (1977, 8; emphasis added)
108 Marchand, 1899, in Germain, 1977, 180
109 Germain, 1977, 29
110 Ibid, 60
111 Ibid, 102
112 This is the main theme of L. Bergeron's *La Charte de la langue québécoise* (1981).
113 Germain, 1977, 165
114 Brecht, 1976

115 B. Brecht, *Die Kleinbürgerhochzeit*, 19–20. For purposes of comparison, we reproduce the following English translation, published by Methuen:
FATHER: Uncle Augustus died of dropsy.
HUSBAND: Cheers.
FATHER: Cheers. Dropsy. First it was just his feet, only the toes actually, then it was up to his knees in the time it takes to start a baby, and the whole thing had gone black. His belly was all swollen, and although they drained it off as best they could ...
HUSBAND: Cheers.
FATHER: Cheers, although they drained it off it was too late. There was the trouble with his heart, and that brought it all to a head. There he lay in the bed I was going to give to you, groaning like an elephant, and looking like one too, the legs anyway. (Brecht, *A Respectable Wedding*, trans. Jean Benedetti, 277–8)
116 Brecht, 1976, 45–6. We have reproduced the spelling in the National Theatre School manuscript.
117 Ibid, 46
118 Ibid, 63
119 Shakespeare, 1962, 877
120 Gurik, 1977, 49
121 Ibid
122 Duvignaud, 1985, 168
123 Levac, 'Avertissement au lecteur,' in Loranger and Levac, 1969, 16; our translation
124 M. Bélair expresses the same idea when he challenges the assertion that the history of Québécois theatre can be traced back to the period of French colonization, as the previously quoted work by Jean Béraud suggests. Evoking the 'anecdotal nature' of the latter, Bélair tersely resolves the fate of three centuries of theatre: '325 years of quasi-imitations' (1973, 19). Of the twenty-five years discussed by Godin and Mailhot, Bélair retains only five as being deserving of the epithet 'Québécois.' According to Bélair, the preceding twenty-five years were a 'sort of pre-history of Québécois theatre' (21). The criterion that dates Québécois theatre from 1968 is the 'problematic' inspired by 'a new awareness of what could be termed québécitude' (20), that is to say, a theatre that is directly or indirectly a theatre of protest, illustrating the present and past alienations of Québécois society. This should be 'articulated by a Québécois language' (35), that is to say, 'joual' (32).
125 Bélair, 1973, 68
126 Ibid, 69–71

3: Shakespeare, Québécois Nationalist Poet: Perlocutory Translation

1 Shakespeare, 1962, 847
2 Shakespeare, 1978, 19. Page references for subsequent citations from Shakespeare's original text and from the Québécois translation are provided in the text. Emphasis is ours, unless otherwise indicated.
3 Searle, 1974, 25
4 Compare Bakhtin, 1994, 84. The chronotope is a *discursive* space–time. To simplify matters, we have classified the spatio-temporal indices according to whether they refer to Shakespeare's mythical Scotland or (also) to New France. The space–time (real and no longer mythical) of the reception fuses these two dramatic chronotopes in the target text, which is itself part of a cultural field, an organized discursive space, which makes it possible for the receiver to integrate the three levels semantically.
5 See Eagleton, 1978, 64–8; in particular, the opposition between text and representation seen from an ideological point of view.
6 The protagonists undergo similar losses. Their role becomes more vague and commonplace, with the characters frequently stripped of their position in the aristocratic hierarchy.
7 Shakespeare, 1977, 157
8 Shakespeare, 1959, 55
9 The use of 'vous' to translate the 'me' of the original text should not be surprising. In the previously cited work by Wright and Lamar, the following note appears: 'Turns me: i.e., turns. Me indicates only the speaker's interest in the circumstances described, a construction known as the "ethical dative"' (1959, 55).
10 Shakespeare, 1977, 156
11 Shakespeare, 1983, 90–1
12 R.-J. Poupart (1976, 77) describes the 'surdestinateur' as 'the conjunction of complementary interpretations of the director and actors in a play.' The translator would therefore also enter into the category of 'surdestinateur.'
13 Shakespeare, 1977, 13
14 Shakespeare, 1983, 153; our translation
15 Shakespeare, 1977, 16; our translation; emphasis added
16 Shakespeare, 1977, 184–206; 1983, 110–23; 1985, 94–104
17 Shakespeare, 1985, 100
18 Leyris's translation (1977, 197) is as follows: 'Ah! Je le reconnais cette fois. Dieu clément, / Ruine ce qui nous rend étrangers l'un à l'autre!' (Oh! I recognize him this time. Merciful God, / Destroy whatever makes us strangers to each other). Y. Bonnefoy (1983, 118) translated the passage as follows: 'Je le

reconnais à présent. Grand Dieu, délivre-nous vite / De ce temps qui nous rend étrangers l'un à l'autre!' (I recognize him now. Almighty God deliver us quickly / From time that makes us strangers to each other).

19 Shakespeare, 1977, 205
20 Shakespeare, 1985, 122
21 Laroche, 1969, 91
22 Belleau, 1963, 82
23 Chamberland, 1969, iii
24 Brault, 1965, 51
25 Miron, 'La braise et l'humus,' in 1970, 53
26 G. Godin, 'Mal au pays,' in 1975, 45
27 Chamberland, 1969, 21
28 The notion 'target discourse' is derived from the term 'target language,' which refers to the language into which a text is translated. We use the term 'target discourse' to emphasize the fact that translation is a function of a preconstituted discourse, that is to say, a set of systemic processes operating not only at the level of language, in the sense linguists use the term, but also at the level of sociocultural codes created by the users of the discourse, in which systems of ideas and values should be included.
29 Vanier, 1974, 30
30 Miron, 1970, 59–61
31 Brault, 1965, 63
32 Miron, 1970, 50
33 Giguère, 1965, 17
34 Miron, 1970, 56–9
35 Major, 1969, 117
36 Lapointe, 1971, 198
37 Vanier, 1974, 35–43
38 Chamberland, 'Les nuits armées,' in 1985, 30
39 Miron, 1970, 58
40 Lapointe, 1971, 198
41 Chamberland, 'Raison de vivre ou de mourir,' in 1985, 49
42 Miron, 1970, 49
43 Lapointe, 1971, 19
44 Brault, 1965, 50
45 This theme, which forms the basis of J.-C. Germain's *A Canadian Play* ..., is also to be found in Garneau's poetry: 'ma race / enlisée dans la grande crétinerie violente / des gestes vendus de vendus aux vendus / qui nous tuent / TOUS' (my race / stuck in the violent stupidity / of sold-out gestures of the sold-out to the sold-out / that kill us / ALL OF US), in *Langage 5* (1971).

46 Brault, 1965, 51
47 See Laroche, 1969, 94–105.
48 Chamberland, 1969, 10–21
49 It is clearly no accident that the translation of this scene is so close to Chamberland's poem-manifesto, nor that, in its thematic and rhetorical cohesion, it is closer to Chamberland than to other poets. Before becoming a dramatist, Garneau was himself a poet, and was particularly inspired by Chamberland. In his poem 'Que c'est ça l'avenir,' which dates from the same period as the translation of *Macbeth*, references to Chamberland, or 'popaul,' are explicit; 'avec popaul / l'été / on chantait: / *je fais confiance à la totalité du réel / j'attends la pluie et le beau temps / et j'ai le temps et j'ai le temps* / c'est popaul, chamberland qui avait écrit ça' (1972, n.p.; emphasis in original). In this poem, which is interspersed with lines from Chamberland's work, the obsessive question is: 'où c'est ça l'avenir? / c'est-y par en avant?' (ibid) (Where is the future? / is it ahead of us?). This question makes it even clearer that the translation of a play like *Macbeth* has a doxological function in the discursive field of Quebec.
50 Chamberland, 1969, 18
51 H. Meschonnic provides a counter-example to this approach in his criticism of A. Vialatte's translations of Kafka. Meschonnic fails to see the origin of the discrepancies he finds, apart from calling them an 'ideology of literature,' the definition of which is not clear. This type of analysis, which is purely normative, fails to take into account the various institutional constraints that influenced Vialatte's translation. It is these very constraints that ensured the legitimacy of this translation. Cf. 1985, 83–98.
52 Angenot, 1978, 95
53 This idea is repeated obsessively in the work of Québécois writers: 'Literature is a sign that we exist' (M. Dubé, quoted by A. Parizeau, 'Marcel Dubé,' in *La Presse*, 8 Aug. 1986, B-2). See also, C. Levac, 'When Quebécois dramatists find a framework, a theatrical structure which is our own, which really expresses our uniqueness, we will have not only our own authentic drama but also a country' in Loranger and Levac, 1969, 16; our translation.
54 After G. Szanto, A.P. Foulkes's authoritative work demonstrated the illocutionary effect of dramatic writing. See, in particular, his analysis of *The Crucible* (1983, 83–107). Theatre translation reinforces and adds to the ideology already interwoven in the source text.
55 Gobin, 1986, 73; our translation
56 Andrès and Lefebvre, 1979, 80; our translation
57 Cf. G. Deleuze, 'Avenir de linguistique,' in Gobard, 1976, 3. This 'coefficient of territorialization' (which could also be termed a 'doxological coefficient') can be applied particularly well to theatrical production and its criticism. One of

the best examples of this phenomenon is provided by Monique Englebertz (1989); in her work we find passages such as the following: 'The most important theoretician of the new Québécois theatre is without doubt, Jean-Claude Germain ... When he called his troupe "Les Enfants de Chénier" and his theatre "Le Théâtre d'Aujourd'hui" ... he put his brilliance, his knowledge, and his experience at the service of a concept of art which supports the people in its struggle for reappropriation of its rights' ... ' This is a desire to get away from the influence of a *corrupt power*, to rise up against *a corrupt art* which is subjected to it, to open one's eyes to the *dangers concealed in that art*, in particular to the *maintaining of the people in a state of ignorance*' (49; our translation, emphasis added). A few lines above these comments, Englebertz provides a list of so-called dangerous and corrupt authors: 'Anouilh, Claudel, Corneille, Aeschylus, Euripides, Giraudoux, Marivaux, Molière, Musset, Racine, and Shakespeare.'

4: The Search for a Native Language: Translation and Cultural Identity

1 Jakobson, 1969, 353
2 Mounin, 1963. See also Ladmiral's synthesis (1979, 85–114).
3 Mounin, 1963, 165
4 These very questions were raised by T. Savory: 'Cervantes published *Don Quixote* in 1605; should that story be translated into contemporary English, such as he would have used at the time had he been an Englishman, or into the English of today? There can be, as a rule, very little doubt as to the answer, for, in most cases, a reader is justified in expecting to find the kind of English that he is accustomed to. If a function of translation is to produce in the minds of its readers the same emotions as those produced by the original in the minds of the readers, the answer is clear. Yet there is need to notice in passing the possibility of exceptions whenever the original author is read more for his manner than for his matter. We may read the speeches of Cicero, for example, chiefly that we may have an opportunity to appreciate his eloquence. Of recent years the most eloquent speaker of English has been Sir Winston Churchill, and Churchill's style was not Cicero's style. Should a speech by Cicero be so translated as to sound as if it had been delivered by Churchill? No' (1968, 56–7).
5 'Gaweda' is a synthesis of several registers, the styles of nineteenth-century Polish story-tellers and of seventeenth-century Sarmatian Baroque. In his novel *Trans-Atlantyk*, Gombrowicz re-creates 'the sound of a stylized way of speaking ..., deliberately rustic (an affectation comparable to the language Proust gave to the Guermantes) ... a mixture that conjures up a "Polishness" of

former times.' After explaining how an invented language is used to expose the archaeological layers of this nostalgic Polishness, C. Jelenski demonstrates how translators of the novel managed to deal with what appeared to be deficiencies in the target language: 'It seemed futile to look for ... a coherent French model. In cases where there was an archaically colourful word in the Polish text, we turned to writers such as Madame de Sévigné, Saint-Simon, or even La Fontaine, and simply borrowed expressions similar to the ones in the original. These expressions played the same role in the French text (contrast between contemporary and past time periods, witty allusion to quaint former times) as their equivalent in the Polish text. On occasion, a dated syntactic device enabled us to render the fin-de-siècle colour of certain passages, that kind of mocking, humorous distinction used to describe particularly superficial characters in the novel' (Gombrowicz, 1976, 20; our translation).

6 E. Nida has found a practical answer to this difficult question: the speech of women should have priority because it is women, not men, who are responsible for educating the children. The proselytizing objective that motivates Nida's translation of the Bible explains this 'pragmatic' solution to a fundamentally linguistic problem (Nida and Taber 1982, 32). In more common cases of bilingualism or diglossia, Nida and Taber's choice of priorities is similarly motivated: '... priority is given to the larger of two languages, or to a language designated as national or official, or to a language spoken by an appreciable number of people who cannot communicate effectively in any other language ... With respect to the level of language to be used in the translation, priority is given to common language or popular language translations over translations made in literary language' (ibid, 176–7).
7 Berman, 1984, 46–7; our translation
8 Quoted by C. Bruneau, 1955, 126
9 Du Bellay, *Deffense et illustration de la langue françoyse*, Book I, Ch.V (quoted by Mounin, 1955, 14). We should not forget, however, that Du Bellay rejected and impugned translation as an agent of this transformation.
10 Gobard, 1976, 34; our translation
11 Ibid
12 Trudeau, 1982, 122
13 Bergeron, 1980
14 S. Robinson and D. Smith, *Practical Handbook of Canadian French* (Toronto: Macmillan 1973), i
15 Ibid, 1, 6, 102, 72, 74
16 Bergeron, 1981, 11; our translation
17 Ibid, 9
18 Ibid, 8

19 This is how Nida defines adaptation (1982, 134).
20 Lalonde, 1979, 21; our translation
21 On the construction of 'memory-screens' and reinterpretations made by nationalist historiographers of the Conquest, which is portrayed as 'the initial catastrophe of French Canada, the *Apocalypse Now* that plunged a country happy under the French, into subjection and humiliation,' see Weinmann, 1987, 277–88.
22 Rioux, 1974, 17; our translation
23 Here is how the authors, both university professors, describe the goal of the *Practical Handbook of Canadian French*: 'It is the authors' hope that it will aid communication and understanding between the two main language groups and also demonstrate the richness of expression of French-Canadian speech, a language attuned to our Canadian reality' 1973, back cover.
24 Lalonde, 1979, 53
25 See, in particular, Marcel, 1982 and Trudeau, 1982.
26 Rossi-Landi, 1983, 87; emphasis in the original
27 Dubois, 1978, 44–5; our translation
28 Lalonde, 1979, 53; our translation
29 Ibid, 15
30 J. Éthier-Blais, 'Sept auteurs en proie au mal québécois,' in *Le Devoir*, 20 Feb. 1988, D-8; our translation, emphasis added
31 Garneau, 1974; our translation
32 Lalonde, 1979, 53. In an article by J. Godbout, entitled 'Ma langue, ma maison,' we find the same theme of the impurity introduced by the immigrant: 'In the villages and towns of Quebec, there are particularly ugly neighbourhoods where buildings, besides being covered in multicoloured neon lights, are decorated in an astonishing variety of styles ... The passer-by sees in these places the delirious expression of a shattered culture where styles, inspired by the traditional Canadian house, the Spanish castle, or by Victorian turrets, remind us that here, in our country, people can reconstruct their universe as they wish ... Why has Montreal been disfigured? To build American sky-scrapers. To build Italian white-brick buildings in red-brick streets. Could the Greeks have been forbidden to put blue paint on the grey stones and could the Portuguese have been told not to transform slate roofs into rainbows? ... We should perhaps perceive bilingualism in this way. A single language is harmony, more than one language is war ... But since language is the architecture of emotions and thought, there are places on the verge of madness. We are living in one': *L'Actualité*, July 1987, 104.
33 J.-P. Faye uses the expression 'cette inconnue énigmatique' in his preface to Lalonde, 1979 (p. 6).

34 Miron, 1970, 118
35 Ibid, 118, 124
36 Ibid, 118
37 Weinmann, 1987, 315
38 Miron, 1970, 118
39 'The desire for a State, to be constituted in a Nation-State, thus corresponds necessarily to the desire that motivates certain individuals or certain groups within a society to impose their interpretation of the national interest on all members of the society ... When the former take over the power of the State, you may expect the national interest they invoke to be represented as all the more urgent and at the same time all the more objective, so great will be the desire for power that motivates them, and so imperious their determination to impose on all of society a conception of itself that is destructive of its habitual way of living and thinking' (Morin and Bertrand, 1979, 138–9).
40 Gobin, 1978, 107; our translation, emphasis in the original
41 Lalonde, 1979, 12
42 Ibid, 13
43 Ibid
44 Ibid, 15
45 Chamberland, 1969, 69; our translation
46 Ibid
47 Lalonde, 1979, 20. The incest theme is also found, interestingly, in Michel Tremblay's *Bonjour là, bonjour* (1974). The theme appears in a number of plays, but Tremblay uses it as a metaphor and not just to evoke a social problem.
48 Lalonde, 1979, 13
49 Ibid, 18
50 Ibid, 164
51 Ibid, 166
52 Lalonde, 1974, 'poème-affiche' (protest-poem)
53 Luther, quoted in Berman, 1984, 45; our translation
54 M. Garneau, production notes for *Macbeth* at Le Théâtre de la Manufacture; quoted by Andrès and Lefebvre, 1979, 84
55 Ibid
56 M. Garneau, 'AG, aile gauche,' in 1974
57 Shakespeare, 1978, 41. The original text is as follows: 'I have given suck, and know / How tender 'tis to love the babe that milks me. / I would, while it was smiling at my face, / Have plucked my nipple from his boneless gums / And dashed the brains out, had I sworn as you / Have done to this' (Shakespeare, 1962, 851).
58 Andrès and Lefebvre, 1979, 84; our translation

59 The following appears on the back cover of the play by J.-C Germain, 1972): *Diguidi, diguidi, ha! ha! ha!* followed by *Si les Sansoucis s'en soucient, ces Sansoucis-ci s'en soucieront-ils? Bien parler, c'est se respecter!*
60 Chekhov, n.d., 2
61 'V dome Prozorovyx. *Gostinnaja s kolonnami, za kotoroj viden bol'šoj zal.* Polden'; na dvore solnečno, veselo. V zale nakry-vajut stol dlja zavtraka': Chekhov, 1984, 307; emphasis added.
62 Brecht, 'La Bonne Âme de Se-Tchouan,' unpublished, trans. Gilbert Turp. The extract is quoted directly from the manuscript, deposited with the National Theatre School library. The following is the original text (p. 1). 'EST IST ABEND, WANG, DER WASSERVERKAÜFER, STELLT SICH DEM PUBLIKUM VOR. WANG – Ich bin Wasserverkaüfer hier in der Haupstadt von Sezuan. Mein Geschäft ist mühselig. Wenn es wenig Wasser gibt, muss ich weit danach laufen. Und gibt es viel, bin ich ohne Verdienst. Aber in *unserer Provinz* herrscht überhaupt grosse Armut. Es heisst allgemein, dass uns nur noch die Götter helfen können. Zu meiner unaussprechlichen Freude erfahre ich von einem Vieheinkaüfer, der viel herumkommt dass einiger der höchsten Götter schon unterwegs sind und auch hier in Sezuan erwartet werden dürfen. Der Himmel soll sehr beunruhigt sein wegen der vielen Klagen, die zu ihm aufsteigen': Brecht, 'Der gute Mensch von Sezuan,' in *Die Stücke von Bertolt Brecht*, 595; emphasis added
63 Editor's note in Brecht, 1975, 11
64 French translations use the reverse procedure. The 'marchand d'eau' expresses himself as if he were a member of high society: 'WANG – Je suis marchand d'eau, ici, dans la capitale du Se-Tchouan. Mon commerce est pénible. Quand il n'y a pas beaucoup d'eau, je dois aller loin pour en trouver. Et quand il y en a beaucoup, je suis sans ressources. Mais dans notre province règne généralement une grande pauvreté. Tout le monde dit que seuls les dieux peuvent encore nous aider. Joie ineffable, j'apprends d'un maquignon qui circule beaucoup que quelques-uns des dieux les plus grands sont déjà en route et qu'on peut aussi compter sur eux au Se-Tchouan. Le ciel serait très inquiet du fait des nombreuses plaintes qui montent vers lui': ibid, 7.
65 Brecht, 1976, 30
66 Ibid, 31
67 Tremblay, 1969, 3
68 Ibid
69 Tremblay, program for *L'Effet des rayons gamma sur les vieux garçons*, quoted in *Cahiers de la Nouvelle Compagnie Théâtrale* 1 (October 1974), 10
70 O'Neill, *Desire under the Elms*, in 1959, 57
71 O'Neill, n.d., 81

72 Ibid, 100
73 R. Balibar (1985, 280–98) has analysed the procedures used by French novelists to create local colour. She notes in particular that textual elements employed to create a rural effect often appear in italics and must be read in a different tone and treated differently from the main body of the text. A novel like *Jeanne* by G. Sand, in which there is an attempt to defend a dialect, the old French of Berri, was a failure. Balibar points out that the use of the dialect in the same context as the national language had no influence on French thought of the time. She attributes this failure to the contemporary ideological atmosphere, the Republican ideal being to promote communication among citizens with different mother tongues. The legitimate language was the language of the state, and every effort had to be made to eradicate differences.
74 Chekhov 1967, 373; 1983, 44–5
75 This situation can be applied to a country like Israel. In this respect, see G. Toury, 1980.
76 Turp, 1984, 3; our translation
77 Krysinski, 1983, 10–11; our translation, emphasis added. This observation is similar to M. Bataillon's analysis of the translation of *Platonov* by E. Triolet; the analysis ends with the following observation: 'The translation trap in Elsa's work is that she is splendidly fluid.' This 'polished' translation, adds Bataillon, 'corresponded exactly to what was happening in the theatre of the fifties': *Sixièmes assises de la traduction littéraire* (Arles: Actes Sud 1989), 82–5.
78 Marsolais, 1977, 11; our translation
79 Ibid
80 Krysinski, 1983, 11
81 Strindberg, 1985, 13
82 Ibid, 14
83 MacDuff, 1984, 14
84 Marsolais, 1977, 12
85 Ibid
86 Strindberg, n. d., 52
87 Ibid, 5, 8

Conclusion

1 Derrida, 1987, back cover
2 Lafon, 1988/1989, 422; our translation
3 Cf. Simon, 1988, 82–7

Bibliography

Andrès, Bernard. 1986. 'Québec: émergence de l'institution littéraire et parodie des codes français.' *Études littéraires* 19/1 (Spring-Summer), 141–52
Andrès, Bernard, and Paul Lefebvre. 1979. '"Macbeth." Théâtre de la Manufacture.' *Jeu* 11, 80–8
Angenot, Marc. 1977. 'Présupposé, topos, idéologème.' *Études françaises* 13/1–2, 11–34
– 1978. 'Fonctions narratives et maximes idéologiques.' *Orbis Litterarum* 33, 95–110
– 1979. *Glossaire pratique de la critique contemporaine.* Montreal: Hurtubise HMH
– 1983. *La Parole pamphlétaire.* Paris: Payot
– 1989. *1889. Un État du discours social.* Montreal: Le Préambule
Assises de la traduction littéraire (Arles, 1989), Traduire le théâtre. 1990. Arles: Actes Sud
Athayde, Roberto. 1975. *Mademoiselle Marguerite.* Trans. M. Tremblay. Montreal: Leméac
Audet, Noël. 1969. 'La Terre étrangère appropriée.' *Voix et images du pays* 2, *Cahiers Sainte-Marie* 15, 31–42
Bakhtin, Mikhaïl. 1973. *Marxism and the Philosophy of Language.* Trans. Ladislav Matejka and I.R Titunik. New York and London: Seminar Press
– 1984. *Rabelais and His World.* Trans. Hélène Iswolsky. Bloomington: Indiana University Press
– 1994. *The Dialogic Imagination.* Trans. Cary Emerson and Michael Holquist. Austin: University of Texas Press
Balibar, Renée. 1985. *L'Institution du français.* Paris: Presses Universitaires de France
Bassnett-McGuire, Susan. 1985. 'Ways through the Labyrinth: Strategies and Methods for Translating Theatre Texts.' In *The Manipulation of Literature,* ed. T. Hermans, 87–102. London: Croom Helm

Bélair, Michel. 1973. *Le Nouveau Théâtre québécois*. Montreal: Leméac
Belleau, André. 1963. 'La Littérature est un combat,' *Liberté* 5/2, 82
- 1981. 'Le Conflit des codes dans l'institution littéraire québécoise'. *Liberté* 23/2 (March–April), 15–19
- 1984. *Y a-t-il un intellectuel dans la salle?* Montreal: Éd. Primeur
Béraud, Jean. 1958. *350 ans de théâtre au Canada français*. Montreal: Cercle du Livre de France
Bergeron, Léandre. 1980. *Dictionnaire de la langue québécoise*. Montreal: VLB
- 1981. *La Charte de la langue québécoise*. Montreal: VLB
Berman, Antoine. 1984. *L'Épreuve de l'étranger*. Paris: Gallimard
- 1985a. 'Traduction ethnocentrique et traduction hypertextuelle.' In *Les Tours de Babel*, ed. G. Granel, 48–64. Mauvezin: Trans-Europ-Repress
- 1985b. 'La Traduction et la lettre ou l'auberge du Lointain.' In *Les Tours de Babel*, ed. G. Granel, 31–150. Mauvezin: Trans-Europ-Repress
- 1986. 'La Terre nourrice et le bord étranger.' *Communications* 43, 205–21
Bérubé, Renald. 1969. 'Les Grands Départs de Jacques Languirand ou la mise à l'épreuve de la parole.' *Voix et images du Pays* 2, *Cahiers Sainte-Marie* 15, 63–75
- 1975. '*Le Cid* et *Hamlet*: Corneille et Shakespeare lus par Ducharme et Gurik.' *Voix et images du Pays* 1/1, 35–56
Bouthillette, Jean. 1972. *Le Canadien français et son double*. Montreal: L'Hexagone
Brassard, Jacques, and Michel Tremblay. 1969. *Lysistrata*. Montreal: Leméac
Brault, Jacques. 1965. *Mémoire*. Montreal: Librairie Déom
Brecht, Bertolt. 1966a. *Der Gute Mensch von Sezuan*. Frankfurt: Suhrkamp
- 1966b. *Die Kleinbügerhochzeit*. Frankfurt: Suhrkamp
- 1970. 'A Respectable Wedding.' In *The Collected Plays*, vol 1. London: Methuen
- 1975. *La Bonne Âme du Se-Tchouan*. Trans J. Stern. Paris: L'Arche
- 1976. 'Le Buffet impromptu ou la nôsse chez les propriétaires de bungalow.' Adapt. J.-C. Germain. Unpublished manuscript, National Theatre School
- 1979. *La Noce chez les petits bourgeois*. Trans. J.-F. Poirier. Paris: L'Arche
- n.d., 'La Bonne Âme de Se-Tchouan.' Trans. G. Turp. Unpublished manuscript, National Theatre School.
Bruneau, Charles. 1955. *Petite Histoire de la langue française, I*. Paris: Armand Colin
Cardinal, Marie. 1986. *La Médée d'Euripide*. Montreal: VLB
Chamberland, Paul. 1969. *L'Afficheur hurle*. Montreal: Éd. Parti Pris
- 1985. *Terre Québec*. Montreal: L'Hexagone
Châtelet, François. 1979. *Questions Objections*. Paris: Denoël-Gonthier
Chekhov, Anton. 1967. *Oeuvres*. Paris: Gallimard
- 1983. *Oncle Vania*. Trans. M. Tremblay and K. Yaroshevskaya. Montreal: Leméac
- 1962. 'Tri sestry.' In *Izbrannoe rasskazy, povesti, p'esy*. Moscow: Prosveščene, 505–68

- n.d. 'Les trois soeurs.' Trans. R. Lalonde. Unpublished manuscript, National Theatre School
Colbert, François. 1979. *Le Marché québécois du théâtre*. Quebec City: Institut Québécois de Recherche sur la Culture
- 1988. *Conjonctures, le Québec et l'autre* 10–11 (Fall)
Corneille, Pierre. 1961. *Théâtre choisi*, Ed. M. Rat. Paris: Garnier
Dagenais, Angèle. 1981. *Crise de croissance: Le théâtre au Québec*. Quebec City: Institut Québécois de Recherche sur la Culture
Darbelnet, Jean. 1984. 'La Responsabilité du traducteur: Quel est son objet?' *Informatio* 13 2–3 (April-June), 19–20
Delisle, Jean. 1986. 'Dans les coulisses de l'adaptation théâtrale'. *Circuit* 12 (March), 3–8
- 1980. *L'Analyse du discours comme méthode de traduction*. Ottawa: Ottawa University Press
- 1989. *Translation: An Interpretative Approach*, Abridged ed. Trans. M. Creery and P. Logan. Ottawa: University of Ottawa Press
Derrida, Jacques. 1987. *Psyché. Inventions de l'autre*. Paris: Galilée
D'Hulst, Lieven. 1987. *L'Évolution de la poésie en France: Introduction à une analyse des interférences systématiques 1780–1830)*. Louvain: Presses de l'Université de Louvain
Dimić, Milan, and Marguerite K. Garstin. 1988. 'The Polysystem Theory: A Brief Introduction, with Bibliography.' In *Problems of Literary Reception/Problèmes de réception littéraire*, eds E.D. Blodgett and A.G. Purdy, 177–96. Edmonton: University of Alberta Press
Dubois, Jacques. 1978. *L'Institution de la littérature*. Paris: Fernand Nathan
Ducharme, Réjean. 1967. 'Le Cid maghané.' Montreal. Unpublished manuscript, National Theatre School
Duval, Étienne-F. 1983. *Le Jeu de l'histoire et de la société dans le théâtre québécois, 1900–1950*. Trois-Rivières: Éd. E.-F. Duval
Duvignaud, Jean. 1985. *Le Propre de l'homme*. Paris: Hachette
Eagleton, Terry. 1978. *Criticism and Ideology*. London: Verso Press
Englebertz, Monique. 1989. *Le Théâtre québécois de 1965 à 1980. Un théâtre politique*. Tübingen: Niemeyer
Erdman, Nicolaï. 1986. *Le Suicidé*. Trans. M. Vinaver. Arles: Actes Sud
Even-Zohar, Itamar. 1978. 'The Position of Translated Literature within the Literary Polysystem.' In *Literature and Translation: New Perspectives in Literary Studies*, ed. J. Holmes et al., 117–27. Leuven: Acco
- 1979. 'Polysystem Theory.' *Poetics Today* 1/1–2, 287–310
Foucault, Michel. 1972. *The Archaeology of Knowledge*. Trans. A.M. Sheridan Smith. London: Tavistock
Foulkes, A.P. 1983. *Literature and Propaganda*. New York: Methuen

Frank, Armin P. 1984. 'Theories and Theory of Literary Translation.' In *Literary Theory and Criticism*, ed. J.P. Strelka, 203–21. New York: Peter Lang
Garneau, Michel. 1973. *L'Animalhumain*. Montreal: Fédération des coopératives Étudiantes
- 1974. *Langage 5*. Montreal: L'Aurore
Genette, Gérard. 1982. *Palimpsestes*. Paris: Seuil
Germain, Jean-Claude. 1972. *Diguidi, diguidi, ha! ha! ha!, suivi de, Si les Sansoucis s'en soucient, ces Sansoucis-ci s'en soucieront-ils? Bien parler, c'est se respecter!* Montreal: Leméac
- 1977. *Les Faux Brillants de Félix-Gabriel Marchand*. Montreal: VLB
- 1983. *A Canadian Play/Une Plaie canadienne*. Montreal: VLB
Giguère, Roland. 1965. *L'Âge de parole*. Montreal: L'Hexagone
Giraudoux, Jean. 1946. *La Folle de Chaillot*. Paris: Grasset
Gobard, Henri, 1976. *L'Aliénation linguistique*. Paris: Flammarion
Gobin, Pierre. 1978. *Le Fou et ses doubles*. Montreal: Presses de l'Université de Montréal
- 1986. 'Macbête à la foire. De quelques traitements de Shakespeare en français.' *Études françaises* 19/1, 67–79
Godin, Gérald. 1975. *Libertés surveillées*. Montreal: Parti Pris
Godin, Jean-Cléo, and Laurent Mailhot. 1980. *Le Théâtre québécois II*. Montreal: HMH
- 1981 [1970]. *Le Théâtre québécois*. Montreal: HMH
Gogol, Nikolaj. 1968. 'Revizor.' In *Izbrannye proizvedenija*. Leningrad: Lenizdat
- 1980. *The Government Inspector*. Trans. Milton Ehre and Fruma Gottschalk. Chicago: University of Chicago Press
Gombrowicz, Witold. 1976. *Trans-Atlantique*. Trans. C. Jelenski and G. Serreau. Paris: Denoël
Graham, Joseph F. 1985. *Difference in Translation*. Ithaca: Cornell University Press
Gruslin, Adrien. 1981. *Le Théâtre et l'État au Québec*. Montreal: VLB
Gruslin, Adrien, and Jean-Pierre Lamoureux. 1983. 'Entretien avec Louise et Jean-Ducepppe.' *Jeu*, 29, 98–112
Gurik, Robert. 1977. *Hamlet, prince du Québec*. Montreal: Leméac
Hauser, Arnold. 1968. *Mannerism: The Crisis of the Renaissance and the Origin of Modern Art*. Cambridge, MA.: Harvard University Press
Herbert, John. 1971. *Aux yeux des hommes*. Trans. R. Dionne. Montreal: Leméac
Hermans, Théo, ed. 1985. *The Manipulation of Literature: Studies in Literary Translation*. London: Croom Helm
Holmes, James S., José Lambert, and Raymond Van Den Broeck, eds. 1978. *Literature and Translation: New Perspectives in Literary Studies*. Leuven: Acco
Humanitas, Les 'ethniques' et les médias. 17 1987. 48–9
Hutcheon, Linda. 1985. *A Theory of Parody*. New York: Methuen

Jakobson, Roman. 1969. 'Linguistics and Poetics.' In *Style in Language*, ed. Thomas Sebeok, 350–77. Cambridge, MA.: MIT Press

Krysinski, Wladimir. 1983. 'Tchekhov, Tremblay, Brassard ou comment changer la vie par le théâtre.' *Avant Première* 9/3, 10–11

Ladmiral, Jean-René. 1979. *Traduire: Théorèmes pour la traduction*. Paris: Payot

– 1986. 'Sourciers et ciblistes.' *Revue d'esthétique* 12, 33–42

Lafon, Dominique. 1988/1989. 'Les Muses étrangères du théâtre québécois; mémoire ou exutoire?' *L'annuaire théâtral, Le theâtre au Québec. Mémoire et appropriation*, Fall 1988 and Spring 1989, 422–33

Lalonde, Michèle. 1974. *Speak White*. Montreal: L'Hexagone

– 1979. *Défense et illustration de la langue québécoise*. Paris: Seghers-Laffont, Coll. Change

Lambert, José. 1980. 'Production, tradition et importation: Une clef pour la description de la littérature et de la littérature en traduction.' *Canadian Review of Comparative Literature* 2, 246–52

Lambert, José, and Hendrik Van Gorp. 1985. 'On Describing Translations.' In *The Manipulation of Literature*. ed. T. Hermans, 42–53. London: Croom Helm

Lanoux, Victor. 1976. *L'Ouvre-boîte*. Adapted by Y. Deschamps and J.-L. Roux. Montreal: Leméac

Lapointe, Paul-Marie. 1971. *Le Réel absolu*. Montreal: L'Hexagone

Laroche, Maximilien. 1969. 'Notes sur le style de trois poètes: Roland Giguère, Gatien Lapointe et Paul Chamberland.' *Voix et images du pays* 2, *les Cahiers Sainte-Marie* 15, 91–106

Lefebvre, Paul, and Pierre Ostiguy. 1978. 'L'Adapatation théâtrale au Québec.' *Jeu* 9, 32–47

Lefevere, André. 1975. *Translating Poetry. Seven Strategies and a Blueprint*. Amsterdam: Van Gorcum

Lemire, Maurice, ed. 1986. *L'Institution littéraire*. Quebec City: Institut Québécois de Recherche sur la Culture

Leonard, Martine, and Françoise Siguret. 1972. 'La "Route de l'expansion road" ou l'impasse de la publicité bilingue.' *Meta* 17/1, 56–71

Lepage, Roland. 1976. '*La Folle du quartier latin*.' Unpublished manuscript, Théâtre du Trident, Quebec City

Lévesque, René. 1982. *Memoirs*. Trans. P. Stratford. Toronto: McClelland and Stewart

Link, Jürgen, and Ursula Link-Heer. 1980. *Literatursoziologisches Propädeutikum*. Munich: Fink Verlag

Loranger, Françoise, and Claude Levac. 1969. *Le Chemin du Roy*. Montreal: Leméac

McDonough, John Thomas. 1974. *Charbonneau et le Chef.* Trans. P. Hébert and P. Morency. Montreal: Leméac
Macduff, Pierre. 1984. 'Monique Mercure/Mère Courage.' *En Scène* 2/2, 14–15
Machiavelli, Nicolas. 1952. *Oeuvres complètes.* ed. E. Barincou. Paris: Gallimard, Bibliothèque de la Pléïade
– 1984. *Mandragola. Clizia.* Ed. G.M. Anselmi. Milan: Mussia editore
Mailhot, Laurent. 1987. 'Traduction et "Nontraduction": L'épreuve du voisin étranger dans la littérature québécoise.' In *L'Altérité dans la littérture québécoise*, 13–59. Bologna: CLUEB
Maillet, Antonine. 1978. *Le Bourgeois Gentleman.* Montreal: Leméac
Major, André. 1969. *Poèmes pour durer.* Montreal: Éd. du Songe
Marcel, Jean. 1982. *Le Joual de Troie.* Montreal: E.I.P.
Marchand, Felix-Gabriel. 1899. 'Les faux brillants.' In *Mélanges poétiques et littéraires.* Montreal: C.O. Beauchemin et Fils; reproduced in J.C. Germain, 1977. *Les Faux Brillants*, 177–295. Montreal: VLB
Marsolais, Gilles. 1977. 'Traduire et monter Mademoiselle Julie.' *Cahiers de la Nouvelle Compagnie Theâtrale* 11/2, 11–12
Martin, Robert, ed. 1978. *The Theater Essays of Arthur Miller.* New York: Viking Press
Meschonnic, Henri. 1973. *Pour la Poétique II.* Paris: Gallimard
– 1985. 'La Femme cachée dans le texte de Kafka.' *Texte* 4, 83–98
Miron, Gaston. 1970. *L'Homme rapaillé.* Montreal: Presses de l'Université de Montreal
Molière. 1963. *Oeuvres complètes.* Paris: Seuil
Morin, Michel, and Claude Bertrand. 1979. *Le Territoire imaginaire de la culture.* Montreal: Hurtubise HMH
Moser, Walter. 1985. 'La Mise à l'essai des discours dans *L'homme sans qualités* de Robert Musil.' *Canadian Review of Comparative Literature*, March, 12–45
Mounin, Georges. 1955. *Les Belles Infidèles.* Paris: Cahiers du Sud
– 1963. *Les Problèmes théoriques de la traduction.* Paris: Gallimard
Müller, Heiner. 1984. *Hamletmachine.* Trans. Carl Weber. New York: Performing Arts Journal Publications
Nardocchio, Elaine. 1986. *Theatre and Politics in Modern Quebec.* Edmonton: University of Alberta Press
Nida, Eugene. 1964. *Toward a Science of Translating.* Leiden: Brill
Nida, Eugene, and Charles Taber. 1982. *The Theory and Practice of Translation.* Leiden: Brill
O'Neill, Eugene. 1959. *Three Plays.* New York: Vintage Books
– 1971. 'Désir sous les ormes.' Trans. R. Ripps and Y. Sauvageau. Unpublished manuscript, National Theatre School
– n.d. 'Désir sous les ormes.' Trans. M. Dumont and M. Grégoire. Unpublished manuscript, National Theatre School

Palimpsestes, Traduire le dialogue. Traduire les textes de théâtre, 1987 (1). Paris: Université de la Sorbonne Nouvelle

Pavis, Patrice. 1987. *Dictionnaire du théâtre.* Paris: Messidor-Éd. sociales

– 1990. *Le Théâtre au croisement des cultures.* Paris: José Corti

Pavlovic, Diane. 1987. 'Cartographie: l'Allemagne québécoise.' *Jeu* 43, 77–110

Piotte, Jean-Marc. 1988. 'Vivre en Québécois.' *Conjonctures* 10–11 (Fall), 41–58

Poupart, René-Jean. 1976. 'Communication théâtrale et traduction.' *Cahiers internationaux de symbolisme*, 31–2, 77–88

Richler, Mordecai. 1974. *Les Cloches d'enfer.* Trans. G. Rochette. Montreal: Leméac

Rioux, Marcel. 1974. *Les Québécois.* Paris: Seuil

Robin, Régine. 1973. *Histoire et linguistique.* Paris: Armand Colin

Robinson, Sinclair, and Donald Smith. 1973. *A Practical Handbook of Canadian French.* Toronto: Macmillan

Ronfard, Jean-Pierre. 1977. *Lear.* Montreal: Trac

– 1982. *La Mandragore.* Montreal: Leméac

Rossi-Landi, Ferrucio. 1983. *Language as Work and Trade: A Semiotic Homology for Linguistics and Economics.* Trans. Martha Adams et al. South Hadley, MA: Bergin and Garvey

Savory, Theodore. 1968. *The Art of Translation.* Boston: The Writer

Searle, John. 1974. *Speech Acts.* London: Cambridge University Press

Sénac, Philippe. 1983. *L'Image de l'Autre.* Paris: Flammarion

Shaffer, Peter. 1976. *Équus.* Adapt. J.L. Roux. Montreal: Leméac

Shakespeare. 1959. *Macbeth.* Ed. Louis B. Wright and Virginia LaMar. Washington, DC: The Folger Shakespeare Library

– 1962. *The Oxford Complete Works.* Ed. W.J. Craig. London: Oxford University Press

– 1977. *Macbeth.* Trans. P. Leyris. Paris: Aubier Montaigne

– 1978. *Macbeth.* Trans. M. Garneau. Montreal: VLB

– 1983. *Macbeth.* Trans. Y. Bonnefoy. Paris: Mercure de France

– 1985. *La Tragédie de Macbeth.* Trans. J.-M. Déprats. Paris: Solin

– 1989a. *Coriolan.* Trans. M. Garneau. Montreal: VLB

– 1989b. *La Tempête.* Trans. M. Garneau. Montreal: VLB

Simon, Sherry. 1987. 'Les Traductions "made in Quebec".' *Circuit* 17 (June), 5–7

– 1988. 'Shakespeare en traduction.' *Jeu* 48 (September), 82–7

– 1989. *L'Inscription sociale de la traduction au Québec.* Quebec City: Office de la Langue Française

Slade, Bernard. 1981. *Chapeau!* Trans. L. de Céspedes. Montreal: Leméac.

Stratford, Philip. 1977. *Bibliography of Canadian Works in Translation.* Ottawa: SSHRC

Strindberg, August. 1985. *Mademoiselle Julie.* Trans. Boris Vian. Paris: L'Arche

- n.d., 'Mademoiselle Julie.' Adapt. G. Marsolais. Unpublished manuscript, National Theatre School
Struve, Gleb. 1971. *Russian Literature under Lenin and Stalin*. Norman: University of Oklahoma Press
Szanto, Georges, 1978. *Theater and Propaganda*. Austin: University of Texas Press
Taguieff, Pierre André. 1985. 'Le Néo-racisme différentialiste. Sur l'ambiguïté d'une évidence commune et ses effets pervers: L'éloge de la différence.' *Langage et société* 34 (December), 69–106
Toury, Gideon. 1980. *In Search of a Theory of Translation*. Tel Aviv: Porter Institute for Poetics and Semiotics
Théâtre/Public, Traduire, 44 (March-April 1982). Ed. G. Banu.
Théâtre Québec. May 1987. Montreal: Centre d'Essai des Auteurs Dramatiques
Tremblay, Michel. 1969. 'L'Intelligence de rire de soi-même.' *L'envers du décor* (II) 1 (November), 3
- 1972. *Les Belles-Soeurs*. Montreal: Leméac
- 1974. *Bonjour là, bonjour*. Montréal: Lemeac
- 1985. *Le Gars de Québec*. Montreal: Leméac
Trudeau, Danielle. 1982. *Léandre et son péché*. Montreal: Hurtubise
Turp, Gilbert. 1984. 'Pourquoi retraduire *Mère Courage et ses enfants?*' *En scène* 2/2
Valesio, Paolo. 1976. 'The Virtues of Traducement: Sketch of a Theory of Translation.' *Semiotica* 18/1, 1–96
Van Den Broeck, Raymond. 1985. 'Second Thoughts on Translation Criticism.' In *The Manipulation of Literature*, ed. T. Herman, 54–62. London: Croom Helm
Vanier, Denis. 1974. *Je*. Montreal: L'Aurore
Vauthier, Jean. 1953. *Théâtre*. Paris: L'Arche
Weinmann, Heinz. 1977. 'Narcisse et l'autre: Pour un ethnotype québécois.' *Voix et images* 3/2 (December), 266–76
- 1987. *Du Canada au Québec*. Montreal: L'Hexagone
Weiss, Peter. 1966. *The Persecution and Assassination of Jean-Paul Marat as Performed by the Inmates of the Asylum of Charenton under the Direction of the Marquis de Sade*. Trans. Geoffry Skelton. New York: Atheneum
Zindel, Paul. 1970. *L'Effet des rayons gamma sur les vieux-garçons*. Trans. M. Tremblay. Montreal: Leméac
- 1971 ... *Et Mademoiselle Roberge boit un peu*. Trans. M. Tremblay. Montreal: Leméac

Index of Proper Names

Adamov, A., 190
Aeschylus, 105, 107, 218
Albee, E., 29, 49, 187
Allen, M., 199
Andreev, L., 45
Andrès B., xxi, 82, 212, 217, 221
Angenot, M., 7, 202, 217
Anouilh, J., 48, 107, 218
Antonelli, L., 44
Arden, J., 186
Aristophanes, 16, 20–5
Arlt, R., 163
Arreola, J.J., 46
Athayde, R., 14, 27
Austin, J.L., 110

Bakhtin, M., xxi, 6, 90, 202, 213, 215
Balibar, R., 188, 223
Barillet, P., 48
Basile, J., 206
Bassnett-McGuire, S., 202
Bataillon, M., 223
Beaulieu, V.-L., 179
Beckett, S., 48
Bélair, M., 36–8, 43, 47, 52–3, 105, 203, 205–6, 214
Belleau, A., xxi, 4, 142, 201–2, 209, 216

Benavente, J., 46
Béraud, J., 36, 205, 214
Bergeron, L., 166–7, 213, 219
Berman, A., xxi, 57, 207, 209, 219, 221
Bertrand, C., 221
Bérubé, A., 74
Bérubé, R., 212
Besré, J., 30
Betti, U., 44, 47
Bocaccio, 73
Boileau, 81
Bonnefoy, Y., xvii, 123, 127–8, 132–40, 153, 215
Bontempelli, M., 44
Borges, J.L., 11
Bouchard, M.M., 198
Bourdieu, P., xix
Bouthillette, J., 208–9
Brassard, A., xxii, 16, 20, 24, 203
Brault, J., 142, 144, 149, 216, 217
Brecht, B., 10, 13, 44–5, 98–9, 101, 167, 184, 213–14, 222
Bruneau, C., 219
Büchner, G., 45, 47
Buissonnau, P., xxii, 43

Calderón, 46

234 Index of Proper Names

Cardinal, M., 21–6, 30, 204
Carrière, J.-C., 48
Céline, L.-F., 83
Cervantes, 163, 218
Céspedes, L., de., 15
Chamberland, P., 68, 142, 150–3, 156–7, 209, 216–17, 221
Châtelet, F., 7, 202
Chaucer, 163
Chekhov, A., 12, 15, 27, 29–30, 45, 110, 167, 183, 188–90, 210, 222–3
Chiarelli, L., 44
Cicero, 163, 218
Claudel, P., 48, 218
Colbert, F., 33, 204
Constantineau, P., 207
Corneille, P., 47, 80–7, 97, 212–13, 218
Crémieux, B., 190
Cyr, R.R., 205

D'Annunzio, G., 44
D'Hulst, L., 201
Dagenais, A., 16, 203
Dante, 163
Darbelnet, J., 208
De Filippo, E., 43
Deleuze, G., 217
Delisle, J., xxi, 3, 201–3
Del Valle-Inclán, R., 46
Déprats, J.-M., 132–6, 138, 153, 202
De Rojas, F., 46
Derome, B., 209
Derrida, J., 195, 223
Deschamps, Y., 15, 30, 106, 204
Di San Secondo, R., 44
Dimić, M., 201
Dionne, R., 14, 19, 203
Disney, W., 83
Dorst, T., 45
Dostoevsky, F., 45

Du Bellay, J., 164, 168, 178, 219
Dubé, M., 16, 217
Dubois, J., 170, 202, 220
Dubois, R.-D., 198
Ducasse, I., 83
Duceppe, J., 27, 30
Ducharme, A., 205
Ducharme, R., 79–89, 97, 212
Ducrot, O., 70, 210
Dumont, M., 187
Duplessis, M., 72, 95, 145
Duras, M., 165
Durham, Lord, 62–5, 69, 208–9
Duval, E.-F., 210–11
Duvignaud, J., 104, 214

Eagleton, T., 215
Engelbertz, M., 202, 218
Erdman, N., 45
Ernst, M., 209
Éthier-Blais, J., 172, 203, 220
Euripides, 21–6, 30–1, 107, 218
Even-Zohar, I., 3, 201

Fabbri, D., 44
Fassbinder, R.W., 44–5
Faye, J.-P., 220
Ferron, J., 181
Feydeau, G., 48
Flaubert, G., 21
Fo, D., 13, 42–3
Foucault, M., 3, 7, 201
Foulkes, A.P., 217
Frank, A.P., 201
Freeman, D., 36
Frisch, M., 44

Gadda, C.E., 163
Gallant, M., 203
García Lorca, F., 46

Index of Proper Names

Garneau, M., xvi–viii, 10, 30, 109–42, 145, 149, 153, 156–7, 159, 160–1, 165, 173, 180–3, 199, 204, 216, 220–1
Garstin, M.K., 201
Gauvin, L., 212
Gélinas, G., 206
Genette, G., 212
Germain, J.-C., 25–6, 38, 60–70, 91–101, 105–6, 182, 185, 194, 204, 208–9, 213, 216, 218, 222
Gide, A., 68
Giguere, R., 145, 216
Giraudoux, J., 48, 71, 105–6
Gobard, H., 165, 217, 219
Gobin, P., 175, 217, 221
Godbout, J., 220
Godin, G., 142, 216
Godin, J.-C., 36, 212–14, 216
Goethe, xv, xviii, 90
Gogol, N., 10, 12, 15, 19–20, 45, 71–2, 210
Goldoni, C., 42–3, 47
Gombrowicz, W., 47, 163, 218–19
Gorky, M., 45
Gozzi, C., 43
Graham, J.F., 202
Grandmont, É. de, 9, 59
Grédy, J.-P., 48
Grégoire, M., 187
Gruslin, A., 33, 50, 204, 206
Guimond, O., 212
Guitry, S., 47
Gurik, R., 101, 103–4, 214

Handke, P., 45
Hauser, A., 206
Hébert, P., xxii, 14
Heine, H., 109
Herbert, J., 14, 17–18, 27, 32, 35, 203
Hermann, P.W., 83

Hermans, T., 201
Hölderlin, F., viii
Hutcheon, L., 82, 212

Ionesco, E., 48

Jakobson, R., 127, 135, 162, 218
Jarry, A., 44, 198
Jasmin, C., 207
Jelenski, C., 219
Jourdheuil, J., 202

Kafka, F., xix, 217
Kaiser, G., 45
Kataev, A., 45
Kleist, H., 44
Knight, L., 207
Kokoschka, O., 45
Krysinski, W., 223

Laberge, M., 198
Labiche, E., 47
Lachapelle, A., 30
Ladmiral, J.-R., 201, 218
Lafon, D., 223
Lafontaine, R., 30
Lalonde, M., 168–9, 176, 178–80, 182, 186, 220–1
Lalonde, R., 12, 110, 183, 210
Lambert, J., xxi, 202
Lamoureux, J.-P., 204
Lanoux, V., 15, 17, 31–2, 48, 204
Lapointe, P.-M., 216–17
Laroche, M., 216–17
Larose, J., 205
Laurier, W., 64, 209
Lavoie, J., 74
Lefebvre, P., 59, 71, 202, 210, 217, 221
Lefevere, A., 210
Lemieux, J.-M., 30

236 Index of Proper Names

Léonard, M., 208
Lepage, R., 29, 74, 198–9, 210
Lescarbot, M., 36
Levac, C., 214, 217
Léveillé, R., 34
Lévesque, R., 32, 95, 202
Lewis, J., 83
Leyrac, M., 30
Leyris, P., xvii, 122–3, 127, 132–8, 153, 215
Lichtenstein, R., 83
Link, J., 201
Link-Heer, U., 201
Loranger, F., 214, 217
Luther, M., 164, 179, 221

McDonough, J.T., 14, 17, 36
Macduff, P., 223
Machiavelli, 12, 73–4
Maheu, G., 198–9, 204
Maiakovsky, V., 45
Mailhot, L., 36, 212–14
Maillet, A., 12, 30, 34, 74–9, 92–4, 211–12
Major, A., 216
Manet, E., 48
Marcel, J., 220
Marchand, F.-G., 25–8, 91, 93–8, 213
Marinetti, F.T., 44
Marivaux, 48, 106
Marleau, D., 198–9
Marsolais, G., 188, 190–4, 223
Martin, R., 206
Maxwell, M., 30
Melville, H., 167
Mercure, M., 192, 213
Meschonnic, H., xix, 4, 201, 217
Michelet, N., 211
Miller, A., 49, 206

Miron, G., xvii, 67–8, 143, 145, 162, 174, 176, 180, 182, 208–9, 216, 221
Mishima, Y., 40
Mitchell, W.O., 36
Molière, 10, 12, 47–8, 74–5, 79, 92–3, 105–6
Monroe, M., 84
Morency, P., 14
Morin, M., 221
Morisset, J., 206
Moser, W., 201
Mounin, G., 162, 218–19
Müller, H., 45, 47, 85–6, 89, 204, 212
Musset, 105–6, 218

Nardocchio, E., 202
Nida, E., 163, 219–20

O'Neill, E., 25, 49, 187, 222
Ostiguy, P., 59, 71, 210

Pannwitz, R., xviii
Pavis, P., 203
Pelletier, D., 30
Petrowski, N., 213
Picard, B., 30
Pinard, D., 213
Piotte, J.-M., 206
Pirandello, L., 42–4, 190
Pitoeff, S., 190
Ponson du Terrail, 92
Pontaut, A., 208
Poupart, R.-J., 215

Queneau, J., 198

Rabelais, F., 90
Racine, J., 47–8, 107, 218
Richler, M., 14, 17–18, 27–8, 205

Index of Proper Names   237

Rioux, M., 106, 207, 220
Ripps, R., 187
Robin, A., xiv
Robin, R., xxi, 3, 201
Robinson, S., 166, 219
Rochette, G., 14
Ronfard, A., 44
Ronfard, J.-P., 12, 24, 30, 73–4, 87–91, 210, 213
Rossi-Landi, F., 220
Roussin, A., 47
Roux, J.-L., xxii, 14–15, 30–1, 204
Roy, G., 34
Ruzante, N., 43

Saint-Laurent, L., 64, 209
Sartre, J.-P., 25
Sastre, A., 46
Sauvageau, Y., 187
Schaffer, P., 14, 27
Schiller, xviii
Schlegel, A.W., xvi
Schnitzler, A., 44
Schwarzinger, H., 202
Schwitters, K., 45, 47, 198
Scola, E., 43
Searle, J., 110, 215
Sénac, P., 211
Shaffer, P., 14
Shakespeare, xvi–viii, 27, 86, 88–90, 101–3, 105, 107, 109–51, 160–1, 163, 167, 182, 199, 214, 216–18, 221
Shaw, G.B., 59
Siguret, F., 208
Simon, C., 165
Simon, N., 49
Simon, S., 29, 202–4, 223
Slade, B., 15
Smith, D., 166, 219

Spengler, O., 209
Spillane, M., 83
Stein, P., 23
Stratford, P., 17, 203
Strauss, B., 45, 198
Strindberg, A., 188, 190, 223
Struve, G., 213
Synge, J.M., xv
Szanto, G., 202, 217

Taber, C., 163, 219
Taguieff, P.-A., 205
Talesnik, R., 46
Tardieu, J., 207
Terence, 73
Tessier, R., 47, 206
Tirso de Molina, 46
Touraine, A., xix
Tournier, M., 165
Toury, G., 3, 201–2, 223
Tremblay, M., 9, 12, 14–31, 45, 59, 71–4, 185–93, 198, 204–5, 208, 210, 221–2
Triolet, E., 189–90, 193, 223
Trudeau, D., 219–20
Trudeau, P.E., 64, 209
Turp, G., 13, 184, 190, 192, 222–3

Valesio, P., 210
Van Den Broeck, R., 202
Van Gorp H., 202
Vanier, D., 143, 216
Vauthier, J., 73, 210
Vialatte, A., xix, 217
Vian, B., 190–2
Vilar, J., 210
Villeneuve, R., 199
Vitez, A., 190, 202
Voss, H., xviii

Wedekind, F., 45
Weinmann, H., 205, 210, 220–1
Weiss, P., 45, 90, 213
Weiss, W., 206
Williams, T., 49, 187
Witkiewicz, S., 47
Wittlinger, K., 44

Yaroshevskaya, K., 15, 190
Yeats, W.B., xv

Zandes, N., 203
Zindel, P., 14, 26–7, 49, 204